FANTASIES

OF THE NEW CLASS

FANTASIES
OF THE NEW CLASS

Ideologies of Professionalism in
Post–World War II American Fiction

STEPHEN SCHRYER

Columbia University Press   New York

Columbia University Press
Publishers Since 1893
New York   Chichester, West Sussex
Copyright © 2011 Columbia University Press

Chapter 3 is reprinted from Stephen Schryer, "Mary McCarthy's
Field Guide to U.S. Intellectuals: Tradition and Modernization
Theory in *Birds of America*," *Modern Fiction Studies* 53:4 (2007),
821–844. © 2007 by the Purdue Research Foundation. Reprinted
with permission of The Johns Hopkins University Press.

Library of Congress Cataloging-in-Publication Data

Schryer, Stephen.
Fantasies of the new class : ideologies of professionalism in
post-World War II American fiction / Stephen Schryer.
p. cm.
Includes bibliographical references and index.
ISBN 978-0-231-15756-8 (cloth : alk. paper)—
ISBN 978-0-231-15757-5 (pbk. : alk. paper)—
ISBN 978-0-231-52747-7 (ebk.)
1. American fiction—20th century—History and criticism.   2. Social
classes in literature.   3. Professional employees in literature.
4. Elite (Social sciences) in literature.   5. Professional
employees—United States—History—20th century.   6. Literature
and society—United States—History—20th century.   I. Title.

PS374.S68S35 2011
813'.54093552—dc22   2010041827

Columbia University Press books are printed
on permanent and durable acid-free paper.

This book is printed on paper with recycled content.
Printed in the United States of America

c 10 9 8 7 6 5 4 3 2 1
p 10 9 8 7 6 5 4 3 2 1

References to Internet Web sites (URLs) were accurate
at the time of writing. Neither the author nor
Columbia University Press is responsible for URLs that may have
expired or changed since the manuscript was prepared.

CONTENTS

ACKNOWLEDGMENTS

Thanks are due, first and foremost, to Michael Szalay at the University of California, Irvine, who read countless early drafts of various chapters from this project. This book would have been unthinkable without his critical guidance. Mary Esteve, who supervised my postdoctoral fellowship at Concordia University, helped give shape to this project in its final stages. The following scholars provided crucial feedback, advice, encouragement, and support at various moments in the writing process: Andrew Hoberek, Sean McCann, Brook Thomas, Mark Goble, Nicola Nixon, and Scott Kaufman. I also thank Philip Leventhal at Columbia University Press for his keenly perceptive editorial advice and for seeing this book through to final publication. Early versions of chapters 1 and 3 appeared in *PMLA* and *Modern Fiction Studies*; I thank those two journals for permission to include the material here. Last, I thank my new colleagues at the University of New Brunswick for their collegiality and intellectual stimulation. This book is dedicated to my wife, Joanne Minor— my model of an ideal, socially conscious professional.

FANTASIES

OF THE NEW CLASS

INTRODUCTION

FANTASIES OF THE NEW CLASS

If he is to think politically in a realistic way, the intellectual must constantly know his own social position. This is necessary in order that he may be aware of the sphere of strategy that is really open to his influence. If he forgets this, his thinking may exceed his sphere of strategy so far as to make impossible any translation of his thought into action, his own or that of others. His thought may thus become fantastic. If he remembers his powerlessness too well, assumes that his sphere of strategy is restricted to the point of impotence, then his thought may easily become politically trivial. In either case, fantasy and powerlessness may well be the lot of his mind.

C. Wright Mills, "The Social Role of the Intellectual" (1944)

In its 1952 "Our Country and Our Culture" symposium, the *Partisan Review* asked participants to respond to the editors' claim that "for better or for worse, most writers no longer accept alienation as the artist's fate in America; on the contrary, they want very much to be a part of American life."[1] With the exception of a few dissenters, such as Norman Mailer and C. Wright Mills, most of the contributors agreed with this assessment. Writers and literary critics, they argued, had entered the mainstream of American culture; they now occupied comfortable teaching positions in the nation's universities, which tended to pacify the aesthete's traditional revolt against bourgeois society. Conversely, significant portions of the American public had in turn become open to literary culture. "In many civilizations," Lionel Trilling argued, "there comes a point at which wealth shows a tendency to submit itself to the rule of mind and imagination, to refine itself, to apologize for its existence with a show of taste and sensitivity. In America the tendency to this submission has for some time been apparent." For Trilling, this submission was the consequence of a demographic shift in U.S. society: the rapid expansion of the professional middle class. American intellectuals often overlooked this shift; they knew little "about the existence and the training and the influence of, say, high school teachers, or ministers, or social workers, the people of the minor intellectual professions, whose stock in trade is ideas of some kind." This educated class, however, was the primary channel through which literary ideas flowed to the rest of the American public. Its members were "at least potentially supporters and consumers of high culture,"[2] and Trilling imagined that they would mitigate the self-interest and acquisitiveness of American society.

Trilling's response adumbrates the central theme of the chapters that follow: post–World War II literary intellectuals' relationship to the new class of university-educated knowledge workers.[3] Buoyed by its essential role in the postindustrial economy and welfare state and by the massive expansion of postsecondary education, the new or professional-managerial class became the fastest-growing occupational stratum in American society in the decades after World War II.[4] Observing this rapid growth, many writers and social critics predicted that the new class would become America's hegemonic elite, counteracting and eventually displacing the moneyed bourgeoisie. In making this claim, these writers echoed a theme that had run through reformist critiques of American society since the late nineteenth century: the idea that qualified professionals would tame free-market capitalism, forcing it to submit to expert guidance.[5] This theme encapsulated the dominant ideology of professionals throughout the Progressive and New Deal eras—an ideology that Steven Brint refers to as "social trustee professionalism." This ideology claimed that professionals transcended the purely pecuniary motives of the capital-owning bourgeoisie. Instead, it highlighted professionals' technical expertise and concern for the public welfare. Social trustee professionalism technically "promised competent performance of skilled work involving the application of broad and complex knowledge, the acquisition of which required formal academic study. Morally, it promised to be guided by an appreciation of the important social ends it served."[6] This ideology was at the center of the version of democratic liberalism that motivated reform efforts throughout much of the twentieth century—what historian Howard Brick refers to as the "postcapitalist vision" of left-of-center U.S. intellectuals. According to Brick, one of the key elements of this vision was the idea that "the social salience of capitalist institutions was steadily declining, including the determining force of market processes, the authority or potency of business wealth, or even the efficacy of economics as the best way to understand, or act on, social affairs."[7] For postcapitalist thinkers, the decline of free-market institutions created the opportunity for intelligent experts, guided by collective values and beliefs, to reorganize society in a more egalitarian fashion.

However, Trilling's response signals a crucial shift in this discourse of professionalism, a shift that was especially important for literary intellectuals writing in the post–World War II era. Trilling did not believe that the expanding new class that he lauded in "Our Country and Our Culture" should engage in social engineering of the kind envisaged by ambitious New Dealers in the 1930s. Indeed, Trilling established his reputation in the 1940s as a critic of progressive liberalism and its impact on U.S. literary culture. In his early criticism, Trilling criticized New Deal liberals' "organizational impulse," which led them to order "the elements of life in a rational way."[8] Echoing the concerns of a growing number of U.S. intellectuals, Trilling claimed that this impulse had culminated in the impersonal bureaucracies of the welfare state. These bureaucracies seemed to mark the triumph of reformist energies that had been building since the Progressive Era. In fact, they marked the rigidification of those energies into administrative and technical routines and thus prefigured the demise of autonomous intellectual work: "we must understand that organization means delegation, and bureaus, and technicians, and that the ideas that can survive delegation, that can be passed on to agencies and bureaus and technicians, incline to be ideas of a certain kind and of a certain simplicity." In contrast, the job of literary criticism is "to recall liberalism to its first essential imagination of variousness and possibility, which implies the awareness of complexity and difficulty."[9] Literary criticism should instill negative capability within the new class—an aesthetic capacity to live with paradox, to keep contraries in play without resolving them.

Trilling thus envisaged a new model of professional reformism, one based on cultural education rather than on institution building. He outlined this new model in his 1947 novel *The Middle of the Journey*.[10] The novel describes the ideological conversion of John Laskell, a New Deal liberal who begins the narrative as an expert in public housing for low-income families. In this role, Laskell "committed himself to the most hopeful and progressive aspects of modern life, planning their image in public housing developments, defending them in long dull meetings of liberals and radicals." However, Laskell undergoes a series of traumatic experiences that lead him to an awareness of variousness and possibility at odds with his reformist sympathies. While mourning the death of his fiancée, he succumbs to a near-fatal case of scarlet fever. Lying in his sickbed, he arrives at an existential self-awareness, "as if being had become a sensation." He describes this new awareness in aesthetic terms, as a consciousness of a phenomenal and moral complexity hitherto invisible to him. He becomes fascinated by a rose on his bedside table: "he could have become lost in its perfection, watching the strange energy which the rose seemed to have, for it was not static in its beauty, it seemed to be always at work organizing its petals into their perfect relation with each other."[11] In Kant's *Critique of Judgment*, flowers are the chief example of "free natural beauties," objects that are utterly purposeless and thus elicit pure judgments of taste. They exemplify the fact that judgments of taste are without interest, that beautiful objects instead provoke a "free play of the cognitive powers" that precedes desire or pleasure.[12] Trilling evokes something similar with Laskell's appreciation for the rose; Laskell experiences a "desire that wanted nothing . . . the removal of all the adverse conditions of the self, the personality living in nothing but delight in itself." This experience forces him to rethink his ideological creed; middle-class progressives, he realizes, continually project their subjective desires on the world, thereby occluding its true complexity. "The future and the present were one," he reflects; "the present could no longer contrive and manufacture the future by throwing forward, in the form of expectation and hope, the desires of the present moment."[13] The bulk of the novel traces Laskell's adherence to this present-oriented creed, which enables him to see through the ideological simplicities of his fellow New Deal liberals.

This altered perspective implies that Laskell's reformist vocation is at an end; it is hard to imagine how he can continue on as a public-housing developer without manufacturing the future. Indeed, *The Middle of the Journey* seems to allegorize a common theme among writers in the late 1940s and 1950s—the idea that intellectuals should retreat from the exigencies of public service in order to cultivate a purely private aesthetic sensibility. This idea has inspired much subsequent criticism of cold war literature, which describes how postwar writers abandoned the collectivist politics of the 1930s in order to cultivate a new sense of embattled individuality.[14] However, the point of Trilling's early criticism and fiction is that negative capability is itself the basis for a new kind of public service, one that consists of disseminating this sensibility to an expanding, educated public, thereby dissolving the ideological and bureaucratic rigidity of the welfare state.[15] This sense of vocation was one that Trilling derived from Matthew Arnold, the subject of his doctoral dissertation and first book. Surveying Victorian society in *Culture and Anarchy* (1869), Arnold argued that it was caught up in mechanistic ways of thinking that interpreted material accomplishments as ends in themselves. This situation prevented the emergence of "Culture," which Arnold famously defined as the "pursuit of our total perfection by means of getting to know, on all the matters which most concern us, the best which has been thought and said in the world, and, through this knowledge, turning a stream of fresh and free thought upon our stock notions and habits." Despite this view of his society, Arnold found hope in the gradual emergence of a new social group, the "aliens" or "saving remnant," consisting of superior persons from each class "who are mainly led, not by their class spirit, but by a general *humane* spirit, by the love of human perfection."[16] Trilling, in his writings of the 1940s and 1950s, retrofitted Matthew Arnold for the cold war era, envisaging aesthetically attuned professionals such as Laskell as a saving remnant who would disrupt the stock notions of the middle class. This saving remnant would transform U.S. capitalism in a more subtle but profound fashion than that imagined by New Deal technocrats.

Trilling thus established the basic pattern followed by many of the writers described in the chapters in this book. He envisioned intellectuals abandoning their technocratic pretensions toward social reform in favor of a different, humanistic model of cultural education oriented toward the educated middle class. According to this model, the intellectual embodies a greater critical intelligence and social authority than ever before. However, this critical intelligence has a mysterious, indirect impact on the society around it. Rather than building institutions, the intellectual improves the culture, driving the expanding new class to adopt more complicated patterns of thinking associated with the practice of professionalism itself. This conception of cultural education marked a shift in the U.S. discourse of professionalism away from the social trustee professionalism typical of early-twentieth-century reformers and toward what I call "new-class fantasy." This new discourse retained the moral and technical claims of social trustee professionalism. New-class fantasists still laid claim to superior moral probity and technical expertise; moreover, they still claimed that they transcended the purely pecuniary motives of the traditional bourgeoisie. However, they now shaped the culture through example rather than through specific social reforms. The result was a conception of professionalism that

6

was fantastic in the sense evoked by C. Wright Mills in this introduction's epigraph. It was a conception that hinged on intellectuals
ignoring or mystifying the "sphere of strategy" within which they
work—the institutions of the post–New Deal state. As a result, new-
class fantasists embraced simultaneously impotent and exaggerated
models of intellectual agency.

POSTWAR LITERATURE
AND CONSENSUS SOCIOLOGY

In developing this thesis, *Fantasies of the New Class* reads U.S. fiction
and literary criticism in tandem with the consensus sociology of the
post–World War II period. In particular, this project of reading literature alongside sociology dominates the early chapters of this book,
which focus on specific debates that took place between literary intellectuals and sociologists during the high tide of consensus social
science—the 1950s and 1960s. Subsequent chapters focus more narrowly on novelists writing in the 1970s and 1980s who extend or
complicate the models of new-class agency outlined in the book's
first half. Consensus sociology is a paradigm that has gone largely
unnoticed by critics of postwar fiction, who have tended to focus on
the work of popular sociologists such as David Riesman, William H.
Whyte Jr., and C. Wright Mills rather than on the institutional social science that influenced government policy. This social science,
best exemplified by Talcott Parsons's structural functionalism, was
one of the key forms in which the technocratic liberalism and postcapitalist vision of the 1930s survived into the 1950s and 1960s.[17]
Parsons's theoretical perspective, especially as elaborated by subsequent modernization theorists interested in third-world development, shaped much of the research that informed domestic and foreign programs during the Kennedy and Johnson administrations.
This transformation of sociology into an important administrative
resource was a relatively new phenomenon, one that depended on

the postwar consolidation of the welfare state. Prior to the 1940s, sociologists often echoed the technocratic idealism expressed in texts such as Herbert Croly's *The Promise of American Life* (1909);[18] however, they rarely got a chance to put their expertise to work.

Post–World War II literary intellectuals responded to sociology's newfound prestige with some trepidation. The New Critics, discussed in chapter 1, explicitly defined their work against the social sciences, institutionalizing a disciplinary conflict between literature and sociology that continues to shape academic literary studies to the present day. Trilling's relationship with the social sciences was more nuanced; he practiced a broadly sociological style of criticism and sympathetically reviewed popular works of sociology such as Riesman's *The Lonely Crowd*.[19] Indeed, Trilling belonged to an intellectual milieu—the New York intellectuals—that prominently featured sociologists such as Riesman, Mills, and Daniel Bell. Overall, however, Trilling argued that mainstream U.S. sociology embodied a deadening instrumentalism—the very tendency toward organizational thinking that humanistic inquiry was supposed to counteract. Hence, Laskell's progressive friends in *The Middle of the Journey* buttress their liberal ideas with various sociological clichés. "Social causes," one explains, "environment, education or lack of education, economic pressure, the character-pattern imposed by society, in this case a disorganized society, all go to explain and account for any given individual's actions."[20] This same sociological determinism underlies Laskell's early career as an urban planner; he assumes that social environment determines human behavior and that changes to the one will improve the other. Trilling's anxiety, articulated in his criticism, was that this attitude would institute a "bland tyranny" of social engineers. "The social sciences in general no longer pretend that they can merely describe what people do," he complained; "they now have the clear consciousness of their ability to manipulate and adjust."[21]

Postwar literary critics thus revived a century-old antagonism between literature and sociology. As Wolf Lepenies argues, for the nineteenth-century humanist "the battle lines are drawn as follows:

sociology is a discipline characterized by cold rationality, which seeks to comprehend the structures and laws of motion of modern industrial society by means of measurement and computation and in doing so only serves to alienate man more effectively from himself and from the world around him; on the opposite side there stands a literature whose intuition can see farther than the analyses of the sociologists and whose ability to address the heart of man is to be preferred to the products of a discipline that misunderstands itself as a natural science of society."[22] Sociology, in other words, seemed to embody a threatening intrusion of scientific expertise into humanistic territory. This intrusion seemed particularly galling for nineteenth-century humanists given that both disciplines shared similar ambitions of speaking about society as a whole. In the United States, this disciplinary conflict never fully materialized until the 1940s. In particular, the predominant novelistic aesthetic of the 1930s was hospitable to sociology. This hospitality was exemplified by the Chicago naturalism of writers such as James Farrell and Richard Wright, who drew on the ethnographic techniques of Chicago school sociologists and in turn influenced their work.[23] Many liberal and leftist literary critics—such as Van Wyck Brooks, Vernon Parrington, and Granville Hicks—similarly applied sociological ideas to the study of literary works, exploring the ways in which literary ideas are shaped by their authors' class origins. In contrast, Trilling and other postwar literary critics reacted against the sociological determinism of the Depression years, which they believed had assimilated too much of the managerial idealism of that era. Naturalist novelists and progressive critics, Trilling complained, were dominated by their "informing idea of the economic and social determination of thought." This idea implied the existence of "a thing called reality; it is one and immutable, it is wholly external, it is irreducible. Men's minds may waver, but reality is always reliable, always the same, always easily to be known."[24] For Trilling, social reality is instead characterized by a continual, dialectical clash of values and ideas. The best writers do not depict social conditions; rather, they record this conflict: "in any

9

culture, there are likely to be certain artists who contain a large part
of the dialectic within themselves, their meaning and power lying in
their contradictions; they contain within themselves, it may be
said, the very essence of the culture."[25] Trilling thus helped establish
the model of literary representation that would soon dominate liberal and leftist humanist criticism: literature highlights ideological
rifts elsewhere invisible in society.[26] This shift in conceptions of reality means that novelists must abandon the illusion of easy mimesis
and that progressive liberals must mitigate the organizational impulse of their political creed. If social reality is multiple, then neither
the social engineer nor the documentary realist has an automatic
purchase on it; he or she has access only to a tendentious version.[27]

This opposition between the literary intellectual and the sociological technocrat runs throughout much postwar fiction and literary criticism, reaching its apotheosis in the Vietnam era in the work
of Norman Mailer and other countercultural writers.[28] Thereafter,
the opposition becomes less pronounced, perhaps due to the decreas-
ing impact of sociology on policy decisions after the Kennedy and
Johnson administrations. However, in rethinking social reality as a
tissue of ideas and attitudes, Trilling and other postwar writers echoed
many consensus sociologists associated with the welfare state. These
sociologists were themselves in the process of abandoning simple
forms of economic determinism in order to focus on the complexities of psychology and culture. Talcott Parsons, discussed in greater
detail in chapter 1, is a case in point. Throughout the 1950s and 1960s,
he was the preeminent U.S. sociological theorist, and he articulated
an unbounded enthusiasm for the welfare state that exemplified many
of Trilling's criticisms of technocratic liberalism. Whereas Trilling
viewed the bureaucratic institutions of the welfare state as a dead cara-
pace generated by the organizational impulses of middle-class reformism, Parsons celebrated them as the functioning organs of a healthy
social system. However, behind this disagreement about the welfare
state lay a basic agreement about the ideal function of the expanded
new class within it. For Parsons, the crucial impact of the educated

middle class does not result from its concrete, technical contributions to society—treating patients in hospitals, analyzing census re-
ports, designing public housing, and so on. Rather, the new class is
the key social stratum that checks the anomie of advanced, industrial society through the cultural attitudes that it embodies. Parsons's sometimes collaborator, the sociologist Edward Shils, summed
up the structural functionalist theory of professionalism as follows.
Every society has a cultural center, within which cultural professionals of various sorts generate ideas and values that are disseminated
outward to the periphery. The center, Shils argued, "is a phenomenon of values and beliefs. It is the center of the order of symbols, of
values and beliefs, which govern the society. It is the center because
it is ultimate and irreducible; and it is felt to be such by many who
cannot give explicit articulation to its irreducibility. The central zone
partakes of the nature of the sacred. In this sense, every society has
an 'official' religion, even when that society or its exponents and in-
terpreters, conceive of it, more or less correctly, as a secular, pluralis-
tic, tolerant society."[29] Parsons and Shils, like Trilling, thus moved
intellectuals and other cultural professionals to the center of U.S.
society and attributed a crucial yet also mysterious agency to them. Intellectuals do not formulate ideas about a better society; they bring
this society into being through their very existence. Hence, in a
pattern that was repeated throughout the postwar era, literary intellectuals such as Trilling rejected the sociological tendencies of 1930s
naturalism and progressive criticism, associating them with the most
technocratic aspects of the liberal tradition. However, in doing so,
they paralleled trends already under way within sociology itself—a tendency to imagine intellectuals rehumanizing the welfare state through
cultural education. *Fantasies of the New Class* shows how postwar writers' late-modernist aesthetic served a transdisciplinary project of
creating a public-minded but antimanagerial cultural elite dedicated
to national education but indifferent or hostile to pragmatic reform.

The resulting education projects were quite diverse, and the chapters here trace out the fault lines dividing postwar writers similarly

[handwritten margin notes: "Cultural center", "intellectuals possessed mysterious agency + center of US culture", "✳", "Thesis"]

invested in new-class cultural politics. New-class fantasy gave rise to celebratory defenses of the welfare state, genteel demands for its reform, and apocalyptic visions of its destruction—all of them couched in terms of intellectuals' ability to divert the new-class psyche away from narrowly technocratic forms of expertise. Indeed, what is striking about new-class fantasy is the extent to which it pervaded the work of writers and sociologists across the political spectrum, forging similarities between the political prescriptions of the radical Left, the liberal Center, and the neoconservative Right. The maverick sociologist C. Wright Mills, probably the single most important influence on the 1960s New Left, is a case in point. Over the course of the 1950s, Mills criticized both Trilling and Parsons as examples of postwar intellectuals' tendency to retreat into aestheticism or to celebrate the current social system uncritically. He rejected Trilling's optimistic assessment of American wealth submitting to the rule of mind and imagination, arguing that Trilling confused "knowledge as a goal with knowledge as mere technique and instrument."[30] He also criticized Parsons's consensus paradigm, instead emphasizing the prevalence of class conflict in the United States.[31] However, in his lifelong engagement with the uses and abuses of sociological expertise, Mills often replicated Trilling's Arnoldian rethinking of professional agency, envisaging the emergence of a new-class saving remnant that might check the welfare state's bureaucratic rationalism. "Liberalism," Mills argued, "has become less a reform movement than the administration of social services in the welfare state; sociology has lost its reforming push; its tendencies toward fragmentary problems and scattered causation have been conservatively turned to the use of corporation, army, and state."[32] In his famous trilogy on American class stratification—*The New Men of Power* (1948), *White Collar* (1951), and *The Power Elite* (1956)—Mills surveyed the major classes of U.S. society, showing how union leaders, routine white-collar workers, and the power elite all participated in this calcification of the welfare state.[33] As a result, none of them could function as effective agents of social change. Instead, in his later work, especially *The Causes* of World War III (1958)[34] and The Sociological Imagination (1959), Mills turned to the emerging knowledge elite—those in charge of what he called the "cultural apparatus," composed of "all of the organizations and milieux in which artistic, intellectual and scientific work goes on, and of the means by which such work is made available to circles, publics, and masses."[35] Critical intellectuals, Mills hoped, would use this apparatus to challenge the welfare state's instrumental rationality. They would do so by disseminating the "sociological imagination": a humanistic capacity embodied in literature and sociology that allows individuals to connect personal problems to broader social structures and historical trends.[36]

Mills's account of the cultural apparatus dramatizes the alternation between impotence and fantasy that he himself diagnosed as a constant temptation for the U.S. intellectual. Critical intellectuals, in his assessment, have been cut off from all other social groups— from the labor movement, from the general public, from those in positions of power. They are also increasingly being cut off from the cultural apparatus itself, which has been co-opted by the power elite. "We, the cultural workmen," he complained, "do not have access to the means of effectively communicating images and ideals; others who own and operate the mass media stand between us and our potential publics."[37] Critical intellectuals, in other words, no longer have any means of translating their ideas into suggestions for social policy. Nevertheless, they can become a revolutionary force by adhering to the standards of professionalism inherent in their disciplinary milieus, without succumbing to narrow forms of specialization. The ideal path of the social scientist who wishes to "realize the value of reason and its role in human affairs," Mills suggested, "is to remain independent, to do one's own work, to select one's own problems. . . . Such a conception prompts us to imagine social science as a sort of public intelligence apparatus, concerned with public issues and private troubles and with the structural trends of our time underlying them both—and to imagine individual social scientists as rational members of a self-controlled association, which we call the social sciences."[38] Intellectuals, in Mills's account, should be less concerned with helping to implement specific reforms and more concerned with cultural provocation.[39] For this reason, Mills pinned many of his political hopes on adult-education programs, which could transform select members of the public into a politically engaged, broadly cultured citizenry.[40] Late in his life, he also found cause for hope in the emergence of the New Left—a political movement of young professionals disaffected from the welfare state's bureaucratic rationalism.

Mills thus exemplifies the extent to which new-class fantasy was at once a response to the knowledge elite's newfound prominence in U.S. society and a reflection of that elite's ongoing powerlessness. The problem with the post–New Deal welfare state, Mills argued, was not its reliance on increasingly complex bodies of knowledge. Indeed, throughout the 1950s, Mills criticized the Eisenhower administration's disconnection from humanistic and scientific learning. "Knowledge and power are not truly united in the ruling circles," he complained, "and when men of knowledge do come to a point of contact with the circles of powerful men, they come not as peers but as hired men."[41] In contrast, he nostalgically evoked a period in American history when knowledge, power, and taste were conjoined in the governing elite: "Once upon a time, at the beginning of the United States, men of affairs were also men of culture. . . . George Washington in 1783 read Voltaire's 'Letters' and Locke's 'On Human Understanding'; Eisenhower, two hundred years later, reads cowboy tales and detective stories."[42] Because of this call for knowledge to be synthesized with power, Mills sometimes echoed the classic, progressive demand for strong government, guided by expert knowledge and capable of realizing the public will in the face of dominant private interests.[43] For Mills, however, the existing welfare state represented the calcification of professional reason into rationalistic expertise. The post–New Deal welfare state was the creation of the new class, was utterly dependent on its services, and rewarded it accordingly. However, it also transformed knowledge workers into cogs in the bureaucratic social machine, which had been co-opted by the power elite. Rather than reviving the eighteenth-century ideal of cultured statesman intellectuals, the welfare state represented the degeneration of mind into routine. For this reason, the critical intellectual's goal was not to extend the reform efforts of the New Deal era. Rather, it was to reenliven the new class's critical imagination.

NEW-CLASS FICTIONS

Chapter 1 of this study explores the New Critics' role in professionalizing literary studies in the 1930s and 1940s, but the rest of the book focuses on novelists who variously grappled with the growing prominence of the new class in U.S. society. This choice of focus is motivated by the fact that the novel is an intrinsically sociological genre, one historically linked to the emergence of bourgeois society and adept at exploring its class divisions. The choice is also motivated by the fact that postwar writers inaugurated a new kind of novelistic aesthetic, one specifically oriented toward representing the pervasive cultural influence of the new class. This aesthetic was chiefly the invention of novelists associated with the New York intellectuals, the group of anti-Stalinist writers and critics clustered around little magazines such as the *Partisan Review*, *Commentary*, and *Dissent*. Critics have often maligned this generation of writers; as Robert Seguin notes, they occupied a transitional period in U.S. literary history, positioned "unfavorably between the great interwar period on the one hand and the exuberant meta-fictional and multicultural bounty of the postmodern era on the other."[44] The New York intellectuals who once dominated the literary field now seem an insular group who dismissed most of the literary innovations that would come to fruition in the 1960s.[45] However, I argue that novelists associated with the New York intellectuals established a distinctive late-modernist aesthetic that adumbrated crucial shifts taking place in the political consciousness of U.S. intellectuals. Indeed, the very insularity of some of their work marked an important change in the class and institutional dynamics of postwar fiction—an emerging sense of the growing prominence of the new class and of writers and other intellectuals' absorption into its institutions. In the fictions of figures such as Ralph Ellison, Mary McCarthy, and Saul Bellow, ideas and the intellectuals who create them move into the center of novelistic representation. All of these writers envisaged their novels as records of conflicts taking place within the cultural center, and they imagined these conflicts as having epochal significance for the rest of U.S. society. Moreover, they bequeathed this belief to the next generation of New Left–inspired and postmodern writers—represented in this study by Marge Piercy and Ursula K. Le Guin's political science fiction and by Don DeLillo's *White Noise*.

This new aesthetic first emerged in the 1930s in the form of a series of literary debates about the respective strengths and weaknesses of 1920s modernism and Depression-era naturalism. As Terry Cooney documents, these debates unfolded within the Communist Party and pitted William Phillips and Philip Rahv, the two cofounders of the *Partisan Review*, against party stalwarts such as Mike Gold and Granville Hicks.[46] Reacting against the socialist realism of the Third International, Phillips and Rahv complained that party critics promoted fiction that was naively mimetic and ideologically doctrinaire. This tendency, they argued, was the product of the critics' "mechanical materialism," which assumes "a direct line between economic base and ideology, and in this way distorts and vulgarizes the complexity of human nature, the motives of action, and their expression in thought."[47] In contrast to these critics, Phillips and Rahv called for radical writers to cultivate a properly dialectical understanding of the relationship between superstructure and base.[48] They envisaged a different kind of radical fiction—one that would synthesize the radical political consciousness of the 1930s with the modernist innovations of the 1920s.[49] This fiction would no longer function as a mouthpiece for party dogma; rather, it would act as an experimental laboratory in which radical ideas could be elaborated and tested. At stake in this debate was the question of literary intellectuals' place within the radical movement. For Hicks and Gold, they should remain in the rear, faithfully depicting social conditions and voicing party policy. For Phillips and Rahv, they should be the vanguard. Citing Lenin, Phillips and Rahv argued that the literary intellectual "marches ahead of the spontaneous movement, points out the real road, and when he is able, ahead of all others, [solves] all the theoretical, political and tactical questions which the 'material elements' of the movement spontaneously encounter. It is necessary to be critical of [the movement], to point out its dangers and defects and to aspire to *elevate* spontaneity to consciousness."[50]

This emphasis on the social function of autonomous intellectuals became central to the alternative aesthetic that New York intellectuals such as Phillips and Rahv began to promote in the late 1930s after their break with the Communist Party.[51] The two editors outlined this new aesthetic in "Literature in a Political Decade" (1937), an essay that they published in the interim between their departure from the party and the relaunch of their journal as an organ for anti-Stalinist literary and social thought. Surveying leftist literature of the 1930s, they argued that it consistently neglected the key role of intellect in U.S. society: "What novelist," they asked, "has created authentic intellectuals embodying the contradictions of conversion, escape, defeat (or, for that matter, any of the attitudes of writers like Anderson, Hemingway, or Dos Passos)? . . . In fact, it has not yet been given to our literature to objectify its reality in terms of its highest expression—the mind." This problem, they suggested, was not merely restricted to the socially conscious literature of the 1930s. Rather, taking aim at the American jingoism of the Popular Front, they argued that it encompassed the entire American tradition. Even the lost generation's modernism "was no more than a cultural veneer glossing the old village furniture" and shared the same "anti-intellectual bias" as the later proletarian novel.[52] Phillips and Rahv thus outlined the attitudes that would guide many of the writers associated with the *Partisan Review* in the 1940s and 1950s. Serious writers should abandon the lower-class subjects of Depression-era novels such as *Studs Lonigan, As I Lay Dying, The Grapes of Wrath*, and *Native Son*. They should instead focus on the expanding educated middle class and on the cultural impact of intellectual work. As Saul Bellow later explained, looking back on the literary debates of the late 1930s, "it seemed to me at a certain point we had gone as far in America as stupidity would get us. We were living in a very sophisticated society— on the technological side, extremely sophisticated—surrounded by all sorts of curious inventions and writers still insisted on sitting on the curb and playing poker and talking about whores."[53]

This changed novelistic focus presaged a shift in U.S. writers and critics' relationship to the new class. As Thomas Strychacz, Louis Menand, Mark McGurl, and others have shown, U.S. writers in the period between 1890 and 1940 were already immersed in the culture of professionalism that was reshaping U.S. society.[54] This was particularly true of the modernists, whose literary innovations the New York intellectuals sought to preserve in the 1930s. As McGurl argues, modernism was "reflective of the notion, associated with professionalism, that there might be pleasure *in* work and, specifically, in the particular kind of intellectual work that reading the difficult modernist text is said to require."[55] However, there was a disjunction between modernist fiction's formal difficulty, which paralleled the technical idiom of many professions, and its representational content. This disjunction gave rise to what McGurl, following William Empson, refers to as modernist fiction's "pastoral structure."[56] Modernists used complex techniques to depict low subject matter and lower-class subjects, a strategy developed in Gertrude Stein's *Three Lives* (1907) and brought to perfection in William Faulkner's *The Sound and the Fury* (1929). This disjunction, McGurl argues, was the product of modernist novelists' dialectical effort to mark off their social distance from the bourgeois middle class while also establishing themselves as an exclusive literary elite.

In the fiction of the New York intellectuals and other postwar writers, this complex class dynamic begins to unravel. With the ab-

sorption of literary intellectuals into new-class institutions such as
the university, writers found it increasingly difficult to imagine
themselves as embattled elitists. They conversely found it easier to
imagine themselves as members of a broadly cultured middle class
educated at the postsecondary level. As Andrew Hoberek remarks,
the postwar institutionalization of literary labor "blurred intellectuals' traditionally antagonistic relationship with the middle-class
mainstream in two ways: by transforming intellectuals into white-
collar employees, and by transforming the rest of the middle-class
into the higher-educated mental laborers that Riesman calls 'demi-
intellectuals.'"[57] This changed sense of class identity was captured
by the *Partisan Review*'s "Our Country and Our Culture" symposium,
which provoked Trilling's vision of schoolteachers and social workers embracing the sensibility and attitudes of literary culture. Philip
Rahv, in his response, outlined the class dimension of writers' assimilation into the U.S. mainstream: "Writers and artists have suc-
ceeded in breaking down the scholastic barriers that kept them out
of university-teaching, and many economists and sociologists have
made their way into government bureaus. . . . We are witnessing a
process that might well be described as that of the *embourgeoisment* of
the American intelligentsia."[58] Among writers associated with the
New York intellectuals, this *embourgeoisment* tended to erase the pastoral structure of previous modernist work. On the one hand, writers such as Ralph Ellison, Mary McCarthy, and Saul Bellow cultivated
a relatively accessible version of the modernist art novel, toning down
many of its formal innovations. On the other hand, they moved
away from the low subject matter characteristic of both the modernists and the Depression-era naturalists, instead exploring the centrality of intellectuals and intellection within postwar society.[59]

This aesthetic shift can be glimpsed in the complex strategies
that one of the most celebrated fictions of the 1950s—Saul Bellow's
The Adventures of Augie March—adopts in order to differentiate itself
from both the modernist art novel and 1930s proletarian fiction. At
first glance, the novel encompasses the "low" subject matter of the

modernist art novel; largely set in the Depression, *Augie March* tells the story of a second-generation Jewish American who grows up in Chicago's immigrant slums, raised by his impoverished single mother in a squalid tenement flat. However, the novel gestures toward modernist pastoralism only in order to collapse its class dynamic. Hence, early in the novel Augie acquires a fire-charred copy of the complete set of *Harvard Classics*, thus beginning the liberal education that allows him to pepper his first-person narrative with learned allusions. Augie becomes a figure who bridges the art novel's class divide between complex narration and simple subject. According to Hoberek's reading of the novel, this synthesis exemplifies postwar writers' desire to bypass the cultural institutions of the welfare state: "*Augie March* is, on one level, a fantasy about acquiring the cultural capital necessary for upward mobility while bypassing the putatively deindividualizing institutions responsible for disseminating it."[60] However, the novel is equally a fantasy about the pervasive cultural impact of these institutions. Harvard president Charles Eliot's educational artifact penetrates the ghetto, reshaping it in the image of university culture. Augie's autodidacticism, in other words, dramatizes the persistent authority of humanistic cultural capital.

Augie March similarly encompasses and negates the 1930s naturalist novel. In particular, much of the novel seems like an homage to the naturalism of James Farrell, whose *Studs Lonigan* (1932–1935) trilogy similarly focuses on a second-generation youth who grows up in Chicago's working-class, ethnic neighborhoods. As Carla Cappetti demonstrates in her book *Writing Chicago*, Farrell's trilogy, like many Chicago fictions, draws on a complex form of social determinism influenced by the Chicago School of Sociology, the dominant sociological paradigm of the 1920s and early 1930s. Midway through *The Young Manhood of Studs Lonigan* (1934), Farrell's Irish American protagonist attends a lecture by John Connolly, "King of the Soap Boxers," at Chicago's Bug Club. Connolly explains the basics of Robert Park and Ernest Burgess's theory of urban development in an effort to tame

the racial violence that Studs and other delinquents have been perpetuating against African American migrants to the neighborhood:

> When the city expanded, it expanded from the center. In Chi-
> cago, the expansion spread out from the Loop. The inner circle
> pushed outwards causing corresponding changes in the concen-
> tric circles. The Negroes coming into the situation as an eco-
> nomically inferior race, had naturally found their habitation
> in the second circle. Since they had located in the slums of the
> black belt, the city had been growing into a bigger and better
> Chicago. The pressure of growth was forcing them into newer
> areas. . . . All these factors produced a pressure stronger than
> individual wills and resulted in a minor racial migration of
> Negroes into the residential districts of the south side. Blather
> couldn't halt the process. Neither could violence or race riots. It
> was an inevitable outgrowth of social and economic forces.[61]

Connolly thus articulates the sociological determinism that Trilling
and other New York intellectuals distrusted in the 1930s. His theory emphasizes the ecological conditions that push immigrant groups
into conflict with each other. Not surprisingly, the speech has little
effect on Studs and his friends, who leave the club reflecting that
Connolly is a "real guy" but go on to terrorize a local black merchant.[62]
They demonstrate that they too are products of "social and economic
forces" and cannot be changed by the "mere blather" of professional
reformers.

Augie March begins by seemingly recapitulating this deterministic
worldview. "All the influences were lined up waiting for me," Augie
reflects. "I was born, and there they were to form me, which is why I
tell you more of them than of myself."[63] This emphasis on Augie's
passivity has led critics such as Donald Pizer to place *Augie March*
within the naturalist tradition. The novel, he argues, "explores with
considerable complexity and depth the naturalistic absorption in the
precarious balance between the conditioning forces of life and man's

desire and need to discover centers of value and affirmation despite the presence of these forces."[64] However, the conditioning forces that affect Augie are not those that affect Studs—the shaping influence of his urban environment and of broad historical trends such as the Great Depression. Rather, the novel goes out of its way to upend conventional historical narratives, to emphasize the ways in which Augie does not fit into a collective history determined by economic changes. For instance, Augie's family is destitute in the booming 1920s but thrives in the 1930s when Augie's brother Simon marries the daughter of a local coal magnate. This is the same era that ruins Studs's father and hastens Studs to an early death. Similarly, Augie is less weighted down by urban ecology than is Studs; he does not remain trapped in his Chicago neighborhood but rather becomes increasingly detached from it, moving in ever-widening circles that connect him to the full panoply of American social classes.

The forces that shape Augie instead originate from the dominating ideas and personalities of those around him. In serial fashion, various charismatic figures literally or figuratively try to adopt him; they want to remake him in their image and impress their personal philosophy on him. In each case, Augie plays along but ultimately resists. "You've got *opposition* in you," one of his would-be mentors tells him. "You don't slide through everything. You just make it look so."[65] This process of resistance culminates in a vision of social reality's being entirely mediated by such mentors and their competing ideas. After a breakup with Thea Fenchel, a wealthy heiress who takes on Augie as a lover but fails to remake him according to her Nietzschean philosophy, Augie muses about humanity:

> It's made up of these inventors or artists, millions and millions of them, each in his own way trying to recruit other people to play a supporting role and sustain him in his make-believe. The great chiefs and leaders recruit the greatest number, and that's what their power is. There's one image that gets out in front to lead the rest and can impose its claim to being genuine with

more force than others, or one voice enlarged to thunder is heard above the others. Then a huge invention, which is the invention maybe of the world itself, and of nature, becomes the actual world—with cities, factories, public buildings, railroads, armies, dams, prisoners, and movies—becomes the actuality. That's the struggle of humanity, to recruit others to your version of what's real. Then even the flowers and the moss on the stones become the moss and the flowers of a version.[66]

If Farrell's world is one in which there are sociological forces that cannot be deflected by "mere blather," then Augie's is nothing but blather. Bellow thus grants an unlimited if loosely defined authority to intellectuals, who play the largest role in inventing and fighting to dominate this ever-shifting medium.[67] Meanwhile, Augie, like most of Bellow's later protagonists, emerges as the ultimate new-class cultural hero, a latter-day member of Arnold's saving remnant. He definitively affiliates with no person or party. Instead, he immerses himself in the Western literary tradition and achieves a knowledge of complexity and difficulty that allows him to resist the ideas that others continually impose on him. *Augie March* thus culminates in the protagonist's achievement of a mystical understanding of a wordless state beyond ideology that is akin to John Laskell's aesthetic apprehension of the rose in *The Middle of the Journey*. "I have a feeling," Augie explains, "about the axial lines of life, with respect to which you must be straight or else your existence is merely clownery, hiding tragedy." These axial lines are an ancient source of wisdom, "older than the Euphrates, older than the Ganges,"[68] which allow human beings to slough off the noise and distraction of their culture.

As in the case of Trilling's criticism, the transition here is not between Farrell's sociological fiction and Bellow's antisociological fiction. Rather, the transition is between two different sociological visions—between Park and Burgess's environmental determinism, on the one hand, and Parsons and Shils's sociology of the cultural center, on the other. In Bellow's case, this shift entailed an explicit choice between two sets of mentors. As an undergraduate, he took courses with Louis Wirth, a Chicago school sociologist who wrote extensively about Jewish American ghettos and recapitulated Park and Burgess's model of urban development.[69] As a mature writer, Bellow was a friend and colleague to Edward Shils, who helped him acquire his tenured position at the University of Chicago's Committee on Social Thought.[70] Bellow's subsequent fiction and nonfiction, which focused on the pervasive impact of intellectual ideas on U.S. society, sometimes recapitulated Shils's basic metaphors and concepts. "What is at the center now?" Bellow asked in his acceptance speech for the 1976 Nobel Prize. "At the moment, neither art nor science but mankind determining, in confusion and obscurity, whether it will endure or go under."[71] By the 1970s, as I argue in chapter 4, Bellow had cultivated a distrust of intellectuals' will-to-power that was akin to the distrust felt by neoconservatives such as Irving Kristol. Nevertheless, his own goal was to reconquer the cultural center, using it to reeducate the American public: "If writers do not come again into the center, it will not be because the center is pre-empted. It is not. They are free to enter. If they so wish."[72] As the chapters in this volume show, this new sociological vision enabled a different kind of postwar fiction—a realism of the cultural apparatus, focused on the fluid medium of ideas and values that Augie evokes in his vision of the reality inventors. It was a realism that mirrored the self-conception of humanistic intellectuals at a key moment in their history and that dramatized both the exaggerated scope and the practical limitations of their political ambitions.

realism
of the
cultural
apparatus

NEW-CLASS FANTASY

In 1979, leftist sociologist Alvin Gouldner published the definitive statement of new-class fantasy. Written as a manifesto in imitation of Karl Marx, *The Future of Intellectuals and the Rise of the New Class* predicted that the new class would become the ruling elite in every industrialized nation. Echoing Trilling's "Our Country and Our Culture" response, published twenty-five years earlier, Gouldner based this prediction on university-based intellectuals' cultural influence on the rest of the new class. The professional stratum, Gouldner argued, was divided into two groups: humanistic intellectuals (including teachers, ministers, social workers, historians, and qualitative sociologists such as himself) and the technical intelligentsia (including practical scientists, engineers, and other technological specialists). The former's interests are "primarily critical, emancipatory, hermeneutic and hence often political." The latter's interests are technical and concerned with improving the means of production. Gouldner imagined, however, that the two groups are united by their joint dependence on the academy and the culture of critical discourse that it fosters. This culture, the institutionalized inheritance of Enlightenment and romantic philosophy, "forbids reliance upon the speaker's person, authority, or status in society to justify his claims. As a result, [the culture of critical discourse] de-authorizes all speech grounded in traditional societal authority."[73] This discourse is intrinsic to the technical intelligentsia's expertise and guarantees that it articulates universalist claims at odds with the capital-owning bourgeoisie. The new class's challenge to the old class depends on the culture of the university, which humanistic intellectuals disseminate beyond its walls in order to reshape the corporate workplace.

Gouldner's manifesto reflects many of the fundamental, salutary changes that the new class helped bring about: changes in gender relations, environmental consciousness, vocational patterns, and child-rearing practices. At the same time, it reads today like one of the worst failed prophecies of the late twentieth century; Gouldner's chief example of the senescence of traditional capitalism is the failure of Ronald Reagan, the representative of the "most politically backward and less educated sections of the old class,"[74] to win the 1976 presidential nomination for the Republican Party. As the events of the 1980s showed, however, the old class was alive and well. It found a powerful voice within the new Right and the rejuvenated Republican

Party, which eradicated many of the reformist measures of the 1970s and 1980s and reaffirmed the centrality of economic capital in U.S. social life. Rather than becoming a ruling elite, large swaths of the new class became proletarianized through phenomena such as corporate downsizing and the proliferation of part-time work. Like the traditional working class, they became a vast, expendable workforce with little job security.[75] Much of this class also abandoned the social trustee ideology that motivated professionals in the early twentieth century. As Brint argues, they instead embraced a newer ideology of expert professionalism, which rejected the social trustee's emphasis on disinterested public service and instead reimagined technical expertise as a salable commodity: "From a sociological perspective, expertise is now a resource sold to bidders in the market for skilled labor. It is no longer a resource that requires an extensive sphere of occupational judgment about purposes."[76]

By the 1980s and 1990s, it seemed obvious that the culture of the university did not pose a fundamental threat to the economic capital of the old class. Rather than humanizing the corporate welfare state, the university became increasingly corporatized, developing closer ties to industry than ever before.[77] At the same time, this private-sector partnership and the concomitant shift to corporate-style management within the university did not infringe on the kind of critical discourse produced by humanistic intellectuals. Within the literary academy in particular, the 1980s and 1990s were a golden age for various kinds of post-Marxist and postmodernist critiques. These radicalized versions of the culture of critical discourse had little impact on the expert professionalism of the technical intelligentsia. Instead, they became specialized discourses perversely adapted to their corporate milieus. As Bill Readings explains in *The University in Ruins*, with the globalization of capital and the concomitant weakening of the nation-state, the stakes of new-class cultural politics have become increasingly negligible. Cultural critique is threatening only when it confronts a robust national culture and challenges the institutions and ideologies by which it is reproduced. "The global system of capital," however, "no longer requires a cultural content in terms of which to interpellate and manage subjects."[78] Gouldner's text comes near the end of the period discussed in the chapters that follow, and it highlights the blind spots shared by many new-class fantasists throughout this period. He exaggerated humanistic intellectuals' ability to influence the technical segments of the professional-managerial class, and he overlooked the ongoing subordination of new-class expertise to traditional economic capital. Throughout the post–World War II period, humanistic intellectuals remained, in Pierre Bourdieu's terms, "a dominated segment of the dominant class,"[79] with all of the anxieties and illusions that stem from that condition. *Fantasies of the New Class* traces the origins and eventual denouement of these anxieties and illusions as writers and sociologists struggled to come to terms with their expanded influence yet ongoing marginality within the new class.

1

THE REPUBLIC OF LETTERS

THE NEW CRITICISM, HARVARD SOCIOLOGY, AND THE IDEA OF THE UNIVERSITY

n the 1930s, two disciplinary paradigms emerged that cannily prefigured the institutional requirements of the post–World War II university and expanding new class: the New Criticism developed by southern poet-critics such as John Crowe Ransom, Cleanth Brooks, Robert Penn Warren, and Allen Tate and the structural functionalism spearheaded by Harvard sociologist Talcott Parsons.[1] Both of these paradigms helped transform their disciplines into erudite yet teachable bodies of knowledge, in ways that seemed tailor made for the mass influx of students that took place in the 1940s and 1950s. In the case of the New Critics, this transformation was facilitated by their promotion of close reading as the discipline's primary interpretive method. John Guillory and Gerald Graff, in their disciplinary histories of English literature, describe the apparently contradictory demands that the New Critics' espousal of close reading fulfilled. On the one hand, Guillory states, it allowed the New Critics to reimagine literary language as an advanced form of cultural capital, one that imparted to texts "a certain kind of *rarity*, the very difficulty of apprehending them."[2] On the other hand, according to Graff, close reading's bracketing of social context seemed "ideally suited to a new, mass student body that could not be depended on to bring to the university any common cultural background."[3] Parsons's structural functionalism fulfilled similar demands. His chief accomplishment was to develop a highly technical theoretical vocabulary, one that lent a veneer of scientificity to the discipline that it had hitherto lacked. At the same time, Parsons's purpose was to thoroughly systematize his discipline in ways that made it more amenable to presentation in postsecondary textbooks.[4]

However, in spite of these pedagogical parallels, the two paradigms seemingly embodied different models of professionalization. In general, as Guillory argues, the humanities and social sciences underwent a process of definition by mutual exclusion in the 1940s and 1950s as each marked off its respective proximity to the hard sciences: "First, the social sciences were led to discard interpretation as much as possible from their methodological repertoire. And second, the humanities came to be identified as the disciplines whose only method was interpretation."[5] For the first generation of U.S. New Critics, who began their careers as Agrarian ideologues opposed to the industrialization of the South, literature was the only remaining counterweight to the triumph of technical rationality within the welfare state. Their cultivation of close reading was in part an effort to isolate this anti-instrumental dimension of literature, to shelter it from the technocratic pretensions of the new class. Hence, the New Critics rejected any approach to literary studies that seemed social scientific. Literary historicism, Allen Tate complained in 1941, "takes its definite place in the positivistic movement which, from my point of view, has been clearing the way for the slave state."[6] If the New Critics tried to make literary studies less sociological, Parsons conversely tried to make sociology less literary. His work represented the apogee of his discipline's technocratic ambitions. He pushed sociology away from the interpretive tendencies of earlier paradigms such as the Chicago school and tried to refashion it as an objective science. The New Criticism and structural functionalism, in other words, pulled their disciplines to opposite poles of the professional spectrum. In Alvin Gouldner's terms, the New Critics cultivated a purist image of themselves as traditional, humanistic intellectuals; sociologists reenvisaged themselves as potential members of the technical intelligentsia.

As I argue in this chapter, the separation of literary studies and sociology that took place under the aegis of New Criticism and structural functionalism masked underlying affinities between the two disciplines' attitude toward the new class that critics and sociologists hoped to train within their classrooms. Both paradigms involved similar deformations of the social trustee ideology that pervaded the professional stratum in the early twentieth century. As we saw in the introduction, this ideology encompassed both technical and moral claims; the social trustee professional was a technically qualified expert dedicated to the public good. Both the New Criticism and structural functionalism attempted to synthesize these claims. The New Criticism was indeed rooted in an overt hostility toward the technocratic tendencies of the sciences and social sciences. However, the effect of the New Critics' work was to reshape literary studies in imitation of these disciplines; the method of close reading, as John Crowe Ransom argued in "Criticism, Inc." (1937),[7] was supposed to make criticism more scientific—that is, more predictable and rigorous. Close reading became the discipline's specialized techne, its claim to professional identity, and the New Critics linked this techne to the imagined moral effects of literature in modern society. Parsons's structural functionalism similarly tried to push sociology closer to the natural sciences by excluding interpretation and fashioning a new technical vocabulary for the discipline. At the same time, his conception of the sociologist's function was essentially humanistic and

31

cleaved to the lineaments of the social trustee ideology. At the heart of Parsons's byzantine theoretical edifice was the notion that social systems are held together by noninstrumental moral values that once originated from the pulpit but today come from the universities. The purpose of sociologists and other welfare-state professionals is to maintain and reproduce these values, which ensure the homeostasis of the social system.

Both paradigms thus exemplify the fracturing of social trustee ideology that took place within the post–World War II academy. In Gouldner's scenario, the university was supposed to be the site where the disciplines would come together to perpetuate a common culture of critical discourse, thereby forging a meritocratic new class that would displace the old bourgeoisie as society's intelligent and moral elite. Among other things, this scenario did not take into account the logic of specialization, which tended to atomize the new class rather than binding it together into a coherent social stratum. As Barbara Ehrenreich and John Ehrenreich argue, "specialization was the [professional-managerial class] member's chief selling point, the quality which justified his or her claim to a unique niche in society, but it acted as a centrifugal force on the class as a whole."[8] In literary studies and academic sociology, this atomization went beyond differences in technique; the social trustee synthesis of techne and morality gave rise to discipline-specific and mutually antagonistic fantasies of cultural education. These fantasies eroded social trustee professionalism's pragmatic impetus, instead narrowly orienting it toward disciplinary self-perpetuation.

THE UNITED STATES AS UNIVERSITY

The differentiation of sociology and literary studies that began in the mid-1930s is particularly striking given that the two disciplines often overlapped in the United States in the early decades of the twentieth century. Before the emergence of the New Criticism and structural functionalism, many sociologists incorporated the methods and assumptions of writers into their work and vice versa. In particular, as Carla Cappetti documents, a rich cross-fertilization of sociology and literature took place in Chicago in the 1920s and 1930s. The dominant sociological paradigm in the United States at this time was the Chicago School of Sociology, generally remembered for its empirical studies of Chicago's ethnic neighborhoods and subcultures. This school relied on qualitative methods, especially ethnographic techniques borrowed from the Boasian tradition in anthropology. According to Cappetti, the Chicago school also borrowed from late-nineteenth- and early-twentieth-century literary naturalism—especially the work of urban writers such as Émile Zola and Theodore Dreiser; this debt was particularly evident in the sociologists' style, which relied on rich description to convey a phenomenal sense of Chicago's communities. The Chicago sociologists in turn influenced the generation of naturalists that emerged in the 1930s—James Farrell, Nelson Algren, and Richard Wright. Hence, as we have seen, novels such as Farrell's *Studs Lonigan* directly incorporated Chicago urban sociology as an explanatory framework. By the late 1930s, says Cappetti, Chicago sociology and literary naturalism were converging toward a common writing practice: "on the one hand the tendency toward a more subjective sociology, a sociology that rediscovered the subjectivity of the individual as a social and cultural being; on the other the tendency toward a more objective literature, a literature that rediscovered the individual's unbreachable ties with the larger cultural and social spheres."[9] This literature also explored the progressive notion that societal problems can be alleviated through broad organizational changes. Wright's *Native Son* (1940), for instance, concludes with Boris Max's vision of the worldwide Communist movement working to demolish the decrepit buildings that crippled Bigger Thomas's development. Similarly, in *The Young Manhood of Studs Lonigan* (1934), the bookish Danny O'Neill finds respite from the environmental forces that destroy Studs and other neighborhood youth by reading Thorstein Veblen's *The Theory of Business Enterprise* (1904) and envisioning "a better world, a cleaner world, a world such as that the Russians were attempting to achieve."[10]

Within sociology, the backlash against this disciplinary conjunction took the form of some sociologists' rejection of the Chicago school. In part, this rejection was regional. Eastern sociologists chafed against the midwestern dominance of their field: Chicago sociologists at this time dominated both the discipline's major professional association (the American Sociological Society, later renamed the American Sociological Association) and its premier journal (the *American Sociological Review*).[11] However, the backlash was primarily against the Chicago school's ostensibly unprofessional tendencies; its sociology seemed too qualitative, too amateurish, and too unscientific. These deficiencies were particularly galling because sociology seemed poised on the brink of becoming a discipline that would be centrally involved in government administration and industrial management; the reaction against the Chicago school thus roughly coincided with the rise of industrial sociology and the increased use of social scientists in the New Deal.[12] In the place of the Chicago school, Talcott Parsons gradually emerged as the discipline's major theorist. He established his institutional base at Harvard University, where he was the leading voice within the influential Department of Social Relations, an interdisciplinary program that brought together sociologists, social psychologists, and cultural anthropologists.[13] By the 1950s, a plurality of sociologists worked within a structural functionalist framework derived from Parsons's second major book, *The Social System* (1951), and from articles written by students such as Robert Merton.[14]

Parsons exemplified sociologists' desire to establish their discipline on a firmer methodological footing by purging from it the literary influences of Chicago sociology. This ambition was announced in his first book, *The Structure of Social Action* (1937),[15] an attempt to create a grand synthesis of preexisting sociological theory through detailed readings of Alfred Marshall, Vilfredo Pareto, Émile Durkheim, and Max Weber. The program announced by the book was the antithesis of everything represented by the Chicago school. The Chicago school sociologists focused on qualitative investigation, sometimes to the detriment of theory. Perhaps because of the influence of Chicago pragmatists such as John Dewey and George Herbert Mead, they treated sociological concepts as tools to be picked up or discarded, depending on the tool's utility for a given project. This pragmatic attitude toward theory can be seen in Robert Park and Ernest Burgess's *Introduction to the Science of Sociology* (1921),[16] which was supposed to be the school's basic theoretical text. In fact, it was a compendium of lengthy excerpts from other nineteenth- and early-twentieth-century social theorists, tied together by the two editors' introductions and conclusions to each chapter.

Parsons's goal, in contrast, was to reemphasize the priority of general theory in sociology. For Parsons, the problem with American sociology was that it was no more than a series of discrete analyses, devoid of any theoretical framework or consistent methodology. Sociology in the hands of the Chicago school had degenerated into an unprofessional and prescientific exercise in observing and recording the social world. Parsons described his alternative methodological position as one of "analytical realism." As opposed to the Chicago school's qualitative empiricism, Parsons argued that theory should come first: "scientific 'theory'—most generally defined as a body of logically interrelated 'general concepts' of empirical reference—is not only a dependent but an independent variable in the development of science. It goes without saying that a theory to be sound must fit the facts but it does not follow that the facts alone, discovered independently of theory, determine what the theory is to be, nor that theory is not a factor in determining what facts will be discovered, what is to be the direction of interest of scientific investigation."[17] For this reason, Parsons's work operated at a greater level of abstraction than that of any previous sociologist; in book after book, he developed an ever more elaborate conceptual apparatus intended to categorize and systematize all possible sociological knowledge.

Even more important in terms of the effect on his discipline, Parsons reinvented the language of sociology. Most members of the

Chicago school had written in a nontechnical style, enriched with lengthy quotations from subjects and evocations of Chicago neighborhoods. This style had been a virtual necessity given the Chicago sociologists' use of participant-observation methods, and it was one of the aspects of their work that so appealed to 1930s naturalists such as Farrell and Wright. Parsons, in contrast, invented a convoluted, technical vocabulary, which many of his students referred to as "Parsonese." It was a style intended to give the reader a sense of the abstract, technical level at which Parsons's sociology functioned. It was distinctly unliterary, and it made few concessions to the lay reader. C. Wright Mills, in *The Sociological Imagination* (1959), cited the following passage from *The Social System* to reveal the stylistic depths to which his discipline had sunk under Parsons: "'A role then is a sector of the total orientation system of an individual actor which is organized about expectations in relation to a particular interaction context, that is integrated with a particular set of value-standards which govern interaction with one or more alters in the appropriate complementary roles. These alters need not be a defined group of individuals, but can involve any alter if and when he comes into a particular complementary interaction relationship with ego which involves a reciprocity of expectations with reference to common standards of value-orientation.'"[18] This style privileged conceptual difficulty for its own sake, and it lent a veneer of professional and scientific dignity to a discipline struggling to defend its position in relation to the hard sciences.

However, as we have seen, if Parsons wanted to professionalize his discipline by liberating it from the literary tendencies of the Chicago school, he also wanted to claim for his discipline the moral concerns typically associated with the humanities. Beginning with *The Structure of Social Action*, he initiated a polemic against the positivistic–utilitarian tradition in the social sciences. This polemic prefigured Trilling's argument against literary naturalism and progressive criticism in *The Liberal Imagination*; Parsons imagined culture, the world of ideas, as a distinct sphere irreducible to economic determination.

Hence, the central effort of *The Structure of Social Action* was to show that Parsons's four theorists—Marshall, Pareto, Durkheim, and Weber—had initiated a paradigm shift in the social sciences away from economic models of social action. Society, all four theorists imagined, exists insofar as all individuals within it are guided by a "common system of value attitudes."[19] These values are fundamentally nonrational, meaning that they cannot be contained within a means–end calculus of the kind imagined by utilitarian thinkers. In Parsons's later social systems theory or structural functionalism, which departed from his early action theory in important ways, he maintained this emphasis on the determining role of culture. At the heart of his later theory, with its description of systems within systems within systems, was the idea that every society has a central cultural system, consisting of its nonrational values and traditions. The purpose of a modern society's social institutions (schools, hospitals, courts of law, and so on) is to integrate these values into the psyche of every individual and to recondition therapeutically anyone who goes astray. This process ensures the *equilibrium* or *homeostasis* of the social system—two of the key terms of Parsons's critical vocabulary.

Throughout his work, Parsons combined this cultural determinism with a new-class fantasy about professionals' function in U.S. society.[20] As Howard Brick documents, in Parsons's sociology of the 1930s he envisaged social reform as a question of cultural education. In claiming that each society depends on a nonrational value consensus, Parsons believed that he had discovered the focus of all future reform efforts. "Since 'political' measures," Brick claims, "depended for their efficacy on a preexisting moral bond secured in social institutions, the real locus of reform lay not in the state but in civil society."[21] This early emphasis on cultural education gave Parsons's early work its reformist edge; he believed that professionals should push back against the profit-oriented, traditional bourgeoisie. Professionals, who were the group in society most attuned to disinterested social ideals, should reshape America's value consensus. Brick argues that over the course of the 1940s and 1950s Parsons became increasingly sanguine about this cultural impact. He believed that professionals were already displacing the old bourgeoisie as America's hegemonic elite and that this displacement was an inevitable feature of the welfare state: "where once Parsons called for critical analysis of the economic order, he now declared the virtual supersession of capitalism as a social system."[22] Professionals do not need to do anything to influence policy or reshape public attitudes; the new-class revolution was quietly taking place anyway.

One of the distinguishing features of this vision of professionals' cultural influence was that it blurred the distinction between humanistic intellectuals and the technical intelligentsia. Echoing Émile Durkheim, Parsons viewed all professionals as agents of socialization, secular priests who shape and incite belief in society's core values.[23] Parsons argued, for instance, that physical illness is not merely a bodily dysfunction but also a form of social deviance that places strain on the social system. Doctors do not merely cure patients; they manage and discipline the sick role, ensuring that patients conform to cultural expectations about sickness and recovery.[24] In addition, Parsons also claimed that humanistic intellectuals' distinctive mode of self-governance was spreading throughout American society, gradually transforming it into an ideal social system. He conceived of professionalism as a mediating term between two of the central concepts of sociological theory—gemeinschaft and gesellschaft. Gemeinschaft, or traditional community, is collectivist and immediate, bound together by face-to-face contacts. Gesellschaft, or modern society, is individualistic and abstract, bound by contractual relations and therefore prone to anomie. The professions combine the best elements of both. In Parsons's terms, they are societal communities—organic villages of experts sprouting up within the impersonal, bureaucratic state. Parsons's preeminent example of this type of association is the academic department: "the collegial pattern is today perhaps most fully institutionalized in the academic world, which contrary to what many have argued, is not giving way to bureaucratization, even though higher education has recently undergone unprecedented expansion.

The basic equality of 'colleagues' in a faculty or department is in particularly sharp and persistent contrast with bureaucratic hierarchy."[25] According to Parsons, this type of organization was spreading throughout the United States as more citizens received a higher education and flooded the marketplace. Academia stood at the center of what he called an educational revolution, akin to the industrial and democratic revolutions of previous centuries. This revolution was in the process of transforming the United States into a massive societal community of free professionals. Even in business, "organizations have become more associational, for it is essential to secure the cooperation of specialists without asserting sheer authority. Much of modern 'bureaucracy' thus verges on the collegial pattern."[26] Prefiguring Gouldner's vision of new-class unity, Parsons imagined that the technical intelligentsia, trained by humanistic intellectuals in the academy, would reform both government and the modern corporation in its image. America was becoming a university.[27]

Parsons's sociology, then, eschewed the literary methodology and discursive style of the Chicago school, treating it as a disciplinary outside that threatened sociology's professional identity; the discipline's essential technique had to be kept pure of anything that seemed like an amateurish import from a humanistic discipline. At the same time, Parsons recuperated many of the concerns of literary intellectuals and other humanists by claiming nonrational moral consensus as the central object of sociological study. This social trustee synthesis of antiliterary technique and humanistic morality was crucial to Parsons's conception of the role of sociologists and other professionals in the welfare state, and it explained the basic conservatism and fantasy element of his position. Parsons's sociology, which New Left sociologists of the late 1960s attacked as a typical example of establishment thinking, was in fact rooted in liberal ideals. He hoped for a greater distribution of educational advantages, greater inclusion of African Americans in the U.S. "societal community," a concerted professional effort to eliminate poverty, and so forth. The problem with these social ideals was that they were rarely coupled with any pragmatic program for their implementation; he assumed his ideals were already embodied in the practice of professionalism and need only await the progress of time to spread throughout the rest of society. Professionals, in other words, are not active reformers; by safeguarding and reproducing their society's already existing central values, they ensure the continuity and homeostasis of the social system.

However, what is most striking about Parsons's project is the extent to which his new-class fantasy contradicted the actual effects his work had on his discipline. According to Parsons's theory, society's central moral values radiate out from the professions to the rest of the social system, but the effect of Parsons's own project was to help transform sociology into an insular discipline disconnected from public discourse. This effect stemmed directly from his methodological rejection of sociology's literary tendencies—in particular, the Chicago school's readable, nontechnical style. Ironically, the sociologists of the 1950s and 1960s who best fulfilled Parsons's new-class fantasy were those who most vehemently rejected his methods—maverick sociologists who cultivated an accessible style and wrote for a nondisciplinary audience, such as C. Wright Mills.

FROM THE OLD SOUTH TO THE ACADEMY OF LETTERS

While most American sociologists after the mid-1930s were trying to distance themselves from the literary-minded Chicago school, American literary critics were involved in a dialectical interplay with their own disciplinary other—the social sciences. The New Critics in particular responded to the same pressures of professionalization as Parsons and created a disciplinary synthesis of technique and morality that became a potent force in the post–World War II academy. For sociology in the United States, the eschewal of literary methods marked the changing of the guard between the University of Chicago and Harvard. With the New Critics, the influence of disciplinary specialization is directly traceable in the dramatic alteration of their theory over the course of the 1930s and 1940s. In the early 1930s, most of the New Critics were political Agrarians chiefly interested in protecting the South from industrialism; by the 1940s, they were formalist aesthetes interested in disseminating the apolitical practice of close reading throughout the academy.

This transition has been the focus of several studies of New Critical professionalization—in particular, Guillory's *Cultural Capital* and Graff's *Professing Literature*. Both studies highlight the essential continuity between the Agrarians' early political ideals and New Critical formalism; hence, Graff argues that "New Critics like Ransom did not think they were turning their backs on the moral and social function of literature. For them, rather, the point was to define these social and moral functions as they operated within the internal structure of literary works themselves."[28] Guillory similarly shows how the Agrarians' interest in social *doxa*—a preconscious commonality of belief that the Agrarians thought was embodied in traditional communities—became translated into their later formalist criticism as an essential quality of literature. Graff and Guillory's identification of this larger continuity underlying agrarianism and New Critical professionalism provides a useful corrective to most accounts of the New Critics' depoliticization.[29] However, it overlooks an important discontinuity in the Agrarians and New Critics' relation to disciplinary specialization, exemplified by their changing attitudes toward the sciences and social sciences. Both the Agrarians and the New Critics engaged in frequent polemics against these technical professions, which they viewed as harbingers of atheist rationalism and technocratic industrialism. However, the Agrarians viewed the sciences and social sciences as cultural rather than disciplinary threats; these disciplines embodied the foreign culture of the North. Resisting them meant becoming aware of one's identity as a southerner; it entailed no particular vigilance toward one's own disciplinary practices. Indeed, many of the Agrarians' early essays exemplify the same intermingling of disciplinary practices that the Chicago school engaged in. Much of this work was not literary criticism at all, but amateur sociology; it dabbled in economics, anthropology, and history to theorize the difference between rural communities and industrial society. This sociological bent changed with the emergence of New Critical professionalism. The New Critics increasingly saw the academy rather than the region as the critic's primary object of identification; in Antonio Gramsci's terms, they came to imagine themselves as an independent class of traditional intellectuals rather than as organic intellectuals intimately connected to the South. It was now the discipline that needed to be defended from outsiders, and this defense could occur only through a process of professionalization—namely, by inventing and disseminating specialized reading techniques that could compete with the technical disciplines. The New Critics thus came to imagine themselves as dissident members of the national new class they had once shunned—members with a special access to aesthetic sensibility and moral values unavailable to the other disciplines. This changed awareness seeped into their work over the course of the 1930s—in particular into the work of John Crowe Ransom, the U.S. New Critics' mentor and chief theorist.

Agrarianism, from the beginning, was a movement of traditional intellectuals; most of the writers and critics associated with it never strayed far from the academy. It got its start at Vanderbilt University in the early 1920s, when Cleanth Brooks, Robert Penn Warren, and Allen Tate were undergraduate students of Ransom. With the exception of Brooks, they were members of a campus-based poetry group called the Fugitives, part of the southern literary renaissance.[30] These poets-critics turned from literature to conservative cultural criticism in the mid-1920s, inspired in part by the "Scopes monkey trial" of 1925. This widely publicized trial of John Scopes, a Tennessee high school teacher charged with teaching evolution against state law, pitted Clarence Darrow, the noted agnostic lawyer, against William Jennings Bryan, the onetime Democratic presidential candidate and representative of Christian fundamentalism. Like the northern reporters who descended en masse on Dayton, Tennessee, to witness the trial, the Agrarians viewed it as an epochal conflict between religious traditionalism and scientific rationalism, only they were on the traditionalists' side. They began to write polemics on behalf of their region, which culminated in the publication of a collection titled *I'll Take My Stand* (1930). This book, the Agrarians' manifesto, condemned the effect of industrialism on the economy, folkways, and racial hierarchy of the Old South.[31]

In this early work, the Agrarians replayed the conflict at the heart of the Scopes trial between scientific and traditional ways of understanding the world. Ransom's first book, published at the same time as *I'll Take My Stand*, was *God Without Thunder* (1930), a philosophical defense of religious fundamentalism that exemplified his early, interdisciplinary approach. In it, he complained that the sciences and social sciences efface the full complexity of lived experience, what he called the "world's body"; "when our thinking is scientific or conceptual, we fail to observe the particular objects as particulars, or as objects which are different, and contain a great many features not at all covered by the given concept. We attend only to what is constant or like among them, or to what has repetition-value."[32] This aesthetic failure, for Ransom, has consequences that are cultural, economic, and moral. Science leads directly to industrialism, which physically manifests the urge to reduce all phenomena to sameness. On the cultural front, industrialism effaces the differences between local regions, dissolving all folk cultures into a universal mass society that is everywhere the same. On the economic front, it treats nature as a resource to be exploited, robbing human beings of their ability to appreciate aesthetically the environment in which they live. On the moral front, it distorts the relations between human beings, leading them to treat each other as means to selfish ends. In this last regard, social science is particularly dangerous because it tries to turn human beings into objects of research and control.

Ransom's solution was to defend traditions and conventions, which place limits on the rapacious energies and conceptual tyranny of industrialism and the sciences. His argument was based on an elaborate series of homologies between poetry, religion, social custom, and economics. Poetry, for instance, relies on the conventional devices of meter, rhyme, and poetic style. These devices introduce linguistic texture into the poem—local variations of meaning that prevent the poem from ever making a direct statement of fact. Poetry, in other words, incorporates a kind of surface complexity that forces the reader to pay attention to the language itself and thus disrupts any illusion of linguistic transparency. However, this distancing enables a new aesthetic appreciation of the lived experience that the poem gestures toward but can never comprehend; Ransom thus developed the paradox that in order to get closer to reality, we need poetic conventions that distance us from it. Social conventions work the same way. A community's ingrained traditions, rituals, and beliefs place limits on social interaction and thus distance the citizen from a crude, materialist relationship to other people.[33] With regard to economics, Ransom similarly argued that agrarian communities are limited systems that open men and women to a more complex, aesthetic appreciation of nature by restricting their relations with it. Ransom's nativist example, from "The Aesthetic of Regionalism" (1934), is a New Mexican Indian pueblo that the critic glimpses through a train window on a journey across the United States. Observing the Indians' threshing with primitive tools, Ransom commented that it "'feels' right, it has aesthetic quality."[34] Once labor becomes conventional, it loses its character as mere work and turns into folk art, liberating the peasant's aesthetic faculties. Moreover, it lends to the society as a whole an aesthetic unity derived from that society's adaptation to its local environment. The agrarian lifestyle, Ransom explained in the introduction to *I'll Take My Stand*, is "not an abstract system, but a culture, the whole way in which we live, act, think, and feel. It is a kind of imaginatively balanced life lived out in a definite social tradition."[35] Ransom's agrarianism culminates in a nostalgic and sociological vision of a perfectly integrated community, which forms the basis for his regionalist version of identity politics.

The Agrarians, then, were distrustful of modern forms of technique, which were destructive of the ontologically richer knowledge embodied in poetry and traditional communities. The opposition the Agrarians constructed was between the humanistic intellectual as traditional craftsman, akin to Ransom's Pueblo Indians, and the technical intelligentsia as mass producer. This notion of humanist as craftsman was connected to the Agrarians' strong sense of regional identity; both the poet and the peasant experience lived particularity by subjecting themselves to their local customs and environment. Already in this early work, however, we can see inklings of the New Critical notion of academic professionalism, which entailed the Agrarians abandoning their early regionalism, reconciling themselves to their position within the new class, and focusing on the cultivation of a pure or intrinsic theory of literary language. They could not become like the Pueblo Indians from Ransom's nativist fantasy, working the land with crude implements. Embedded in the modern university, they were more like Ransom's narrator, watching the vanishing agrarian past through the windows of an industrial-era train as he makes his way to another conference. The proper site for critics was not the Old South but rather the modern academy, a shelter from industrial society in which they could recollect a lost cultural innocence.

This awareness was already implicit in "The Aesthetic of Regionalism," in which Ransom invoked an elaborate architectural analogy to explain the difference between industrialism and regionalism. Industrialism, Ransom argued, produces a debased form of architecture that reflects its effacement of regional particularities. Ransom's example is the state capitol at Baton Rouge. The building accurately represents the "power and opulence" of the state of Louisiana. However, when the state planned the building, it "took its bag and went shopping in the biggest market; it came back with New York artists, French and Italian marbles, African mahogany, Vesuvian lava for the paving." Regional motifs appear only "in some bas-reliefs and statues, and in the alligators, pelicans, magnolias, sugar canes, and cat-tails worked in bronze in the gates and door-panels."[36] In an industrial society, the regional environment no longer determines all aspects of local culture. Rather, the region becomes merely ornamental, etched onto a characterless economic market that is global in scope.[37] Ransom's contrasting example of regional architecture perfectly adapted to its environment is the building in which he first read "The Aesthetic of Regionalism" as a lecture—one of the new buildings at Louisiana State University:

> The old buildings still stand, or at least the "Barracks" do, in the heart of the city; the others had to go, since the city needed their room, and the University, with four thousand students, needed still more room and larger buildings. The old buildings are simple, genuine, and moving; precisely the sort of thing that would make a European town famous among the tourists. When the much larger plant of the new university was constructed it seems probable that buildings on the order of the Barracks but on the new scale would not have been economical, nor successful; therefore the builders conceived a harmonious plan for the campus in a modified Spanish, and it suits the regional landscape, and is not altogether foreign to the regional history.[38]

Unlike the state capitol, the university successfully embodies its region; however, it does so by compromising with the industrial economy that devoured the old campus. The architects' new plan is not a rejection of the city's modernization. Rather, it is an attempt to complement it aesthetically, already an attenuation of Ransom's regionalist ideal. The architecture of Louisiana State University is no more indigenous to Baton Rouge than the architecture of the state capitol is. The buildings to which Ransom refers were designed by a Massachusetts firm in an Italian style in imitation of Stanford University.[39] If they signify anything, it is not the local region but rather the history of the research university in the United States.

This identification of regionalism with the university prefigured Ransom's abandonment of agrarianism. In letters and essays after "The Aesthetic of Regionalism," he increasingly imagined that the academy rather than any particular region is the critic's primary community. In a 1936 letter to Allen Tate, he confessed, "patriotism has nearly eaten me up, and I've got to get out of it." As an alternative to agrarianism, Ransom proposed the development of an "American Academy of Letters," devoted to securing "an objective literary standard" in the United States.[40] This proposal was perhaps an allusion to Samuel Taylor Coleridge's solution to the British Industrial Revolution—the creation of a "Clerisy" or national church devoted to the cultivation of British culture.[41] The Academy of Letters would be a new cosmopolitan community, no longer rooted in region. It would be a community of diverse writers held together by their professional interest in literature. After listing about thirty qualified and almost qualified names (including his own and Tate's), Ransom explained, "[A]n Academy has got to be pretty catholic; a lot of them will necessarily be strange bedfellows. If too many alien persons seem to go into any nationalist list, our only alternative would be a Southern Academy."[42] Ransom's academy thus seems to be the literary equivalent of the state capitol in Baton Rouge—a hodgepodge of writers and critics ranging from Theodore Dreiser to Marianne Moore. Shortly after writing this letter, Ransom put his new eclecticism into practice. He abandoned his regional roots in Tennessee and moved to Kenyon College in Ohio. His primary accomplishment there, editorship of the *Kenyon Review*, approximated his Academy of Letters. One of the reasons this journal was so influential was its inclusiveness; it published nonsouthern critics such as Lionel Trilling, Irving Howe, and Leslie Fiedler. As Ransom explained to Tate in a 1937 letter, his purpose in establishing the journal was to avoid partisan politics altogether; "it seems to me our cue would be to stick to literature entirely. There's no decent consistent group writing politics. . . . In the severe field of letters there's vocation enough for us: in criticism, in poetry, in fiction."[43]

This turn from the Old South to the cosmopolitan academy was the context for Ransom's effort to transform his theory of poetry and method of close reading into a new disciplinary paradigm capable of imitating the rigor and consistency of the sciences and social sciences. "Criticism must become more scientific," he argued in his aptly titled "Criticism, Inc.," "or precise and systematic, and this means that it must be developed by the collective and sustained efforts of learned persons—which means that its proper seat is in the universities." Criticism will never become a very exact science, "but neither will psychology, if that term continues to refer to psychic rather than physical phenomena; nor will sociology."[44] Ransom's basic conception of literature, at this point in the late 1930s, had not changed. Poetry still embodies an ontologically distinct type of knowledge, one that aims at recovering the particularity of lived experience; "We live in a world," he argued in "Wanted: An Ontological Critic" (1941), "that must be distinguished from the world, or the worlds, for there are many of them, which we treat in our scientific discourses. They are its reduced, emasculated, and docile versions. Poetry intends to recover the denser and more refractory original world which we know loosely through our perceptions and memories."[45] However, in his later work, he abandoned the notion that this original world can be recovered by nonprofessionals, such as his Pueblo Indians. Rather, the ontological experience of poetry can be recovered only by the professional critic working within the academy and only through the scientific technique of close reading, whose exactitude enables it to trace the "desperate ontological or metaphysical maneuver" by which poetry evades the conceptual drive of scientific thought.[46]

Ransom's animus against the sciences and industrialism also shifted. He became reconciled to the existence of an industrial economy and thus to the existence of the technical intelligentsia; "without consenting to a division of labor," he argued in a 1945 essay that disavowed his former politics, "and hence modern society, we should have not only no effective science, invention, and scholarship, but

nothing to speak of in art, e.g., *reviews* and contributions to *reviews,*
fine poems and their exegesis." Poetry and criticism, he concluded,
at best constitute "beautiful expiations" for the horrors of industrialism.[47] Instead, his diatribes against scientific rationality began to
focus on threats internal to his discipline. Graff has reconstructed
the debates into which the New Critics inserted themselves in the
mid-1930s. In his account, the discipline at this time was divided
between two groups—literary historians and generalist critics. The
historians embodied the discipline's technique, which consisted of
positivist research into biographical and textual facts. The general-
ists, among whom the New Critics once ranked, embodied its traditional moral concerns. Literary studies, in other words, replicated
within itself Gouldner's distinction between technical intelligentsia
and humanistic intellectuals. The New Critics' accomplishment was
to present both of these groups as insufficiently professional and to
synthesize their competing claims; both the scholars and the critics
neglected the aesthetic dimension proper to poetry itself. For Ransom, these disciplinary others replaced the northern industrialists
and carpetbaggers of his early essays; they threatened the identity of
literary studies in the same way that industrialism, he once believed,
threatened the South. They threatened to dissolve literary criticism's
boundaries, fusing it into the other disciplines, especially the social
sciences.[48] Literary studies could preserve its distinctive disciplinary culture only if it embraced close reading as its new tradition or
custom.

Indeed, in his later work Ransom used much the same language
to describe his new cosmopolitan, literary communities as he had earlier used in his Agrarian polemics. In a late essay, "The Communities of Letters" (1952), written at the height of the New Criticism's
influence in the academy, he imagined that works of art create alternative communities of critics within industrial society: "there comes
into existence among readers, clustered of course round the presid-
ing genius of the author, a community of a sort which could scarcely

have been contemplated in the formal organization of society, a community of letters based on a common sympathy." Because there are many authors, there are also many reader communities, each one akin to "one of those minority cultural groups which have their rights in a free society as surely as individuals do."[49] These communities parallel Ransom and other Agrarians' proposal in *I'll Take My Stand* that the South join together with other regional cultures and minority groups to combat industrialism. In Ransom's later work, however, the reader communities are no longer opposed to industrial society. Rather, they together form another society within society: "if in some rude sense we add all the communities up, we will have, in theory at least, a total community having a peculiar role. It may be regarded as a secondary society, branching off from the formal or primary society, and easing its requirements, compelling its members to approach to the sense of a common humanity."[50] Ransom envisaged the academy as a republic of letters, bound together by the professional activities of a national clerisy consisting of himself and other critics and sheltering the society's common morality from the effects of industrialization.

Ransom's project of disciplinary professionalization, like Parsons's, ends in a fantasy of the academic department as an ideal community. These two fantasies, however, differ in their imagined effects on the broader public. For Parsons, the academic department is a harbinger of a liberal revolution in industrial society, one that will transform society into a perfected form of the modern welfare state. Parsons's model is an evolutionary one; it requires students to leave the academy and transform business and government in its image. In his university, students are trained to become wise and humane professionals ready to take over key positions in society at large. Ransom, in contrast, envisaged the "communities of letters" as retreats from industrial society; the critic escapes into the academy to keep aesthetic experience alive in a society hostile toward it. However, both fantasies involve similar mutations of social trustee professionalism. Both appropriate the social trustee emphasis on technical expertise and its argument that the professional is the caretaker of public morality. But both undercut the essential assumption of the social trustee—the idea that disciplinary knowledge can or should be used to reform society actively in accordance with that morality. Instead, professionalism becomes reflexively oriented toward the self-perpetuation of the discipline itself, which becomes increasingly isolated from other disciplines and from the public it is supposed to educate and reform. Both structural functionalism and the New Criticism exemplify the ways in which professionalism's moral claims became fastened to a process of institutional routinization that often voided those claims of specific content.

The disciplinary consensuses represented by Parsons's sociology and the New Criticism lasted until the mid-1960s, when the next generation of intellectuals rebelled against them in the name of a more politicized sociology and literary studies. These rebellions culminated in the American Sociological Association and Modern Language Association conferences of 1968, each of which was disrupted by a "Radical Caucus" of younger professors and graduate students with ties to the New Left. They also culminated in the publication of a variety of texts that challenged the disciplinary status quo. In sociology, for instance, Gouldner's *The Future of Intellectuals* replaced Parsons's notion of the university as guarantor of social cohesion with Gouldner's own notion of the university as the center of the disruptive culture of critical discourse. Literary critics similarly abandoned the New Critics' fideism, instead emphasizing literature's deconstructive impact on established constructions of social reality. In many ways, these internal rebellions were efforts to revive and radicalize the moral function of professional work and to reconnect with a broader public. As Louis Kampf and Paul Lauter argued in *The Politics of Literature* (1972), one of the texts that emerged from the 1968 Modern Language Association disruption, "our classroom objective is to make literature a vital part of students' lives, rather than an antiquarian or formal study or a means of forcing them into feelings of 'cultural deprivation.' "[51]

The effects of these paradigm shifts on each discipline's politics and imagined relation to the new class cannot be overestimated. In the long term, however, literary critics and sociologists became increasingly skeptical about whether their disciplines did indeed play any useful role in U.S. society or whether they had merely replaced one set of disciplinary fantasies with another. By the 1990s, these doubts had generated an extensive literature in each field. Donald Levine, for instance, describes "a reduction in public deference shown to the social science enterprise, following a period in the 1950s to early 1960s when virtually all branches of the U.S. federal government—from the Supreme Court to Congress to many executive departments—made unprecedented use of social scientists in such areas as the fight against segregation, analysis of foreign elites, international economic development, and domestic antipoverty programs." The backlash against the social sciences, he continues, originated in the sense that their techniques had failed; "the demand for solutions to social problems far exceeded the capacity of the social sciences to deliver them. There grew a sense that the social sciences have not been and do not seem likely to produce the kinds of results their earlier proponents anticipated."[52] Literary critics similarly questioned the continued viability of their discipline in the face of the emergence of expert professionalism and the growing prominence of the technical intelligentsia. As Guillory argues in *Cultural Capital*, there was a "large scale 'capital flight' in the domain of culture"[53] away from the humanities. This capital flight made the political commitments of literary intellectuals seem increasingly unreal.

As the following chapters show, John Crowe Ransom and Talcott Parsons's work prefigured a broad range of cultural education projects that took root throughout the 1950s and 1960s. These projects stemmed from writers and sociologists' idealized sense of their civilizing mission at a historical moment when both the new class and the university seemed to be at the height of their influence within the U.S. welfare state. New-class fantasy pervaded debates about race relations, welfare reform, and foreign policy in ways that shaped the literary aesthetics and sociological imagination of the post–World War II era.

2

"LIFE UPON THE HORNS OF THE WHITE MAN'S DILEMMA"

RALPH ELLISON, GUNNAR MYRDAL, AND THE PROJECT OF NATIONAL THERAPY

In his 1944 review of Gunnar Myrdal's *An American Dilemma* (1944), Ralph Ellison initiated a lifelong polemic against the sociology of race.[1] He took issue with Myrdal's claim that black culture and psychology can be viewed as pathological by-products of white racism. "Can a people," he asked, "live and develop for over three hundred years simply by *reacting*? Are American Negroes simply the creation of white men, or have they at least helped to create themselves out of what they found around them? Men have made a way of life in caves and upon cliffs; why cannot Negroes have made a life upon the horns of the white man's dilemma?" (*CE*, 339, italics in original). The review established the framework for much of Ellison's subsequent aesthetic. Echoing New York intellectuals such as Lionel Trilling, Ellison rejected simplistic forms of environmental determinism.[2] In particular, he criticized the impact of sociology on naturalistic representations of race—including those found in the work of his friend and mentor Richard Wright. He instead developed an aesthetic that focused on the complexities of psychology and culture that transcend environmental causes. As he explained in a 1965 interview, responding to recent sociological surveys of the black ghetto, "there is something else in Harlem, something subjective, willful and complexly and compellingly human. It is that 'something else' that challenges the sociologists who ignore it, and the society which would deny its existence. It is that 'something else' which makes for our strength, endurance and promise. This is the proper subject for the Negro American writer" (CE, 731). This antinaturalist aesthetic was one that Ellison realized in *Invisible Man* (1952),[3] probably the most successful novel of the immediate post–World War II period.

However, Ellison's relationship to the sociology of race was more complex than his explicit arguments against it would suggest. As Kenneth Warren points out, Ellison sometimes reiterated the central claims of the damage theorists whose work he derided; to do otherwise would be to echo white segregationists who claimed that blacks were best off in their place. "Ellison," Warren writes, "was seeking a dynamic, even dialectical account of the Negro that would acknowledge the history of racial repression but not characterize black people as merely prisoners of a repressive environment."[4] Andrew Hoberek similarly highlights the extent to which Ellison echoed a version of postwar sociology concerned with issues of class rather than with issues of race—the white-collar sociology of figures such as David Riesman, C. Wright Mills, and William H. Whyte Jr. "Ellison's adoption of the organization-man narrative," he argues, "allows him to transcend the 'sociological vision of society' . . . even as it itself ironically reproduces another sociological vision."[5] More fundamentally, as I argue in this chapter, Ellison's work was congruent with changes taking place within the sociology of race itself. During the 1940s and 1950s, as we have seen, consensus sociologists such as Talcott Parsons were eschewing simplistic forms of social determinism in order to focus on questions of psychology and culture. The same shift was occurring in the sociology of race largely due to the influence of *An American Dilemma*, the text that prompted Ellison's critique of white sociology. Although Myrdal's study offered a conventionally pathological portrait of black Americans, it also pushed sociologists to consider the cultural context and psychological intricacies of racial prejudice. The race problem, Myrdal argued, was the result of a struggle "in the heart of the American"[6] between two conflicting value systems: the egalitarian American Creed and various racist prejudices. Myrdal believed that through the efforts of intellectuals such as himself, Americans would become aware of this conflict. In particular, he found hope in the expansion of U.S. higher education, which would disseminate universalist belief systems such as the American Creed to a broader audience. *An American Dilemma* thus helped establish the postwar liberal consensus on racial politics; the race problem was the product of prejudice, to be solved through educational programs aimed at reconditioning the racist psyche rather than through economic programs aimed at redistributing wealth to the black community. Far from eschewing this model of U.S. race relations, Ellison refashioned it into his central trope of black invisibility, which became the basis for his novel *Invisible Man*. He also adopted Myrdal's therapeutic solution; the black novelist's task, he argued, was to diagnose the collective neurosis generated by the clash between ideals and prejudice within the American psyche.

Both *An American Dilemma* and *Invisible Man* thus exemplify the turn toward cultural education that, I have argued, was central to the evolving intellectual politics and literary aesthetics of the 1940s and 1950s. Myrdal and Ellison envisaged sociologists and black writers, respectively, as members of a new-class saving remnant capable of refashioning the American psyche. However, both texts also exemplify the strains generated by this effort to extend new-class fantasy to American race relations. Myrdal and Ellison, in spite of their focus on educational solutions to the race problem, could not help but reflect the ways in which racial prejudices are shaped by a complex interplay between cultural attitudes and economic interests. In particular, this tension between Arnoldian cultural politics and economic insight is central to *Invisible Man*. The novel traces its protagonist's transformation from a would-be black professional into an autonomous, humanistic intellectual capable of giving voice to the American Creed. However, the novel also explores the cynical opportunism bred by black professionals' economic dependence on various kinds of white patronage, an opportunism that mirrors that of the new class as a whole. Ellison's emphasis on the pervasiveness of this attitude calls into question the possibility that education projects of the kind that he envisages in his nonfiction can find much purchase within the expanded, educated middle class. *Invisible Man* thus undermines one of the central premises of new-class fantasy—the idea that humanistic cultural capital, which supposedly gives rise to nonpecuniary value systems such as the American Creed, can transcend the new class's own economic interests.

INVISIBILITY AND THE AMERICAN DILEMMA

Ellison's review of *An American Dilemma* marked a crucial turning point in his intellectual development. In Michel Fabre's terms, the text registered a shift in his basic interests "away from the narrowly political and economic toward the cultural."[7] Before writing the essay, Ellison was known in New York circles as Richard Wright's protégé and chief exegete. In this role, Ellison defended the sociological aesthetic that culminated in books such as *Native Son* (1940) and *Black Boy* (1945).[8] Too many critics, he remarked in a review of the latter book, complained that Wright "omitted the development of his own sensibility" and presented "too little of what they consider attractive in Negro life." "Whatever else the environment contained," Ellison noted, " it had as little chance of prevailing against the overwhelming weight of the child's unpleasant experiences as Beethoven's quartets would have of destroying the stench of a Nazi prison" (*CE*, 133). As Warren notes, Ellison thus anticipated some of the more extreme claims of later damage theorists such as Stanley Elkins.[9] Over the course of the late 1940s and 1950s, Ellison gradually distanced himself from this position; instead, he attacked Wright using almost the same terms that he had earlier attributed to his critics. Ellison found it "disturbing," he explained in 1961, "that Bigger Thomas had none of the finer qualities of Richard Wright, none of the imagination, none of the sense of poetry, none of the gaiety" (*CE*, 74).

Ellison partially adumbrated this new position in his Myrdal review, which simultaneously looked forward to his mature aesthetic and backward to his 1930s commitments. On the one hand, the text laid out the antinaturalistic perspective that would dominate Ellison's later work; it criticized in Myrdal many of the qualities that Ellison admired in texts such as *Black Boy*. Myrdal's determinist view of black psychology, he complained, "demonstrates how many Negro personality traits, said to be 'innate,' are socially conditioned, even to types of Negro laughter and vocal intonation" (*CE*, 339). Echoing Joyce's Stephen Dedalus, Ellison instead called for black writers to create "the uncreated consciousness of their race" through a critical appropriation of black culture: "Much of black culture might be negative, but there is also much of great value and richness, which, because it has been secreted by living and has made their lives more meaningful, Negroes will not willingly disregard" (*CE*, 340). On the other hand, as Barbara Foley notes, the essay was largely contiguous with Ellison's earlier proletarian journalism.[10] Indeed, parts of it echo contemporaneous Communist polemics against Myrdal's work, such as Herbert Aptheker's *The Negro People in America* (1946).[11] Hence, if the essay argued that *An American Dilemma* was too deterministic in relation to black culture, it also argued that the text was not determinist enough in relation to white prejudice. In thinking of racism as a psychological conflict in the minds of whites, Myrdal neglected "the economic motivation of anti-Negro prejudice which to an increasing number of Negro intellectuals correctly analyzes their situation"

(CE, 337). What was needed was not just a change in white racist attitudes but rather, first and foremost, a "change of the basis of society" (CE, 340).

This contradictory stance was in part a response to the complications of *An American Dilemma* itself—a massive, one-thousand-page document put together over several years by a team of social scientists working under the direction of Swedish economist Gunnar Myrdal.[12] The text's main tendency was to challenge Marxist and liberal positions on U.S. racism, which diagnosed the causes of race discrimination as essentially economic.[13] For Myrdal, in contrast, the race problem was the result of a complex interplay between economic and psychological factors; the underlying mechanism of U.S. racism was a "principle of dynamic causation," whereby "white prejudice and discrimination keep the Negro low in standards of living, health, education, manners and morals. This, in its turn, gives support to white prejudice. White prejudice and Negro standards thus mutually 'cause' one another."[14] Overlooking this dynamic interaction, Myrdal argued, led Marxists and liberals to develop oversimplified solutions to the race problem. Marxists believed that African Americans' best ally was the white working class, thus downplaying the irrational prejudices that are sometimes most intense among members of this class. Liberals similarly believed that racism would be overcome through the gradual improvement of economic conditions among African Americans. Myrdal, in contrast, argued that any solution to the race problem must intervene at all points in racism's vicious cycle, at once ameliorating conditions for blacks and challenging whites' attitudes. At key points, *An American Dilemma* thus offered a useful corrective to the economic determinism of left-liberal social thought, which paralleled the dialectical understanding of the relationship between superstructure and base articulated by New York intellectuals such as William Phillips and Philip Rahv. This correction dovetailed with Ellison's own efforts to develop a more complex account of U.S. race relations. "In our culture," he argued in his review, "the problem of the irrational, that blind spot in our knowledge of society where Marx cries out for Freud and Freud for Marx, but where approaching, both grow wary and shout insults lest they actually meet, has taken the form of the Negro problem" (CE, 335).

However, although Myrdal tried to synthesize the economic and the psychopathological, this synthesis often fell apart in his specific accounts of black culture and white racism. Hence, in the study's penultimate chapter, Myrdal described black culture as "*distorted development, or a pathological condition, of the general American culture.*" All of the seemingly distinctive aspects of black psychology and culture, from the "emotionalism in the Negro church" to the "provincialism of his political speculation," were symptoms of social pathologies generated by the pressure of living in a racist society.[15] This deterministic account of black social pathology was contiguous with older trends in sociology and influenced the further development of "damage sociology"—the strand of sociology that Ellison criticized throughout his career.[16] Conversely, when Myrdal discussed white prejudice, he tended to downplay the environmental and economic causes of discrimination, instead emphasizing the priority of culture. Myrdal outlined his central thesis as follows:

> The American Negro problem is a problem in the heart of the American. It is there that the interracial tension has its focus. It is there that the decisive struggle goes on. . . . The "American Dilemma," referred to in the title of this book, is the ever-raging conflict between, on the one hand, the valuations preserved on the general plane which we shall call the "American Creed," where the American thinks, talks, and acts under the influence of high national and Christian precepts, and, on the other hand, the valuations of specific planes of individual and group living, where personal and local interest, economic, social, and sexual jealousies; considerations of community prestige and conformity; group prejudices against particular persons or types of people; and all sorts of miscellaneous wants, impulses, and habits dominate his outlook.[17]

Myrdal conceived of the race problem in terms of two competing value systems: the Enlightenment ideals embodied in national rhetoric and the various prejudices rooted in local cultures. This conflict in turn gives rise to a psychopathological conflict within the mind of the individual racist between an egalitarian conscience and a racist id. According to Myrdal, most Americans try to repress this conflict. They do so through the use of rationalizations, stereotypes, and false beliefs; they distort the facts about black experience in order to assuage the American Creed. Through repetition, these false representations eventually become part of social reality itself. Nevertheless, Myrdal argued, at some level even the most racist southern supremacist ultimately believes in the antiracist assumptions of the American Creed.

This theory led Myrdal, in spite of his emphasis on dynamic causality, to privilege educational over structural solutions to the U.S. race problem. Myrdal was more sympathetic to social engineering than were most U.S. sociologists; in the 1930s, he was one of the legislative architects of the Swedish welfare state—the most ambitious European social democracy. In *An American Dilemma*, however, most of his policy recommendations were gradualist; he suggested enfranchising African Americans in stages and slowly desegregating the education system, starting with the graduate schools—both processes already under way in the 1940s. Instead, he cultivated a new-class fantasy of sociologists as national therapists, whose task would be to appeal to the moral authority of the American Creed and tear apart the spurious rationalizations that justify discrimination.[18] He more broadly understood sociologists as engaged in a world-historical process whereby different value systems come into conversation with each other and whittle away the prejudices inherent in each. Value systems, Myrdal argued, come in two varieties. The American Creed is a higher value system, one that has become general, encompassing the nation's many different cultural groups. Its ideals have taken on the character of the Kantian categorical imperative; they have become universalizable. American prejudices, in contrast, are lower valuations—

a chaotic set of local demands rooted in the economic and biological needs of individuals and groups. The conflict between these two types of valuations is a world historical process that will culminate in the universal dissemination of liberal humanism: "The valuations on the higher and more general planes—referring to *all* human beings and *not* to specific small groups—are regularly invoked by one party or the other, simply because they are held in common among all groups in society, and also because of the supreme prestige they are traditionally awarded. By this democratic process of open discussion there is started a tendency which constantly forces a larger and larger part of the valuation sphere into conscious attention. More is made conscious than any single group would on his own initiative find it advantageous to bring forward at a particular moment."[19] Myrdal thus prefigured Gouldner's account of the culture of critical discourse as giving rise to a perfected welfare state. He viewed his own project as a contribution to this process.

It is this model of white prejudice and educational reform that Ellison criticized as insufficiently materialistic in his 1944 review. However, at the same time he also absorbed Myrdal's American Dilemma thesis into his evolving aesthetic, transforming it into his central trope of black invisibility. He began his review as follows: "In our society it is not unusual for a Negro to experience a sensation that he does not exist in the real world at all. He seems, rather, to exist in the nightmarish fantasy of the white American mind as a phantom that the white mind seeks unceasingly, by means both crude and subtle, to lay to rest. Myrdal proves this no idle Negro fantasy. He locates the Negro problem 'in the heart of the [white] American . . . the conflict between his moral valuations on various levels of consciousness and generality'" (CE, 328). This paragraph gets recycled in *Invisible Man* as the narrator's opening lament about his social condition: "you often doubt if you really exist. You wonder whether you aren't simply a phantom in other people's minds. Say, a figure in a nightmare which the sleeper tries with all his strength to destroy" (*IM*, 4). This idea established the basis for Ellison's version of novelistic modernism. In contrast to Richard Wright, he wanted to avoid naturalistic representations of the damaging effects of social environment on the black psyche. Echoing Trilling's "Reality in America," Ellison argued elsewhere that this conception figures social reality as an inert, physical reality; in *Native Son*, "environment is all—and interestingly enough, environment conceived solely in terms of the physical, the non-conscious" (CE, 162). Ellison instead focused on the ways in which black social reality is invisible to whites because of the mediating presence of racist stereotypes; like other postwar writers, he sought to create a higher realism of the cultural apparatus. As he explained, "I would have to approach racial stereotypes as a given fact of the social process and proceed, while gambling with the reader's capacity for fictional truth, to reveal the human complexity which stereotypes are intended to conceal" (CE, 488). The presence of this idea in the Myrdal essay complicates Ellison's later account of the genesis of *Invisible Man*, which he presented as a reaction against sociological representations of American blacks. He arrived at the idea for the novel in 1945 in a moment of inspiration that he described as follows: "one afternoon, when my mind was still bent on its nutty wanderings, my fingers took over and typed what was to become the very first sentence of the present novel, 'I am an invisible man'" (CE, 354). He conceived of the phrase as "a play on words inspired by the then popular sociological formulation which held that black Americans saw dark days because of their 'high visibility'" (CE 355). In fact, Ellison substituted one sociological account of racism for another—a Myrdalian account of racial invisibility for a more traditional account of high visibility.

In essays published after his review of *An American Dilemma*, Ellison thus echoed Myrdal in his efforts to develop the theory of fiction that would pave the way for *Invisible Man*. The black stereotype, Ellison argued in "Twentieth-Century Fiction and the Black Mask of Humanity" (1946), is a "key figure in a magic rite by which the white American seeks to resolve the dilemma arising between his democratic beliefs and certain antidemocratic practices, between his acceptance of the sacred democratic belief that all men are created equal and his treatment of every tenth man as though he were not" (CE, 85).[20] According to Ellison, these stereotypes became central to U.S. fiction during the Jim Crow era, when Americans were trying to forget the failures of Reconstruction. Before this, major nineteenth-century fictions such as *Moby Dick* and *Huckleberry Finn* confronted the conflict between American ideals and practical prejudices in a more open, painful fashion: the "conception of the Negro as a symbol of man," drawn with a full sense of human complexity, "was organic to nineteenth-century fiction" (CE, 88). The Negro stereotype in modern fiction, in contrast, signals American writers' repression of this project; white Americans' inability to resolve the conflict between the American Creed and racist practices compels them "to force the Negro down into the deeper levels of his consciousness, into the inner world, where reason and madness mingle with hope and memory and endlessly give birth to nightmare and dream; down into the province of the psychiatrist and artist, from whence spring the lunatic's fancy and the work of art" (CE, 149). Like all such acts of repression, this one undermines that which it is supposed to protect—a social order ostensibly based on the ideals encoded in the Bill of Rights and the U.S. Constitution. The end result of this erosion of American ideals is the cynical fiction of U.S. modernists such as Ernest Hemingway, whose work "conditions the reader to accept the less-worthy values of society" and "to justify and absolve our sins of social irresponsibility" (CE, 95).

In contrast, Ellison envisaged black novelists as cultural educators and national therapists who would penetrate the black stereotypes that undermine U.S. democratic ideals. Echoing Myrdal's account of the ongoing conversation between value systems, Ellison described American identity as a work in progress, one that was coming into being through a continual conflict between different races and cultures. "Far from being socially undesirable," he argued, "this struggle between Americans as to what the American is to be is part of the democratic process through which the nation works to achieve itself. Out of this conflict the ideal American character—a type truly great enough to possess the greatness of the land, a delicately poised unity of divergencies—is slowly being born" (CE, 83). The privileged terrain of this democratic conflict is the novel itself: "if the ideal of achieving a true political equality eludes us in reality, there is still available that fictional *vision* of an ideal democracy in which the actual combines with the ideal and gives us representations of a state of things in which the highly placed and the lowly, the black and the white, the Northerner and the Southerner, the native born and the immigrant combine to tell us of transcendent truths and possibilities" (CE, 487, italics in original). Ellison thus conceived of black fiction as a crucible within which a new, post–Jim Crow national culture could be fashioned. In his 1953 acceptance speech for the National Book Award, he described *Invisible Man* as an "attempt to return to the mood of personal and moral responsibility for democracy which typified the best of our nineteenth-century fiction" (CE, 151). The novel's unnamed hero narrates the story from within "a building strictly rented to whites, in a section of the basement that was shut off and forgotten during the nineteenth century" (IM, 6). Squatting within the dark recesses of the house of white American fiction, the invisible man brings to light the American Dilemma buried in the work of his contemporaries.

Ellison's conflict with Myrdal had little to do with the former's emphasis on the autonomy of culture versus the latter's economic determinism; both prioritized questions of culture in their respective discussions of race. Indeed, Ellison's understanding of culture tended to be more complexly materialist than Myrdal's and other postwar sociologists'. Ellison sometimes took well-meaning liberals to task for their belief that racism could be eliminated through government-funded education programs or, more forcefully, through legal intervention. Commenting on Howard Zinn's *The Southern Mystique* (1964),[21] Ellison emphasized the intractability of white southern folkways: "while the myths and mysteries that form the Southern mystique are *irrational* and even *primitive*, they are nevertheless real, even as works of the imagination are 'real.' Like all mysteries and their attendant myths, they imply . . . a rite" (*IM*, 575–76, italics in original). Cultures, for Ellison, are materially grounded in customs and rituals; they cannot be reduced to bodiless values and ideas. At times, this position seemed to pull Ellison uncomfortably close to the work of nineteenth-century sociologist William Graham Sumner. For Sumner, whom Myrdal criticized throughout *An American Dilemma*, folkways are largely unconscious, rooted in local practices and customs, ritualistically performed rather than theoretically defined. Sumner thus established the theoretical foundation for both right- and left-wing versions of identity politics, including the Agrarian politics embraced by the early New Critics; he emphasized the extent to which cultural differences determine a people's entire way of being. "Folkways," Sumner wrote, "are not creations of human purpose and wit. They are like products of natural forces which men unconsciously set in operation, or they are like the instinctive ways of animals."[22]

Warren, as we have seen, argues that Ellison evaded the deeply conservative implications of this Sumnerian position by strategically invoking the sociological determinism he elsewhere condemned. However, most of the determinist moments that Warren cites come from early essays influenced by Wright, such as Ellison's review of *Black Boy*. Ellison more frequently called for the cultivation of new rituals and imaginative works that would materially embody and transform white and black experiences without reproducing the shallow interpretation of culture characteristic of postwar sociology. This is the point of Ellison's early short story "In a Strange Country" (1944), about a black sailor beaten by white servicemen while on shore leave in Wales. Rescued by a group of Welshmen, the protagonist attends a concert in which they ritualistically enact their national unity, singing songs that bridge the performers' class divisions. "When we sing, we are Welshmen," one of them claims, explaining how union officials, mine owners, and miners can create harmony together. Later, when the Welshmen launch into a performance of the American national anthem, the protagonist viscerally experiences the sense of unity they describe, in ways that reveal his disturbing coidentity with the white soldiers who earlier attacked him. "It was as though," he reflects, "he had been pushed into the horrible foreboding country of dreams and they were enticing him into some unwilled and degrading act, from which only his failure to remember the words would save him."[23]

Because of this emphasis on the ritual enactment of value systems, Ellison's teleological account of the development of American identity was much more dialectical than Myrdal's. For Myrdal, modernization is a distillation process; local cultures interact with each other in order to give rise to a single, culturally transcendent value system. This value system subsumes and eliminates all of the local cultural variations that give rise to it. Hence, both white southern culture and African American culture are pathological distortions of the more general American culture and are slated for eventual assimilation. For Ellison, in contrast, the local variations persist. As the nation "works to achieve itself," however, these variations acquire what might be called an aesthetic unity, which is perhaps why it can be glimpsed only in performances such as the black novel and the Welshmen's song. Indeed, Ellison's account of American identity as a "delicately poised unity of divergencies" (CE, 83) echoes the most prominent aesthetic theory available to him in the late 1940s—the New Critical definition of poetry. The poem, Cleanth Brooks argued in The Well-Wrought Urn (1947), "unites the like with the unlike. It does not unite them, however, by the simple process of allowing one connotation to cancel out another nor does it reduce the contradictory attitudes to harmony by a process of subtraction. The unity is not a unity of the sort to be achieved by the reduction and simplification appropriate to algebraic formula. It is a positive unity, not a negative; it represents not a residue but an achieved harmony."[24] The chief aesthetic sin for the New Critics is the heresy of paraphrase—the substitution of a prose approximation for the poem itself. Myrdal's model of national development seems, from Ellison's perspective, like a heresy of this sort, a prosaic paraphrase of the evolving national culture that Ellison hoped to delineate in his fiction.

PATHOLOGIES OF THE BLACK PROFESSIONAL

However, the novel that Ellison completed in his lifetime complicates this account of fiction as a textual enactment of an ideal democracy. *Invisible Man* concludes by invoking Myrdal's American Creed. While hiding in his underground cellar, the invisible man affirms "the principle on which the country was built," which Americans "had dreamed into being out of the chaos and darkness of the feudal past, and which they had violated and compromised to the point of absurdity even in their own corrupt minds" (*IM*, 574). This affirmation coincides with the invisible man's transformation into a Trillingesque saving remnant who reveals the complexity and difficulty of American social experience. Through his written narrative, he explores the "beautiful absurdity of their American identity and mine" (*IM*, 559), which the novel's Marxists, black nationalists, and other ideologues neglect. This patriotic affirmation of American pluralism, which adumbrates the major themes of Ellison's nonfiction, has since divided the novel's critics; in particular, literary intellectuals associated with the Black Arts movement in the 1960s defined their version of identity politics against Ellison's universalism.[25] What is most striking about *Invisible Man*'s affirmative conclusion, however, is its almost total disconnection from the narrative that precedes it.[26] The conclusion evokes the humanist idealism that Ellison attributes to nineteenth-century American literature in "Twentieth-Century Fiction and the Black Mask of Humanity." The rest of the narrative, however, explores the hard-boiled cynicism that he associates with Jim Crow–era writers such as Hemingway. This cynicism is summed up by the grandfather's deathbed advice that haunts the invisible man throughout the novel: "I want you to overcome 'em with yeses, undermine 'em with grins, agree 'em to death and destruction, let 'em swoller you till they vomit or bust wide open" (*IM*, 16). Until the last pages, the invisible man interprets this advice as a description of the trickster strategies that enable African Americans to survive in a racist society. As the mad veteran from the Golden Day counsels him, "Play the game, but play it your own way—part of the time at least. Play the game, but raise the ante, my boy. Learn how it operates, learn how *you* operate" (*IM*, 153–54, italics in original). As soon becomes apparent, this cynical ethos pervades all levels of U.S. society. Hence, in a disorienting moment, the invisible man reflects that Rinehart, a Harlem confidence man who seemingly embodies the grandfather's advice, is little different from the respectable white bigots whom the invisible man remembers from his youth: "Hadn't I grown up around gambler-politicians, bootlegger-judges and sheriffs who were burglars; yes, and Klansmen who were preachers and members of humanitarian societies?" (*IM*, 510).

This disconnect between the American Creed and the everyday texture of U.S. social life presents an obvious contrast with Gunnar Myrdal, for whom the creed was firmly grounded in U.S. culture and institutions. In particular, for Myrdal, the continued survival of the American Creed was guaranteed by the fact that it appealed to a particular class stratum: the most educated segments of the professional middle class. Differences in adherence to the American Creed, he argued, "can be observed today within our own society among the different social layers with varying degrees of education and communication with the larger society, stretching all the way from the tradition-bound, inarticulate, quasi-folk societies in backward regions to the intellectuals of the cultural centers."[27] One of the best solutions to the race problem was to produce more educated citizens; relations between African Americans and southern police officers, for instance, could be improved if all officers attended college.[28] Myrdal thus prefigured some of the central ideas of later new-class theorists such as Alvin Gouldner; he imagined that educationally acquired, humanistic cultural capital would allow the new class to break free of the particularistic interests that dominate other classes in U.S. society and fuel racist prejudice. Hence, one of the reasons why Myrdal offered so few policy recommendations is that he believed that structural transformations were already taking place in U.S. society that would bring about the changes he desired. He lauded the "growing intellectualization" of America—the emergence within it of an expanding knowledge elite open to universalist value systems.[29]

For Ellison, in contrast, the educated middle class was the social stratum that most fully embodied the cynical opportunism that threatened to erode the American Creed. *Invisible Man* is, above all else, a middle-class bildungsroman that traces the education and disillusionment of a would-be black professional and that highlights the persistence of particularistic interests within new-class institutions. This dimension of the text is one that Hoberek helpfully illuminates in his reading of the novel's connection to the "organization man" literature of the 1940s and 1950s. *Invisible Man*, he argues, "shares the plot of such popular treatments of white-collar angst as *The Fountainhead* and *The Man in the Gray Flannel Suit*: a man, anxious to find creative and fulfilling mental labor, instead encounters mystified, conformist organizations that threaten to rob him of his individuality, agency, and autonomy."[30] In particular, this connection becomes obvious through the novel's emphasis on role playing, which echoes accounts of white-collar alienation in texts such as David Riesman's *The Lonely Crowd* and C. Wright Mills's *White Collar*. In Mills's terms, "When white-collar people get jobs, they sell not only their time and energy but their personalities as well. They sell by the week or month their smiles and their kindly gestures."[31] As Hoberek points out, *Invisible Man*'s distinctiveness vis-à-vis other organization man narratives lies in its focus on the black bourgeoisie, a class stratum typically relegated to the lowest reaches of the white-collar world or excluded from it altogether. However, this exceptionality in fact transforms *Invisible Man* into a cannier novel about the dynamics of white-collar work than other organization man narratives from the same period. The black bourgeoisie, because of its marginal position, embodies anxieties about white-collar proletarianization that are invisible to the white middle class. As E. Franklin Frazier argued in *Black Bourgeoisie* (1955, France; 1957, United States), the first major sociological study of the black middle class, this stratum's efforts to differentiate itself from other African American classes was typically hampered by its lack of economic capital. This lack gave rise to various kinds of make-believe as members of the black middle class tried to cultivate "status without substance" in an exaggerated parody of white middle-class behavior.[32]

In *Invisible Man*, this economic marginality short-circuits the cultural education project that Ellison outlines in his nonfiction. As represented in the novel, the black professional is a heteronomous being, forced into a psychologically crippling dependence on white patronage and incapable of embodying higher value systems such as the American Creed. Indeed, in spite of Ellison's stated desire to transcend the economic determinism of naturalists such as Richard Wright, his novel relentlessly portrays the ways in which middle-class black psychology is shaped by economic factors. As we have seen, new-class fantasy was often facilitated by the illusion that educationally acquired capital transcends economic capital; this illusion was at the center of Myrdal's cautiously optimistic assessment of the future of U.S. race relations. *Invisible Man*, in contrast, continually punctures this illusion through its focus on the special circumstances of black professionals; the novel is filled with images of educated blacks scrambling for white-owned resources. Moreover, as Hoberek notes, this desperate scramble parallels that of the white middle class. Hence, when the invisible man visits Wall Street after his arrival in Harlem, he identifies with the black couriers chained to briefcases full of their bosses' money. Ellison equates the couriers with black chain-gang prisoners and thus with the race-specific legacy of slavery. However, the couriers' lack of agency is also emblematic of Wall Street as a whole; the streets are "full of hurrying people who walked as though they had been wound up and were directed by some unseen control" (*IM*, 164).

This heteronomy first becomes evident in the battle royal that initiates the invisible man's professional education. In this section, the white businessmen of the invisible man's small southern town invite him to deliver a speech on social responsibility in exchange for a briefcase and a scholarship to Dr. Bledsoe's college—the tokens of new-class identity that he carries with him throughout the novel. Prior to his speech, however, he must participate in a ritualistic, blind-folded boxing match that reinforces the cultural presuppositions of the southern caste system. This ritual pits the invisible man against the lower-class blacks whom he hopes to rise above. "I felt superior to them in my way," the invisible man reflects, "and I didn't like the manner in which we were all crowded together into the servant's elevator" (*IM*, 18). There are nine of these youth, which literally makes the invisible man a member of W. E. B. Du Bois's talented tenth. As the whites make clear, this class distinction is their own creation; the purpose of the invisible man's participation in the battle is to drive home the fact that his hoped-for professional status depends on their patronage. "We mean to do right by you," one of them explains, "but you've got to know your place at all times" (*IM*, 31). The battle royal is replete with reminders of the invisible man's economic dependence, such as the electrocuted fake coins that he collects after the fight.

As a result of this dependence, the professional status that the invisible man seeks has little to do with the egalitarian national con-science that Myrdal associates with it in *An American Dilemma*. Indeed, the cost of the invisible man's entry into this class is his renunciation of the claim for "social equality" that he accidentally sputters out in blood during his speech. This blood drips onto his new briefcase, forming "a shape like an undiscovered continent" (*IM*, 32)—one of many parodic symbols of the American Creed that Ellison associates with the invisible man's career. Instead, the professional mindset that the invisible man cultivates is more like a racialized version of the tyrannical, Freudian superego. Freud, in describing the superego in *The Ego and the Id* (1923), explains that "its relation to the ego is not exhausted by the precept: 'You *ought to be* like this (like your father).'

It also comprises the prohibition: 'You *may not be* like this (like your father)—that is, you may not do all that he does; some things are his prerogative."[33] Black professional identity, for Ellison, embodies the same double bind. Black professionals must try to emulate the whites who fund them but must never become too much like them. They must yearn for the promise of social equality latent in their professional identity but realize that this promise will never be fulfilled. As a result, the would-be black professional is left in the position of the invisible man at the end of the chapter, when a dream reveals the true import of the day's events: "Keep This Nigger-Boy Running" (*IM*, 33). As in the case of Freud's scenario, at the center of this double bind is a sexual taboo; the black professional must not intermarry with whites and interfere with their monopoly over inherited capital and positions of power. The whites reinforce this taboo through their incorporation of the white stripper into the battle royal ritual. The American flag tattooed above her forbidden vagina functions as another parodic symbol of the creed, evoking both desire and terror.

Dr. Bledsoe's college—Ellison's portrait of Tuskegee Institute— similarly promotes a distorted model of professional development due to its dependence on white economic capital. Not coincidentally, the invisible man's account of his experiences at the college focuses on events surrounding one of the annual ceremonies, "the black rite of Horatio Alger" (*IM*, 111), that the school enacts for the white multimillionaires who fund its operations. This ceremony is an institutionalized version of the ritual that the invisible man performs for his small-town benefactors. The blind orator, Homer T. Barbee, offers an extended paean to Booker T. Washington's philosophy of responsibility, while Dr. Bledsoe adroitly negotiates the double bind imposed by the white philanthropists. This mastery of the double bind is evident in Dr. Bledsoe's professional dress, which at once highlights his aspiration to imitate the trustees and the ineffaceable differences that remain between them: "Like some of the guests, he wore striped trousers and a swallow-tail coat with black-braided lapels topped by a rich ascot tie. It was his regular dress for such occasions, yet for all its elegance, he managed to make himself look humble. Somehow, his trousers inevitably bagged at the knees and the coat slouched in the shoulders" (*IM*, 114). This ritualistic self-degradation highlights the heteronomy of Bledsoe's college, which was typical of segregated black colleges in the Jim Crow era. Although these colleges were beginning to change in the 1920s and 1930s, they still held on to vestiges of the missionary model of education instituted in the post–Civil War years, with its emphasis on moral reform and black humility. White trustees controlled what could and could not be taught and established Puritan codes of conduct more rigid than those found at most white colleges.[34] As Ellison puts it, Bledsoe's philanthropists are "trustees of consciousness" (*IM*, 89), charged with the moral discipline of the black race.[35] Black colleges in the Jim Crow era could therefore be called "lumpen professional institutions"; they lacked the relative autonomy from the marketplace that supposedly characterizes higher education and bolsters its claims to embody enlightened value systems such as the American Creed.

Dr. Bledsoe's college instead breeds two different responses to the professional double bind institutionalized on its campus. The first is the cynical pragmatism exemplified by Dr. Bledsoe. As becomes clear in his interview with the invisible man, Bledsoe himself has no illusions about his pseudo-professional status. "I had to be strong and purposeful to get where I am," he explains; "I had to wait and plan and lick around. . . . Yes, I had to act the nigger!" (*IM*, 143). Bledsoe thus emerges as the first of several African Americans in the novel who adopt the role-playing strategies proposed by the invisible man's grandfather. The second response is madness, which itself envelops a cynical awareness of the double bind. Hence, the road from the college leads directly to the black asylum where many of its graduates eventually find their home. As the invisible man reflects of the inmates, "many of the men had been doctors, lawyers, teachers, Civil Service workers. . . . They were supposed to be members of the professions toward which at various times I vaguely aspired myself" (*IM*, 74). The black veteran whom the invisible man encounters in the Golden Day exemplifies the fate they have suffered. Trained as a brain surgeon and then conscripted into a war ostensibly fought in defense of America's egalitarian principles, he is nearly lynched when he tries to practice in America. He has been driven insane by the same set of injunctions that Dr. Bledsoe masters: "You must become a white professional. / You cannot become a white professional."

These twin options, opportunism and madness, pursue the invisible man throughout the narrative. In particular, the long section devoted to the Brotherhood, the novel's version of the Communist Party, recapitulates most of the institutional tensions of the invisible man's college experience. As a revolutionary organization devoted to eradicating the various forms of dispossession experienced by blacks and other Americans, the Brotherhood seems to embody the American Creed excluded from conventional middle-class institutions. Hence, the promotional material that the invisible man designs for the Brotherhood—a subway poster depicting the interracial "Rainbow of America's future" (*IM*, 385)—seems like a banalized version of Ellison's pluralist model of U.S. identity. Moreover, as Hoberek notes, the invisible man at first conceives of the Brotherhood as an ideal professional workplace; it grants him an "anomalously managerial position"[36] at odds with the menial work performed by most of the novel's African American characters. The point of the section, however, is to show that the Brotherhood's black members remain lumpen professionals, dependent on white economic capital and denied the capacity for autonomous decision making. The anonymous letter that the invisible man receives reminds him of the differences that remain between him and the white members: "Keep working for the people but remember that you are one of *us* and do not forget if you get too big *they* will cut you down. You are from the South and you know that this is a *white man's world*" (*IM*, 383, italics in original). As in the case of the college chapters, Ellison explores both madness and opportunism as responses to this institutional subordination. Tod Clifton, the Brotherhood's youth leader, chooses madness and futile protest; the invisible man tries to become a revolutionary incarnation of Dr. Bledsoe.

Given this pervasive double bind, the problem with sociology is not so much the fact that it reduces African Americans to their social environment. Ellison's novel itself offers a complex sociological analysis of black professionals, one that prefigures many of the insights of Frazier's *Black Bourgeoisie*. Rather, the problem with sociology is that it serves as an institutional reminder that blacks are typically the observed objects rather than the observing subjects of professional discourse. As Roderick Ferguson highlights in his reading of the college chapters of *Invisible Man*, Ellison originally incorporated a section in which a gay instructor reiterates Ellison's critique of Robert Park and Ernest Burgess's *Introduction to the Science of Sociology* (1921), which infamously characterized the Negro as the "lady among the races."[37] Ellison first encountered this textbook during his education at Tuskegee and subsequently commented on it in his Myrdal review. The presence of this textbook in the syllabus of a black college, Ferguson argues, reinforces the institution's traditional, missionary purpose, which consists of both "locating African Americans outside of [white] heteropatriarchal norms"[38] and reinforcing those norms more solidly among the student population. In the finished novel, Ellison displaces this reminder of African Americans' status as pathologized objects of social scientific knowledge onto the figure of Jim Trueblood—the black sharecropper who impregnates his own daughter. After his disgrace, white professionals develop a fascination with Trueblood's crime and transform him into a case study in sociological damage theory. "Some of 'em was big white folks, too," Trueblood explains, "from the big school way cross the State. Asked me lots 'bout what I thought 'bout things and 'bout my folks and the kids, and wrote it all down in a book" (*IM*, 53). Trueblood, eager for white patronage, participates in their construction of him as a damaged victim of his environment, emphasizing the social and economic conditions that contributed to his crime: "You see, suh, it was cold and us didn't have much fire. Nothin' but wood, no coal. I tried to git help but wouldn't nobody help us and I couldn't find no work or nothin'. It was so cold all of us had to sleep together; me, the ole lady and the gal. That's how it started, suh" (*IM*, 53). When the invisible man reaches the nadir of his own professional development—after he is injured in his proletarian job at the paint factory—he suffers a similar fate. Strapped inside a glass-and-metal box in the hospital factory, he too becomes an object of professional scrutiny; the doctors view the invisible man as a pathological "case" that "has been developing for some three hundred years" (*IM*, 237). One of Ellison's chief complaints against the Brotherhood is that it similarly imposes this social scientific perspective on the black population it hopes to incorporate into its political program. Hence, Brotherhood theoreticians discuss Harlem's black population as the product of broad historical forces. "The old ones," Brother Jack explains, "they're agrarian types, you know. Being ground up by industrial conditions" (*IM*, 290). Echoing Trilling's conflation of Stalinism with U.S. social science, the invisible man reflects that such exercises in dialectical materialism make him feel as if he is trapped once again in the hospital machine (*IM*, 505).

Hence, in order to sustain the new-class fantasy that resonates throughout *Invisible Man*'s epilogue, Ellison must separate his intellectual hero from the institutions that have fashioned him—a separation dramatized by the invisible man's retreat into his underground room at the novel's end. Like many young black intellectuals in the 1940s and 1950s, the invisible man evades the middle-class double bind by becoming a bohemian hipster, attuned to the black vernacular culture excluded from his college education.[39] This attempt to differentiate black artists and intellectuals from black bourgeois society is a recurring theme in African American literature. It originated in the Harlem Renaissance, when younger black writers rebelled against the genteel Negritude promoted by NAACP intellectuals such as Du Bois. Publications such as the journal *Fire!*—edited by Wallace Thurman and featuring contributions by Zora Neale Hurston and Langston Hughes—challenged bourgeois sensibilities by focusing on lower-class material deemed injurious to the black community's public image: slang, rural folklore, representations of black sexuality and violence, and so on.[40] Other writers, such as Nella Larsen, precisely anatomized the pathologies of the black bourgeoisie; Larsen's *Quicksand* (1928),[41] in particular, prefigures Ellison's college chapters in its depiction of Tuskegee as "Naxos," an institution oriented toward repressing its students' individual ambitions and perpetuating a garbled version of Anglo-Saxon values. In Ellison's case, he pushes this opposition to an exaggerated extreme. The invisible man's underground room represents his complete disconnection from the white economic patronage that generates the cynical pragmatism of successful black professionals such as Dr. Bledsoe. In this room, the invisible man still performs intellectual labor—the writerly work that produces the narrative that we read. However, this work now depends on theft rather than on patronage; he lights his workspace with electricity stolen from Monopolated Light and Power. This newfound autonomy, the novel suggests, allows the invisible man to give voice to the democratic idealism and aesthetic sensibility blocked by his previous entrapment within new-class institutions.

This transformation contrasts with Ellison's own development during the 1940s and 1950s. Whereas many black artists in this period were excluded from institutionalized forms of patronage, Ellison was not. Indeed, as Arnold Rampersad documents in his recent biography, the publication of *Invisible Man* transformed Ellison into the first black institutional writer who earned a generous living from various universities and foundations, in spite of the fact that he never completed his second novel.[42] More fundamental, it is not clear in *Invisible Man* whether independent black artists can indeed separate themselves from the cynical ethos that affects the black bourgeoisie. Instead, all of the artists that we encounter in the novel are popular entertainers who, like Dr. Bledsoe, are not averse to "acting the nigger" (*IM*, 143) in order to sustain themselves. The best example of this tendency is Jim Trueblood. In Houston Baker's famous reading of the Trueblood episode, Trueblood emerges as a figure for the commercial black artist who transforms his expressive folk culture into a commodity for white consumption: "What the farmer is ultimately merchandizing," Baker notes, "is an image of himself that is itself a product."[43] This account of black artistic compromise also extends to the figure whom the invisible man associates with his own artistic agency: Louis Armstrong. As described by the invisible man, Armstrong's music gives expression to the many-in-one identity that Ellison ascribes to the American novel. His performance embodies Ellison's dialectical aesthetic; he refuses to throw "old Bad Air out, because it would have broken up the music and the dance, when it was the good music that came from the bell of old Bad Air's horn that counted" (*IM*, 581). This aesthetic transforms Armstrong's music into a nationalistic ritual that incorporates the entirety of U.S. national experience—evoked by the multilayered vision that the invisible man achieves while listening to "So Black and Blue." However, through his well-known public persona as a commercial artist, Armstrong also exemplifies the trickster strategies first articulated by the invisible man's grandfather: that of grinning one's audience to death and destruction by self-consciously performing a minstrel act. In terms of the novel's logic, the group that implements Ellison's therapeutic project is potentially compromised by the same dependence on white patronage that elsewhere erodes the American Creed. If Myrdal, in other words, too easily identifies U.S. idealism with the experiences of a particular class stratum—the educated new class— then Ellison locates it nowhere. The American Creed can be uttered only in an imaginary space, impossibly isolated from society.

Midway through the novel, in a scene that inaugurates the invisible man's transformation into a political activist within the Brotherhood, he encounters an elderly black couple being evicted from their apartment. Echoing the antinaturalist turn first adumbrated in Ellison's Myrdal review, the invisible man interprets their eviction in cultural terms, finding a parallel between their material dispossession and his own detachment from his racial heritage: "it was as though I myself was being dispossessed of some painful yet precious thing which I could not bear to lose; something confounding, like a rotted tooth that one would rather suffer indefinitely than endure the short, violent eruption of pain that would mark its removal" (*IM*, 273). What *Invisible Man* documents, however, are the psychological effects of a much more prosaic dispossession affecting black professionals and the new class as a whole. Because of this intense perception of middle-class dispossession, Ellison's novel at once reinforces and undercuts the new-class fantasy that lay at the center of the civil rights era and that was inaugurated by *An American Dilemma*: the idea that writers and other intellectuals could reshape American race relations through a national project of cultural education. Echoing Ellison's nonfiction, the novel imagines the black artist as an inventor of new rites and rituals that can synthesize black and white experiences in order to give voice to egalitarian principles at odds with the prevalent materialism of American social life. As such, the novel reiterates an Arnoldian theme that pervades the work of post–World War II literary intellectuals: the idea that artists cultivate forms of cultural capital that negate the instrumental rationality associated with technical expertise and economic wealth. At the same time, through its anatomization of black intellectuals' dependence on white economic capital, the novel calls this cultural idealism into question.

3

MARY McCARTHY'S FIELD GUIDE TO U.S. INTELLECTUALS

TRADITION AND MODERNIZATION THEORY IN *BIRDS OF AMERICA*

"I am in a state of doubt and dismay about Vietnam," Mary McCarthy wrote to Hannah Arendt on April 2, 1965; "if he [President Johnson] bombs Hanoi, that is the end, as far as I am concerned. I would not find it acceptable to be an American any more."[1] For McCarthy, as for many other U.S. intellectuals, the escalating Vietnam War signaled that something was amiss with postwar liberalism. In the words of popular historian David Halberstam, the Kennedy and Johnson administrations were supposed to represent the rule of "the best and the brightest"—government by experts, idealistically committed to reviving the progressive goals of the New Deal at home and to exporting American political freedoms abroad.[2] However, the advice of Kennedy's and Johnson's scholars in fact contributed to the further involvement of the United States in Vietnam; the best and brightest helped bring about one of the nation's greatest military and humanitarian disasters. McCarthy thus felt compelled to use her newfound celebrity as a best-selling author to speak out against the war and U.S. intellectuals' responsibility for it; it would have been hypocritical for her not to, given that her novel in progress, *Birds of America*, which wouldn't be published until 1971,[3] was about a young American of draft age. She set aside her novel to visit South and North Vietnam, and her experiences culminated in three books of nonfiction highly critical of U.S. foreign policy: *Vietnam* (1967), *Hanoi* (1968), and *Medina* (1972).[4] She took aim, in particular, at the mainstream social scientists who helped direct counterinsurgency programs in the region: modernization theorists such as Walt Rostow, Eugene Staley, and McGeorge Bundy. These figures applied the cold war sociology of scholars such as Talcott Parsons and Edward Shils to the problems of third-world development, envisaging the developing world as a collection of particularistic societies whose premodern peasants needed to be culturally reconditioned in order to help them evolve into modern, democratic citizens. In contrast, McCarthy highlighted the role of traditional humanists such as herself who were alienated from postindustrial society and therefore dedicated to preserving local traditions abroad against the onslaught of U.S. modernization.

In trying to understand the problems of the Vietnam era, McCarthy thus reiterated the disciplinary conflict between literary intellectuals and consensus social scientists that also shaped the work of John Crowe Ransom and Ralph Ellison. In McCarthy's account, traditional humanists such as herself were critics of the instrumental rationality embodied in modern mass society. They were the new class's saving remnant, dedicated to sheltering the nonrational in an era dominated by rational technique. Consensus social scientists, in contrast, were Panglossian optimists who celebrated American liberal democracy as the best of all possible societies and hoped to reshape other cultures in its image. As we have seen, this apparent conflict disguised the fact that both writers and modernization theorists were similarly invested in the idea that intellectuals would use the expanded cultural institutions of the welfare state to create a morally astute, critical citizenry. Nevertheless, for McCarthy, the conflict was fundamental, and she incorporated it into *Birds of America*, the fiction that she interrupted in order to speak out against the war. The novel describes the maturation and disillusionment of Peter Levi—an idealistic young man of upper-middle-class, professional background spending his junior year at the Sorbonne in the fall of 1964. Over the course of the narrative, he falls under the influence of two figures who embody the disciplinary fault lines that McCarthy identified in her reporting. The first is Peter's mother, Rosamund Brown, a musicologist and concert harpsichordist with a string of academic exhusbands. She is the character who most resembles McCarthy, and she embodies the Arnoldian leftism of the New York intellectuals. The second is Peter's academic advisor, Dr. Small, a sociologist who believes that the "market mechanism" (304) will usher in an egalitarian, global society. Through these two characters, McCarthy tries to take stock of the intellectual resources of her generation—to discover what, if anything, it should pass on to the next generation of New Left idealists represented by Peter.

Birds of America and McCarthy's political reporting unfortunately marked the decline of her critical reputation. For most of McCarthy's contemporary readers, both works seemed naive attempts to apply the culture criticism of the cold war era to the political problems of the 1960s. Helen Vendler, in a dismissive review, criticized *Birds of America*'s reiteration of 1950s anxieties about mass culture, as exemplified by Rosamund's obsession with the decline of American cuisine. "Mary McCarthy again her own heroine," the article announced, "frozen foods a new villain."[5] In general, McCarthy's Vietnam-era work fell prey to the obliquity that overcame much New York intellectual criticism and fiction in the late 1960s—a period when, as David Laskin notes, "[t]he Vietnam War, the New Left, and Black Power cut their [the intellectuals'] politics to shreds. . . . *Their* culture was no longer *the* culture."[6] This sense of disconnection threatened the New York intellectuals' new-class fantasies, which had been predicated on the notion that they communicated with a broad, educated public made possible by the expansion of the postwar university. It also contributed to the dramatic splintering of the anti-Communist consensus that the New York intellectuals helped establish in the 1940s and 1950s. McCarthy, pushed to the left by the events of the 1960s, wrote sympathetically about North Vietnam's Communist government in her wartime reporting. Saul Bellow, pushed to the right by the perceived excesses of the counterculture and New Left, echoed the cultural attitudes of the emerging neoconservative movement.

As I argue here, *Birds of America* nevertheless offers a crucial metacommentary on the new-class fantasies of the post–World War II era at a time when those fantasies were being put under pressure by the altered political landscape of the 1960s. In particular, *Birds of America* subjects the basic, postwar distinction between traditional humanists and establishment social scientists to a searching scrutiny, revealing many of the underlying affinities between the two positions. The novel demonstrates that the nostalgia for tradition that animates culture critics such as Rosamund and antiestablishment idealists such as Peter rests on a confused notion of traditional societies that renders their critique of modernization incoherent. The premodern customs preserved or recovered by the traditional humanist are always commercial constructs that easily fit into the world envisaged by the modernization theorists. This self-criticism is legitimated by McCarthy's aesthetic theory as articulated in her career-spanning body of literary criticism. McCarthy, like other New York intellectuals, believed that fiction embodies a peculiar type of intellection inaccessible to the social sciences, which allows it to subject ideas to dialectical critique. This idea was crucial to the New York intellectuals' efforts to create a literature of the cultural apparatus. Hence, *Birds of America* is a novel of ideas in which various ideological positions, embodied by different types of intellectuals, are dialectically played off each other in order to reveal their limitations and hidden affinities. However, the novel is *also* a metacommentary on this theory of fiction, one that reveals it to be mired in the same conceptual distinctions (nature, tradition, and the humanities versus technology, modernity, and the social sciences) that McCarthy puts into dialectical play in her narrative. In particular, as the book's taxonomic title suggests, the New York intellectual understanding of fiction may be inseparable from the social scientific rationality it supposedly transcends. Once read in this way, the novel becomes one of the most penetrating explorations of the disciplinary conflicts of the 1950s and 1960s—at once a guide to the main varieties of U.S. intellectuals and a critical reflection on the possibilities and limitations of intellectual fiction.

MARY MCCARTHY'S CULTURAL POLITICS

McCarthy's antiwar politics in the 1960s followed a path marked out by her early writings and immersion in the New York intellectual social milieu. In the late 1930s, she was one of the original editors of the reinvented, anti-Communist *Partisan Review*; as the journal's theater reviewer, she played an important role in helping to push that journal away from the documentary naturalism and dogmatic Marxist criticism championed by the Stalinist Left. Like other writers associated with the journal, she instead sought to develop a new-class fiction focused on the mores and customs of America's educated elite. McCarthy became the chief chronicler of the New York intellectuals themselves, writing scandalous *romans à clef* that satirized the group's habits, intellectual conflicts, and sexual affairs. In constructing this fiction, she was influenced by the peculiar synthesis of Marxism and 1920s literary modernism that distinguished the New York intellectuals from other literary leftists in the 1930s. In Harvey Teres's terms, many of the New York intellectuals were "Eliotic leftists"[7] who tried to adapt T. S. Eliot's cultural conservatism into a leftist critique of U.S. society.[8] This cultural conservatism became particularly obvious in their critique of the instrumentalism of Marxist and progressive liberal thought. Through Eliot, Trilling argued in "'Elements That Are Wanted'" (1940), we learn that "man cannot be comprehended in a formula," that politics must be guided by a "sense of complication and possibility, of surprise, intensification, variety, unfoldment, worth."[9] This sense of complication was a product of Eliot's emphasis on the importance of tradition, which must guide a people if they are to recover the sense of complication and mystery obscured by modern positivism. For Eliot, this tradition was Christian—in his case, the Anglicanism of his adopted country, England. For the New York intellectuals, who were mostly secular Jews (with the exception of McCarthy, a secular Catholic, and Dwight Macdonald, an Ivy League WASP), it was literature and art, which they counterposed against the blandishments of American mass culture. What the New York intellectuals took from Eliot's social thought, in other words, was his Arnoldian humanism. Eliot, Trilling argued, "continues the tradition of Coleridge and, after Coleridge, of Newman, Carlyle, Ruskin and Matthew Arnold—the men who, in the days of Reform, stood out, on something better than reasons of interest, against the philosophical assumptions of materialistic liberalism."[10]

This Eliotic strand of New York intellectual thought was especially crucial to McCarthy's Vietnam-era writing. As Sabrina Abrams argues, this work expressed "a disillusionment with American, capitalist culture and a longing to return to a pre-industrial, pastoral past."[11] By the mid-1960s, McCarthy viewed the United States as an overtechnologized country that had destroyed its native traditions and replaced them with a debased mass culture that it was in the process of exporting abroad. In her hands, this argument took on an environmentalist emphasis; the worst feature of capitalism is its destruction of nature, which is the ontological basis of the world's various traditional cultures. These cultures, McCarthy argued, acquire their distinctive characteristics from their immediate natural environment; traditional societies, in other words, are like animal species, each adapted to its ecological niche: "A peasant's thatched cottage, like a bird's nest, was not designed by an individual but by the species. And the form and materials of the dwelling at once identify the species of the occupant, just as with birds: the conical white-washed *trulli* of Apulia, the bamboo and straw huts of Indochina, the chinked log-cabins of the North. . . . This is only another way of saying that the design is traditional and that local resources—brick, wood, tufa, reeds—have been taken advantage of."[12] The threat of modern mass society is that it effaces these species differences, creating a culture that is worldwide in scope and nowhere organically linked to its environment. Once this connection between human beings and nature is severed, ethics and aesthetics—the means by which human beings articulate their sense of belonging in the world—begin to disappear. "If nature," she explained in a 1971 interview, "in the beautiful form that we normally think of it: that of the outdoors, plants, farms, forests—if this were to disappear, which it is doing, there'd be nothing left to stand on, no ground for ethics. Then you'd really be in a Dostoevskian position: why shouldn't I kill an old pawnbroker—because there's no longer a point of reference or a court of appeals."[13] With nature dead, human beings fall prey to instrumental thinking, learning to treat others as means rather than as ends in themselves. By the late 1960s, this argument highlighted McCarthy's affinity with parts of the American counterculture that similarly celebrated both nature and non-Western, traditional cultures.[14] It also echoed arguments made forty years earlier by the most famous group of Eliotic social critics in the United States—the southern Agrarians. As we have seen, they too were concerned with the uniqueness and particularity of local cultures, which they argued were the products of a similar kind of natural adaptation.

In her political reporting from this period, McCarthy counterposed this position, which she identified with the worldview of artists and writers like herself, against another position typical of the mainstream, celebratory social science of the cold war era: modernization theory, an approach that viewed modernization as a linear progression from traditional to modern societies. As Michael Latham argues in his study of this paradigm's influence on the Kennedy administration, modernization theorists "placed Western, industrial, capitalist democracies, and the United States in particular, at the apex of their historical scale and then set about marking off the distance of less modern societies from that point. Convinced that the lessons of America's past demonstrated the route to genuine modernity, they stressed the ways the United States could drive 'stagnant' societies through the transitional process."[15] The mainstream social science of the postwar years therefore seemed diametrically opposed to the cultural politics promoted by New York intellectuals such as McCarthy; it seemed like the epitome of the kind of positivism that humanists in the Arnoldian tradition had been fighting since the nineteenth century. In fact, as I have been arguing, postwar social scientists were involved in their own revolt against positivism, one that led them to place greater emphasis on cultural as opposed to economic factors in the development of first and third world countries. However, their theory was indeed a kind of reverse Eliotism insofar as it derided the traditional and the local as narrow-minded cultural identities that needed to be overcome in the transition to the superior form of culture embodied in Western liberal democracy. In particular, Talcott Parsons articulated the difference between traditional and modern societies in ways that ruled out nostalgia for the former. The two types of society, he argued, embody entirely different ethical systems. Traditional societies are particularistic, in the sense that individuals identify with circumscribed families, clans, or villages and exclude outsiders; modern societies are universalistic, meaning that individuals identify with the nation or the human species as a whole.[16] This latter form of identification entails a radical change in the nature of modern ethics—the emergence of universalistic ethical systems that assert identical rights and obligations for all peoples.

This theory implied that the status quo should be maintained in domestic politics ; the United States already embodied the cultural preconditions for its transformation into an ideal societal community. The same was not true for postcolonial development. As Nils Gilman explains, "the United States was deemed a modern country, and therefore in need of little profound reform . . . while colonial countries were considered 'traditional' and therefore in need of change."[17] For political scientists influenced by Parsons, such as Walt Rostow and Eugene Staley, cultural change from traditional to modern societies was both an effect of contact with Western democracies and a precondition for successful economic development. This change was perilous because the dissolution of traditional societies entailed psychological dislocation for third-world peasants as tightly knit, particularistic cultures disappeared. For this reason, the first world had to guide the third world as expeditiously as possible toward the superior form of social integration associated with Western universalism, reeducating the populace so as to prepare them for capitalism and liberal democracy. This careful guidance was especially important in regions menaced by communism, which for modernization theorists was a social disease that preyed on countries during the transition period.[18] Consensus social scientists such as Parsons, Rostow, and Staley thus endorsed homeostasis at home, disequilibrium abroad.

In McCarthy's first book of Vietnam reporting, she focused on one of the most notorious examples of this theory's implementation as policy—the Strategic Hamlet Program, a response to the Viet Cong's infiltration of peasant villages. The basic idea, worked out in tandem between the Ngo Dinh Diem and Kennedy administrations, was to relocate peasants forcibly from their villages into more concentrated settlements surrounded by barbed wire, ditches, and bamboo stakes. There, the peasants would be resocialized; aid workers would train them in modern agricultural techniques and liberal democratic attitudes and instill in them a patriotic identification with Diem's government and its American supporters. The ultimate purpose of the program, as the Kennedy administration's taskforce put it, was to "bring the rural people of Vietnam into the body politic,"[19] to integrate them into the South Vietnamese state. The Strategic Hamlets were supposed to accelerate the process of cultural change described by modernization theorists; in a matter of months or years, participating peasants would be torn from their traditional culture and thrust into liberal democratic modernity. The program—half exercise in civic education, half concentration camp—inevitably led to draconian excesses. Hamlet residents were subjected to constant surveillance and control in an effort to ferret out Viet Cong sympathizers. Hamlets had strict evening curfews, and transgressors were sometimes shot on sight. Peasants, after having been forcibly evacuated from their ancestral villages (their houses and crops burned so that they could never return), were put to unpaid work constructing their hamlet's defenses. The logic used to justify these excesses was that the temporary suffering of the displaced South Vietnamese was a necessary step toward their integration into the global capitalist economy. The very intensity of American violence in South Vietnam, Harvard political scientist Samuel P. Huntington argued in 1968, could be viewed positively as a catalyst toward that country's modernization.[20]

The Strategic Hamlet Program therefore seemed like the epitome of McCarthy's fears about the effects of modernization on local folkways. Americans had tried to stamp their universalistic, modern culture on Vietnamese peasants immersed in a particularistic, traditional culture. In particular, one of the main purposes of the Strategic Hamlets was to introduce the Vietnamese to entrepreneurship and free-market economics. This effort was emblematized, for McCarthy, by one marine officer's plan to build a seven-foot-high bronze dollar sign in the center of his proposed hamlet—a symbol of American values.[21] The dollar sign highlighted, for McCarthy, the true nature of American universalism. It was not, as Parsons believed, the dissemination of a Kantian ethics embodied in documents such as the Universal Declaration of Human Rights. Rather, it was the dissemination of an instrumental rationality that undermined all traditions and ethical systems and a missionary precursor to the intrusion of Western economic capital into the third world. At the same time, the Americans had fractured the Vietnamese's relationship with their natural environment—most dramatically through their chemical defoliation of the jungles, but also through a more subtle destruction of the landscape. "Before the Americans came," McCarthy wrote, "there could have been no rusty Coca-Cola or beer cans or empty whiskey bottles. They had brought them. It was this indestructible mass production garbage floating in swamps and creeks, lying about in fields and along the roadside that made the country, which must once have been beautiful, hideous."[22] These two types of destruction were intimately related for McCarthy; in changing the land, you simultaneously destroy a culture.

By way of contrast, in *Hanoi* McCarthy praised North Vietnamese efforts to improve their country. "This is a moral, ascetic government, concerned above all with the *quality* of Vietnamese life,"[23] she wrote about Pham Van Dong's government, ignoring North Vietnam's atrocities against internal dissidents throughout the 1950s. In particular, McCarthy was impressed with the intellectual leadership of North Vietnam—a group that, she noted, were mostly university-educated professionals from minor mandarin families. In a letter to Dwight Macdonald, McCarthy wrote that North Vietnam "[is] the only people's democracy I've ever seen that's run on aristocratic principles and largely by aristocratic persons with a traditional code of manners and morals."[24] This ruling class was exemplified, for McCarthy, by a surgeon that she visited at Hanoi University Surgical Hospital, who was trying to fuse Western with traditional Vietnamese medicine. It was a case, he explained, of "progress through deliberate and controlled regression, i.e., by rediscovery,"[25] typical of the Vietnamese approach to developing their country. The modern innovations introduced by the Communists—new crop varieties, brick walkways, camouflaged schools and infirmaries—were incorporated aesthetically into the landscape and local hamlets. McCarthy saw the North Vietnamese elite as an ideal counterpart to the technocratic academics in the Kennedy and Johnson administrations. They were,

for her, an Eliotic elite, a clerisy attuned to local ecology and the traditions of their people. Indeed, McCarthy approvingly contrasted
Vietnamese intellectuals to Western humanists such as herself. The
latter could offer only fruitless criticism of an unchangeable social
system: "a free press is livelier than a government-controlled one, but
access to information that does not lead to action may actually be
unhealthy, like any persistent frustration, for a body politic."[26]

In her Vietnam reporting, McCarthy thus offered a stark alternative between two models of intellectual influence. On the one hand,
there were establishment social scientists such as Rostow and Staley,
dominated by instrumental logic and a teleological model of historical development. On the other hand, there was the dictatorial elite
of North Vietnam, whose wise guardianship of their land and people was enabled by their immersion in a shared tradition. This dichotomy is not as idiosyncratic as it may at first appear to be; throughout the late 1960s, writers and activists associated with the New
Left idolized third-world, antidemocratic revolutionaries such as
Fidel Castro and Ho Chi Minh. These leaders' harsh measures were
supposedly justified by the fact that they were at one with their
people, embedded in a common, nonrational tradition like an animal species in its ecological niche. At the basis of McCarthy's idealization of North Vietnam, in other words, is a kind of identity politics
akin to William Graham Sumner's turn-of-the-century sociology; a
regime's worst atrocities can be excused as long as they are contextu-
alized within a foreign culture. By this logic, condemning the North
Vietnamese government for killing its dissidents would be like condemning the bird for building her nest; each is doing only what's
natural to the species. The differences between McCarthy and the
modernization theorists she abhorred are therefore as follows: although both establish a fairly rigid dichotomy between modern and
traditional societies, and, for both, the former transcend the cultural
particularism of the latter, they do so in different ways. For the modernization theorists, this transcendence moves in the direction
of establishing a universalist ethic rooted in liberal democracy; for

McCarthy, it moves in the direction of a universal instrumentalism that destroys ethics altogether. Faced with this prospect, McCarthy's solution is to affirm the cultural particularism rejected by Parsons and others like him—to embrace local cultures as natural adaptations to their time and place and therefore immune to outside critique. This is the position that McCarthy radically rethinks in *Birds of America*; she shows that her own nostalgia for the traditional and the natural is intimately related to the derogation of these things implicit in consensus social science.

THE COMMERCIALIZATION OF TRADITION

At first glance, however, *Birds of America* seems like a relatively straightforward allegorization of McCarthy's Eliotic leftism; in particular, the novel establishes a series of characters who mirror the main positions established in her Vietnam reporting. Hence, Rosamund Brown, a thinly veiled self-portrait, replicates much of McCarthy's cultural politics. She is the focus of the novel's first two chapters, which detail two visits that Rosamund and her son make to Rocky Port, New England—an isolated cottage community that Rosamund envisages as one of the last remaining bastions of America's preindustrial past. These chapters, like McCarthy's account of the Strategic Hamlets, demonstrate the impact of modernization on traditional folkways. Rosamund predictably discovers that Rocky Port has been absorbed into the modern world economy and has become little more than a tourist trap. Residents now insist on affixing historical notices to their homes—at once marking their disconnection from their past and their willingness to market it. Rosamund nevertheless tries to revive and preserve the village's authentic New England traditions—ostensibly an act of resistance against the dissemination of mass culture. The other side of the novel's dialectic is represented by Dr. Small, a technocratic social scientist akin to the modernization theorists that McCarthy criticizes in *Vietnam*. He is a

Panglossian optimist who celebrates the process of modernization regardless of its effects on particularistic traditions. "Capitalism," he explains, "has shown itself to be the most subtle force for progress the world has ever known. In its pre-industrial phase, an insidious, awesome force. Boring from within the old structures, leveling, creating new dreams, new desires, and having the technical know-how and dynamism to satisfy them" (301–2).[27] The novel's central scene with Dr. Small takes place in the Sistine Chapel, which he is investigating as part of a sociological study of mass tourism. Like Rocky Port, the Sistine Chapel has become a tourist destination; once a site of worship and the expression of a particular culture, it has instead become an item of curiosity for international crowds of distraction-seeking tourists. Tourism thus exemplifies the process of modernization that Dr. Small celebrates and Rosamund abhors; by opening all parts of the world to commercial exploitation, tourism tends to make them all the same.

The figure who mediates between these two positions is Rosamund's son, Peter, a young nature lover and political idealist with membership cards for various civil rights organizations. In the fall of 1964, he travels to Paris on a study abroad program and begins to distance himself from his mother's politics. He does this by embracing a universalistic, Kantian ethic similar to the one that modernization theorists such as Parsons believed was the cultural endpoint of the modernization process. "Behave as if thy maxim could be a universal law" (131), Peter repeatedly tells himself. However, he finds himself drawn back into his mother's orbit after several long discussions with Dr. Small. His universalist ethics continually comes into conflict with his distaste for modernity, and he eventually joins his mother's quixotic struggle against modern conveniences. The novel ends pessimistically, with Peter learning that the United States has dropped its first bombs north of the seventeenth parallel and that he may soon be drafted into the war. This event coincides with a near-fatal attack on him by a black swan at the Jardin des Plantes, which symbolizes for him that the natural order has been thrown into disarray. As he recuperates in a hospital bed, the spirit of Immanuel Kant visits him in a fever-induced hallucination. "Nature is dead, *mein kind*" (344), Kant tells him—the novel's apocalyptic last words. This pronouncement echoes McCarthy's concerns about the destruction of the natural environment and its effect on all ethical systems; she evokes the triumph of instrumental reason that, she argued in her reporting, is exemplified by the Vietnam War.

However, *Birds of America* in fact parodies Rosamund's and thus McCarthy's cultural politics, disarticulating the connection between nature and tradition that animates their shared nostalgia for the premodern. McCarthy's strategy for carrying out this parody is announced in the novel's epigraph from Kant: "to attempt to embody the idea in an example, as one might embody the wise man in a novel, is unseemly for our natural limitations, which persistently interfere with the perfection of the idea, forbid all illusion about such an attempt." In the rest of this quotation, which McCarthy leaves out, Kant concludes by noting that such efforts cast "suspicion on the good itself—the good that has its source in the idea—by giving it the air of being a mere fiction."[28] Throughout its pages, *Birds of America* illustrates this tendency for ideas to become unseemly when embodied in fictional examples; the novel's continual movement is from Rosamund and Peter's abstract ideas to the banal realization of these ideas. Hence, much of the novel's comedy comes from Peter's application of the categorical imperative to insignificant ethical dilemmas— for instance, whether to clean the excrement out of his hostel's communal toilet. As in the Kant quotation, this example redounds on the theory it is supposed to illustrate. Peter realizes that the Kantian imperative gets stymied in this instance because whether the dirty bowl even registers as an ethical problem is mostly a function of each resident's childhood training—an empirical factor supposedly irrelevant to pure practical reason. "Could humanity be divided into people who noticed and people who didn't?" Peter asks. "If so, there was no common world. That thought really depressed me. If there was no agreement on a primary matter like that, then it was useless to look for agreement on 'higher' principles" (156).

McCarthy uses the same strategy to parody Rosamund's nostalgia for tradition. Throughout the early chapters, Rosamund's resistance to the modernization of Rocky Port takes the form of her trivial obsession with authentic U.S. cuisine; for her, the intrusion of processed and frozen foods into Rocky Port is the most damaging sign of its absorption into a national and international economy. She therefore establishes a regime of American cooking: "The rules of the Rocky Port kitchen were that every recipe had to come out of Fannie Farmer, had to be made entirely at home from fresh—or dried or salted—ingredients, and had to be, insofar as possible, an invention of the New World" (32). This food purism was an obsession that McCarthy shared with her character; indeed, it was central to her notion of tradition as expressed in her political reporting.[29] Echoing the southern Agrarians, McCarthy understood tradition to be ontologically grounded in its natural environment; local cultures adapt to their environment and are in turn shaped by it. Within this schema, food stands out as the most obvious interface between culture and nature; at the center of McCarthy's cultural politics is the identitarian adage that "we are what we eat." An ideal, traditional world would be made up of distinctive cultures, each defined by the sustenance it derives from the land. Conversely, the modern world is one in which foods and cultures are indiscriminately mixed together or else technologically processed beyond the point of recognition. Hence, McCarthy frequently draws on culinary analogies to describe what is wrong with American society and the industrial mass culture it exports abroad. Modernization, in her account, is like a blender or food processor. Many of the long sentences in her Vietnam reporting imitate its effects:

The samples of U.S. technology that had been showered on the North were mainly in bomb form, yet the simplest Vietnamese

could perhaps see a connection that eludes many American intellectuals between the spray of pellets from the "mother" bomb
and the candy hurled at children in the South by friendly G. I.'s,
between the pellets and the whole *Saran-wrapped* output of American industrial society which can no longer (at least this is my
conclusion) be separated into beneficial and deleterious, "good"
and "bad," but has been *homogenized*, so that "good"—free elections, say—is *high-speed blended* with commercial TV, opinion-
testing, buttons, streamers, stickers, *canned* speech-writing, *instant*
campaign biographies, till no issues are finally discernible, having been *broken down and distributed in tiny particles throughout the suspended solution*, and you wonder whether the purpose of having
elections is not simply to market TV time, convention-hall space,
hotel suites, campaign buttons, and so on, and to give employ-
ment to commentators and pollsters.[30]

This blended culture is McCarthy's restaging of the universalism
touted by modernization theorists such as Parsons, Rostow, and
Staley. Once again, it is a culture entirely dominated by instrumentalism, such that the good elements of the Western democratic tradition have been subordinated to the market economy.

However, as in the case of Peter's application of Kantianism to
toilet etiquette, this application of McCarthy's agrarianism trivial-
izes the idea it is supposed to exemplify. Rosamund, in her efforts to
institute her cooking regime, continually comes into conflict with the
other residents of Rocky Port, who are eager to embrace the culinary
conveniences of modern society. The novel highlights the relative
insignificance of this conflict in comparison to the more important
crises of U.S. society. In the midst of a failed effort to find tapioca
pudding in local stores, Peter reflects, "in this sinister summer of
race riots, church-burnings, civil-rights workers vanishing in Mississippi, in New York, a cop, off duty, shooting to kill at a Negro kid,
the fact that tapioca pudding, his old love, had kicked the bucket
ought not to matter. Yet if he said that to his mother, she felt he was

abandoning her" (70). Indeed, Rosamund arranges her and Peter's second visit to Rocky Port as a substitute for a planned trip, vetoed by his biological father, to join the Freedom Riders in Mississippi. Peter and Rosamund's conflict with the townsfolk thus displaces the conflict that could have taken place between Peter and southern segregationists over the more burning issues of 1964. The triviality of this substitution is highlighted when Rosamund and Peter end up in prison on the last day of their visit. Rosamund infuriates her landlady by taking down the historical notice on her rented home in the midst of a commemorative jamboree, indicating that she will live in history rather than participate in a pageant. When the local constable demands that she put it up again, Peter has a chance to use the passive-resistance techniques he learned from the civil rights groups on campus. The incident exemplifies the way in which many cold war humanists' focus on mass culture distorted their perception of the era's more crucial problems of poverty and race discrimination.

Even more radically, Rosamund's culinary experiment illustrates the incoherence of McCarthy's identitarian critique of modernity; in particular, it illustrates the impossibility of recovering any tradition that does not already register within itself a history of commercialization, technological processing and cultural heterogeneity. Hence, when deciding what to cook from Fannie Farmer, Rosamund has trouble deciding what does and does not constitute a New World dish. She concludes that a dish "did not have its citizenship papers if it had been cooked in America for less than a hundred years" (32) and sends Peter on library research trips to determine when specific ethnic groups arrived in the country. Rosamund, in other words, tries to fabricate a tradition through an effort in artificial historicism that parallels Rocky Port's own attempt to catalog and market its historical past. This research effort will never recover an original culture born out of the people's relationship with their land; her own Puritan ancestors were migrants who brought foreign technologies and ingredients to New England, as did the Native Americans before them.[31] The problem revealed by Rosamund's failure to recover an original American cuisine is the arbitrariness of any cultural politics that tries to distinguish between traditional and modern societies on the basis of their geographical particularism versus their nongeographical universalism. These politics always end up defining and inventing traditions, arbitrarily delineating which technologies and customs do and do not belong in them. Hence, Rosamund reshapes the New England culture she constructs in her household. "She was strong for the traditional," Peter reflects, "and whenever she made an innovation, it became part of the tradition, something that had 'always' been" (27).

This nostalgia for a tradition she can never inhabit highlights the fact that Rosamund, like all of the novel's other peripatetic intellectuals, is a tourist. She is in many ways the ideal consumer of Rocky Port—someone who takes seriously its claim to embody New England's past. Her problem is not that her demands for historical authenticity and cultural distinctiveness clash with Rocky Port's efforts to market itself. Rather, it is that she is too discriminating in these demands. In terms of a distinction that Peter uses to separate himself from the other tourists in the Sistine Chapel, she is a "class" rather than a "mass" (284) tourist—a tourist who is aesthetically attuned to the place she visits as opposed to visitors who are less educated and thus supposedly undeserving. Class tourism, in other words, is a strategy whereby the educated tourist distinguishes herself from the masses who make every place look the same. However, as Peter realizes, mass tourism and class tourism are in fact inseparable; the promise of class tourism is essential to the ways in which tourist destinations market themselves: "There's a logical contradiction in the whole tourist routine. . . . 'Oh God, tourists!' you hear them moan when they look around some restaurant and see a bunch of compatriots with Diners Club cards who might as well be their duplicates. Sort of a blanket rejection that, if they sat down and analyzed it, would have to include themselves. Only nobody does. They can't. Instead, in the Sistine Chapel, you start thinking of the reasons why *you* have the right to be there and all the rest don't"

(294, italics in original). Once this distinction between class tourism and mass tourism collapses, an even greater problem arises with Rosamund's critique of modernization. She is not only a consumer of class and therefore mass tourism, but as a concert harpsichordist and musicologist who preserves and performs music from an extinct musical tradition, she is also a *producer* of that tourism. Traditional humanists such as Rosamund and McCarthy, in other words, inevitably market cultural products to a select audience of fellow intellectuals, thereby creating the illusion that they are class rather than mass consumers of a cultural tradition. Traditional humanists thus embody a paradox implicit in the kinds of tourism that Rosamund derides—although tourism makes all times and places look the same, it always does so in the name of preserving local differences and making them accessible to others. Rosamund therefore misses an important moment of self-realization when her landlady reveals that she is an avid fan of Rosamund's recordings. As in the case of Rocky Port's use of historical markers, the very urge to preserve tradition is a sign that one is irrevocably alienated from it and engaged in its destruction.

This implicit critique of tradition in *Birds of America* means that its apocalyptic conclusion, Kant's invocation of the death of nature in the face of the Vietnam War, opens itself to contrasting interpretations. The obvious interpretation, the one that corresponds to McCarthy's nonfictional statements about nature and ethics, is that human beings have destroyed nature and with it the ontological ground for all ethics and aesthetics. This interpretation is suggested by the Kantian ethics that Peter expounds throughout the novel. In the Kantian system, the experience of natural beauty is supposed to bridge the gap between theoretical knowledge of nature and practical knowledge of ethics—the respective domains of the first two critiques. As Peter sums up in his hallucination, the beautiful things in the world prove "that man is made for and fits into the world and that his perception of things agrees with the laws of his perception" (343). Natural beauty therefore undergirds Kant's theoretical edifice. The problem, suggested by Kant's cryptic remark to Peter, is that nature has been so ravaged by human beings as to have become unrecognizable to them. However, the full context of Kant's warning suggests a different interpretation:

> "Excuse me, sir, you have something to tell me, don't you?" The tiny man moved forward on the counterpane and looked Peter keenly in the eyes, as though anxious as to how he would receive the message he had to deliver. He spoke in a low thin voice. "God is dead," Peter understood him to say. Peter sat up. "I *know* that," he protested. "And you didn't say that anyway. Nietzsche did." He felt put upon as though by an impostor. Kant smiled. "Yes, Nietzsche said that. And even when Nietzsche said it, the news was not new, and maybe not so tragic after all. Mankind can live without God." "I agree," said Peter. "I've always lived without him." "No, what *I* say to you is something important. You did not hear me correctly. Listen now carefully and remember." Again he looked Peter steadily and searchingly in the eyes. "Perhaps you have guessed it. Nature is dead, *mein kind*." (343–44, italics in original)

Kant, in other words, may be proclaiming the death of nature in precisely the same way that Nietzsche proclaimed the death of God. With the development of modernity, we are forced to recognize that nature, like God, never functioned metaphysically in the way that we once thought it did.[32] This seems to be the position enacted by McCarthy's novel.

SOCIOLOGY AND THE NOVEL OF IDEAS

This critique of the twin notions of nature and tradition is a thematic concern that goes beyond *Birds of America*. It also functions as a metacommentary on the New York intellectuals' theory of the novel of ideas. This theory is adumbrated in McCarthy's opening quotation from Kant about the unseemliness of embodying ideas in fiction. Pure ideas, Kant argues, continually run up against our natural limitations, which betray their perfection. As McCarthy explains in *Ideas and the Novel* (1980), the very strength of the novel is in fact its ability to test out and check abstract conceptual thought by confronting it with natural complexity. Ideas, she argues in the context of a discussion of Charles Dickens's *Hard Times* (1854), "are formed in consciousness with a regulatory aim, which is to gain control of the swarming minutiae of experience, to give them order and direction."[33] Hence, one of the efforts the novel makes is to debunk bad ideas that impose this control too tightly. *Hard Times*, for instance, illustrates the inadequacy of utilitarian philosophy through its parody of Mr. Gradgrind, whose name connotes his desire to grind up and destroy the confused welter of experience; in McCarthy's account, he is the prototype for the social scientists she writes about in her reporting and fiction. The novel, in contrast, tries to remain true to the complexity of experience: "the novelist's effort—any artist's effort—to impose shape and form on that mass of particulars while maintaining their distinctness has something in common with the mind's will to absolute rule through the synthesizing process. They are similar but they are not the same. The artist's concern (and especially, I should say, the novelist's) must be to save the particulars at all costs, even at the sacrifice of the perfection of the design."[34] The novel thus tries to imitate natural beauty as defined by Kant in the *Critique of Judgment*; its goal is to become a legible reminder that the free activity of the human mind is not necessarily at odds with the phenomenal world. In Lionel Trilling's terms from *The Liberal Imagination*, good novels reveal the "complexity and possibility" obscured by the ideological formulations of the intellectual class.[35] This theory legitimates McCarthy's effort in *Birds of America*; she wrote the book in order to test both her own theories about modernity and tradition as well as the theories of modernization proponents such as Dr. Small. In the process, she discovered that both theories are overly intellectualized constructs that conflict with experience.

McCarthy's theory, however, rests on the same distinction between tradition and modernity that she disarticulates in *Birds of America*; in all of her essays on the novel, she offers a historical narrative about the impact of modernization on the genre. This narrative aligns novels with the traditional folkways whose disappearance she laments in her political reporting. In "The Fact in Fiction" (1960), for instance, she describes the process whereby novelists incorporate the phenomenal world into their work by assimilating hard nuggets of social and natural fact. In particular, the novelist builds her fiction out of the facts of scandal—petty conflicts within a delimited milieu that reveal a society's underlying class structure: "the scandals the novelists are primed with are the scandals of a village, a town, or a province—Highbury or Jefferson, Mississippi, or the Province of O—; the scandals of a clique—the Faubourg St. Germain, of a city—Dublin or Middlemarch; or of a nation—Dickens' England; or of the ports and hiring offices—London or Nantucket."[36] The novelist is therefore like the agrarian peasant that McCarthy describes in *Writing on the Wall*: her work is built out of local, found materials. The problem with the contemporary novel, McCarthy argues in "The Fact in Fiction," is that modernization is effacing all local cultures, blending them together into one homogeneous global culture. In such a world, the relevant facts and scandals are no longer local. Rather, they are worldwide and as such resistant to literary representation; "it is impossible, except for theologians, to conceive of a world-wide scandal or a universe-wide scandal; the proof of this is the way people have settled down to live with nuclear fission, radiation poisoning, hydrogen bombs, satellites, and space rockets." Instead, the task of representing the scandals of the world devolves on social scientists such as Dr. Small and Dickens's Mr. Gradgrind, whose abstract discourse mimics the processed homogeneity of the new, global society. In the twentieth century, McCarthy complains, "*Middlemarch* becomes *Middletown* and *Middletown in Transition*, the haunts of social scientists, whose factual findings, even in the face of Auschwitz or a space-satellite, have a certain cachet because they are supposed to be 'science.'"[37]

Moreover, McCarthy argues, this transfer of novelistic authority to social scientists has been facilitated by novelists themselves; in the face of the growing prestige of the world's Gradgrinds, novelists have given up the effort to confront abstract ideas with the complexity of the phenomenal world. Instead, they have turned to various kinds of novelistic formalism. In *Ideas and the Novel*, McCarthy describes the decline of the European realist novel, beginning with the art novels of Henry James and Virginia Woolf. These writers modernized the novel by purging both nature and ideas from it, reducing it to splendid, meaningless form. For James, the novel "stood beautifully apart, impervious to the dry rot affecting the brain's constructions and to the welter of factuality."[38] McCarthy thus suggests a perverse affinity between social science and certain kinds of literary modernism, an affinity that she makes explicit in *Birds of America*. In the scene with Peter and Dr. Small in the Sistine Chapel, the novel contrasts their different reactions to Michelangelo's fresco on the ceiling. Peter subscribes to McCarthy's aesthetic. For him, what matters are the fresco's details, each of which has iconographic significance and must be studied carefully in order to grasp the meaning of the whole. Works of art, for him, are rooted in their unique historical and geographical context; they are products of the artist's immersion within a particular culture. Dr. Small, in contrast, champions an aesthetic akin to that which McCarthy attributes to James and Woolf, one that abstracts the work of art from its cultural context and voids it of all content. Small thus dismisses Peter's use of guidebooks to ferret out Michelangelo's historical meaning: "What he [Michelangelo] really cared about, being an artist, was form, line, color. For him, the whole cycle might as well have been an abstract design" (276). This attitude, McCarthy suggests, is one best suited to the era of mass tourism and modernization celebrated by Dr. Small. The conclusion that McCarthy drives toward is that she is one of the last exemplars of a dying art—one that has gone the way of butter churners and fresh fish and may no longer be possible in the modern world. "I've just finished the first section of my novel," she wrote to Arendt about her progress on *Birds of America*, "which ought to make me cheerful. But I am sagging with doubts and apprehensions. The traditional novel, which this is, is so undermined that one feels as if one were working in a house marked for demolition."[39]

This conclusion, however, is complicated by *Birds of America*'s metacommentary on tradition. One of the difficulties involved in aligning the novel with tradition, rather than with modernity, is highlighted by its title, which refers to Peter's Audubon field guide and to the pervasive presence of birds throughout the novel. For Peter, ornithology is one of the last remaining descriptive sciences, one that seeks to obtain knowledge from nature through pure observation; "birds in nature were left to themselves, apart from human interference. The most you might do was to band them or coax them to show themselves" (167). In contrast, the modern sciences seek to meddle with and transform their subject matter. As Peter's first stepfather, a nuclear physicist, explains, "taxonomy, useful in its day, had no place in the curriculum of a modern university, where biology and genetics were acting *on* Nature, like modern physics and chemistry, disturbing its inmost processes, forcing it to answer questions, smashing its resistance" (166). McCarthy's title similarly suggests that she wants to offer a naturalist's guidebook to the various species of Americans that Peter encounters in his travels, one that lets them remain in their natural habitat and merely observes their habits and manners. The novel thus consistently analogizes human beings to birds. Peter describes Rosamund as being "like an American bird—the rose-breasted grosbeak, for instance, modest and vivid" (21)—and later refers to the "flyways" of American tourists, their patterns of migration and typical destinations (292). This comparison seems to reflect McCarthy's interest in rejuvenating literary realism. Hence, in "Characters in Fiction" (1961), she laments that few contemporary novelists have tried to describe the various character types that have emerged in postwar U.S. mass society; "it is as though a whole 'culture' of plants and organisms had sprung into being and there were no scientists or latter-day Adams to name them."[40]

However, this comparison between novel writing and ornithology also entails a very different account of realism from the one that McCarthy offers in *Ideas and the Novel*. Although literary realism may be a taxonomic science, one that observes and preserves the various cultural species of the world, it is still a product of modern, secular rationalism. The novelist as naturalist is not really like the peasant who builds his hut out of local materials; she never immanently lives within a tradition, accepting its customs as self-obvious, natural, and therefore immune to analysis. Rather, the novelist is closer to Mc-Carthy's Dr. Small or Dickens's Mr. Gradgrind—a social scientist who collects the data of experience and imposes categories on them. She takes myriad, unique individuals and reduces them to a type: the mainstream social scientist or the traditional humanist. Indeed, *Birds of America* could just as easily be the title of Dr. Small's sociological study of mass tourism, which similarly compares U.S. tourists to species of birds for analytical purposes. Homosexuals, Dr. Small explains to Peter, are "nest-builders" who travel in pairs; they have migration patterns that "could be understood in terms of the food supply, if that was interpreted in a broad sense to mean readily available adolescent boys" (293). Because of this analytical impulse, the realist novel is a modern, universalistic genre, one of the technologies used to destroy parochial village sentiment and instead create a more cosmopolitan consciousness.

Hence, *Birds of America* is not really an expression of the Eliotic leftism articulated in McCarthy's nonfiction. Rather, it is a more complicated book about the traditional humanist's underlying affinity with the celebration of modernization found in the mainstream social science of the 1960s. The culture critic's nostalgia for tradition, the novel suggests, is inseparably linked to the social scientist's Panglossian optimism—especially when the humanist ends up packaging this nostalgia for mass consumption. Novel writing, moreover, as a technique for describing the "manners and morals" of society, cannot be meaningfully distinguished from the social sciences. Both are empirical disciplines linked to the rise of modern, scientific worldviews. This affinity between the novelist and the social scientist was one with which McCarthy was intimately familiar. While she was writing *Birds of America* and criticizing U.S. modernization efforts in South Vietnam, her husband, James West, was director of information for the Organization for Economic Cooperation and Development, an international agency that collected statistics on third-world development for the U.S. and other first-world governments. McCarthy's husband, in other words, was a crucial participant in the U.S. government's increasing use of academic expertise and especially modernization theory to guide foreign policy. Literally wedded to the social scientific establishment, McCarthy could not help but see that the disciplinary schisms that divided her generation of cold war anti-Communists were not absolute.

4

SAUL BELLOW'S CLASS OF
EXPLAINING CREATURES

MR. SAMMLER'S PLANET AND THE RISE
OF NEOCONSERVATISM

In the opening of Saul Bellow's *Mr. Sammler's Planet* (1970), the elderly protagonist wakes up in his bedroom and reflects that he is surrounded by "the wrong books, the wrong papers."[1] The scene encapsulates the novel's central theme. The bedroom, like the novel itself, is cluttered with the tokens of the Western intellectual tradition. Artur Sammler's books and papers are symptoms of the fact that "intellectual man has become an explaining creature. Fathers to children, wives to husbands, lecturers to listeners, experts to laymen, colleagues to colleagues, doctors to patients, man to his own soul, explained" (3). Sammler is also a member of this explaining class; he too has "a touch of the same—the disease of the single self explaining what was what and who was who" (280). These explanations, however, conflict with the "natural knowledge" (3) of the human soul—the soul's innate understanding of its moral duty, given to it via an original contract with God. The soul, Sammler explains, sits "unhappily on superstructures of explanation, poor bird, not knowing which way to fly" (3). The metaphor evokes Hegel's Owl of Minerva, which looks back on the history of Western thought from the vantage point of its completion. Here, however, this history has become an unfamiliar landscape, one in which the soul can no longer find its way. The history of Western thought has culminated in a cultural nihilism that, Sammler believes, finds expression in the social and political chaos of 1960s New York.

Sammler articulates a sociological perspective that influenced the work of many post–World War II writers: the idea that social reality is determined by ideas and values disseminated by intellectuals within the rapidly expanding new class. In the 1940s and 1950s, New York intellectuals such as Lionel Trilling found both peril and hope in this situation. The educated middle class, Trilling argued in *The Liberal Imagination*, was attracted to the "organizational impulse" that pervaded the New Deal welfare state. However, this class was also an ideal audience for the humanistic attunement to "complexity and difficulty" cultivated by literary intellectuals such as himself.[2] By the 1960s, however, many New York intellectuals had reformulated the dangers facing the new class in ways that were central to their gradual transformation from leftist Trotskyites to Reagan Republicans. According to Trilling, the corrosive attitude that he recommended in his early criticism had itself calcified into a new, institutionalized set of stock notions. Since the nineteenth century, he noted in *Beyond Culture* (1965), the dominant trend in Western literature and social thought has been antiestablishment and antibourgeois: "It is a belief still pre-eminently honored that a primary function of art and thought is to liberate the individual from the tyranny of his culture in the environmental sense and to permit him to stand beyond it in an autonomy of perception and judgment." This capacity for liberation is essential when confined to a limited milieu of artists, philosophers, visionaries, and idealists. In the mid–twentieth century, however, he says, it has become the worldview of a growing faction of humanistic intellectuals comfortably established within the university: "Between the end of the first quarter of this century and the present time there has grown up a populous group whose members take for granted the adversary culture." This group now disseminates this antinomian culture to a mass-educated public unprepared for the rigors of intellectual life, threatening to replace all established customs and traditions with a banalized version of bohemian dissent. The Arnoldian project of rehumanizing bourgeois society seems outmoded in "a society drenched with art and with newspaper gossip about the arts."[3]

For the neoconservatives, the group of New York intellectuals associated with *Commentary* and *The Public Interest*, this adversarial culture was responsible for the cultural excesses of the 1960s.[4] The neoconservatives referred to Trilling's humanist intellectuals as the "liberal elite" or "new class." As Barbara Ehrenreich notes, they did not use these terms with much sociological precision; the new class designated an arbitrary "slice of the professional middle class: in particular, a slice calculated to exclude people, such as corporate employees and professionals in private practice, who may indeed be likely, by virtue of their occupations, to be pro-business and antiliberal."[5] In effect, the term *new class* referred to any professional who also happened to hold left-of-center political beliefs. This group, the neoconservatives argued, wielded enormous power due to its influence within cultural institutions, and it was bent on destroying bourgeois society. "In any naked contest with the 'new class,'" Irving Kristol argued in the *Wall Street Journal*, "business is a certain loser."[6] In responding to this threat, the neoconservatives developed an updated version of new-class fantasy, an adaptation of the Arnoldian politics that the New York intellectuals originally espoused in militating against the progressive liberalism of the 1930s. Recognizing that they too were humanistic intellectuals, the neoconservatives recast themselves as new-class dissidents who would disseminate ideas and values more conducive to social order. "The modern world,"

Kristol argued in 1973, "and the crisis of modernity we are now experiencing, was created by ideas and by the passions which these ideas unleashed. To surmount this crisis, without destroying the modern world itself, will require new ideas—or new versions of old ideas—that will regulate these passions and bring them into a more fruitful and harmonious relation with reality."[7] In this search for alternative ideas, the neoconservatives hoped to cultivate an alliance with America's business elite, who supposedly embodied values of hard work and sexual continence threatened by the liberal elite. Corporations, Kristol noted, should "give support to those elements of the 'new class'—and they exist, if not in large numbers—which do believe in the preservation of a strong private sector."[8] Beginning in the late 1960s and early 1970s, the neoconservatives thus established the basic argument that would guide them through the culture wars of the 1980s and 1990s.

In this chapter, I argue that *Mr. Sammler's Planet* adumbrates this neoconservative cultural politics.[9] The novel is committed to a social vision derived from conservative political philosophers such as Joseph Schumpeter in which capitalist society is destroyed by its "petted intellectuals" (34). This vision in turn derives from Bellow's sense that "mental capital" (212) is more potent than economic capital, that the new class had displaced the old bourgeoisie as America's dominant elite. In arguing this point, I highlight a series of class concerns in Bellow's work often unnoticed by critics focused on the novel's troubling racial and sexual politics—in particular, its crude parodies of second-wave feminism and the Black Power movement.[10] However, rather than dismissing *Mr. Sammler's Planet* as a reflection of late 1960s political reaction among Bellow's generation of Jewish American intellectuals, I argue that the novel also explores many of the contradictions implicit in the neoconservatives' emerging cultural vision. In particular, it examines the inherent conflict between their thoroughgoing cultural determinism and their efforts to imagine a political coalition between conservative intellectuals and business leaders. Bellow foregrounds this potential alliance through the novel's central, homosocial relationship between Sammler and his dying nephew, Elya Gruner—a doctor turned real estate mogul whom Sammler holds up as an embodiment of this-worldly virtue. The entire text drives toward a reunion of these two characters, as Sammler struggles to return to Elya's deathbed but is distracted by the antics of his nephew's spoiled children, who have been corrupted by their new-class education. However, the novel also emphasizes the tensions inherent in this coalition; Sammler's devotion to the knowledge of the soul, the novel suggests, is incompatible with Elya's devotion to commerce. This revelation of the businessman's complicity with the adversary culture complicates Bellow's effort to depict intellectuals as the villains of the modern age. Furthermore, it points beyond his neoconservative cultural politics toward a more complex reading of U.S. class relations otherwise latent in his work.

NEW-CLASS DISSIDENTS

Bellow's fiction is everywhere marked by the fact that he imagined himself as a dissident new-class humanist. Like Ralph Ellison, he was one of the key 1940s and 1950s writers to negotiate the shift from literary naturalism to the novel of ideas called for by critics such as Lionel Trilling, William Phillips, and Philip Rahv. As in Ellison's case, this shift did not so much entail a rejection of sociological fiction as a transition toward a new social scientific perspective: the sociology of the cultural center pioneered by Bellow's colleague and mentor Edward Shils. Bellow's verbose novels increasingly transformed the act of intellection itself into the central object of fictional representation, replacing conventional plot with long expositions of their protagonists' ideas. They also increasingly focused on new-class subjects, leaving behind the lower-class autodidacts that populated early books such as *The Adventures of Augie March*. After *Herzog* (1964), almost all of Bellow's protagonists were scholars, writers, or literary journalists, often associated with one or another university. In this, they imitate their author, who was similarly attached to universities throughout his career—most notably the University of Chicago, where he taught in the Committee on Social Thought from 1962 to 1993. However, Bellow's protagonists also express a profound disgust for and desire to transcend the intellectual stratum to which they belong. They worry that intellectuals have done more harm than good to society; intellectuals, Sammler reflects, "are the people who set the terms, who make up the discourse, and then history follows their words. Think of the wars and revolutions we have been scribbled into" (213). They worry, furthermore, that intellectual work is devoid of moral seriousness, that it is a massive evasion of the soul's natural knowledge. They struggle, therefore, to tear apart the edifice that they have built or inherited from other thinkers. This ambivalence reflects Bellow's own attitude toward the university and the new class that it has fostered. In essays and interviews, he inveighed against American higher education, which he believed had become a home for trendy relativist theories and political extremism rather than an institution devoted to pursuing the truth. "By consenting to play an active or 'positive,' a participatory role in society," Bellow complained in his preface to Bloom's The Closing of the American Mind (1987), "the university has become inundated and saturated with the backflow of society's 'problems.' Preoccupied with questions of Health, Sex, Race, War, academics make their reputations and their fortunes and the university has become society's conceptual warehouse of often harmful influences." By contrast, Bellow argues, he has always treated his vocation as a tenured teacher differently. "For me, the university has been the place of divestiture where I am able to find help in the laborious task of discarding bad thought."[11] Bellow, in this account, was in but not of the university; he used it to free himself from its bad effects.[12]

Of all of Bellow's heroes, Sammler is the most extreme expression of this ambivalent attitude toward humanistic intellectuals. From the beginning of his life, Sammler was marked out to be an intellectual; he was born in Krakow to a family of secular Jews who named him after Schopenhauer and gave him a copy of *The World as Will and Idea* for his sixteenth birthday. In the 1930s, he lived in London as a reporter and formed attachments with the Bloomsbury group and H. G. Wells, whose utopian social philosophy he helped promulgate. The climax of his early career was his involvement in Wells's Cosmopolis project for a World State. This project, he explains, was

> based on the propagation of the sciences of biology, history, and sociology and the effective application of scientific principles to the enlargement of human life; the building of a planned, orderly, and beautiful world society: abolishing national sovereignty, outlawing war, subjecting money and credit, production, distribution, transport, population, arms manufacture et cetera to world-wide collective control, offering free universal education, personal freedom (compatible with community welfare) to the utmost degree; a service society based on a rational scientific attitude toward life. (41)

Sammler thus embraced an ambitious version of social trustee professionalism, an ideology with which he became disenchanted by the subsequent events of World War II. Indeed, through Sammler, Bellow constructs an allegory of the decline of progressive liberalism of the kind popularized by cold war liberals in the 1940s and 1950s. In a return visit to Poland, Sammler and his wife were captured by invading Nazis and thrown into a mass grave; only he survived. This brush with death functions in the same way as John Laskell's sickness in Trilling's *The Middle of the Journey*; it renders Sammler skeptical of all future-oriented philosophies aimed at improving society. Sammler instead become a postideological sage; with his one remaining eye, he reads only the Bible and Meister Eckhart, which he regards as timeless sources of wisdom at odds with contemporary intellectual fashion.

In the novel's present, Sammler lives in New York—which, in the neoconservative imagination, is a center of new-class degeneracy because of its generous welfare system and publishing industry. There,

Sammler encounters what he believes are the long-term effects of his generation's progressive liberalism. On the positive side, the rationalism implicit in Wells's World State has led to ambitious technological projects such as the space program, which echoes Wells's fantasies about moon travel; the events of the novel shortly precede the launch of *Apollo 11*. On the negative side, 1930s liberalism has culminated in the U.S. welfare state, which, if not as ambitious as Wells's socialism, has nevertheless created a degree of affluence that allows everyone to live in relative comfort: "In the gutters, along curbs was much food, eaten, as he saw at three a.m., by night-emerging rats. Buns, chicken bones, which, once, he would have thanked God to have" (138). The problem with this state of affluence is that it has also liberated New York's residents from the bourgeois work ethic, creating a city of criminals such as the black pickpocket whom Sammler sees at work on the city buses and indolent pleasure seekers such as the novel's oversexed youth; "the labor of Puritanism now was ending," Sammler reflects, "the dark satanic mills changing into light satanic mills. The reprobates converted into children of joy, the sexual ways of the seraglio and of the Congo bush adopted by the emancipated masses of New York, Amsterdam, London" (32).

Echoing Trilling's generational argument, Sammler claims that the chief symptom of this cultural degeneracy is the emergence of a new generation of would-be intellectuals who have embraced the utopianism inherent in his generation's progressive liberalism but at the same time abandoned its rationality. This generation is made up of the various youths whom Sammler encounters throughout the novel—spoiled children of the upper middle class who read Bataille, Marcuse, and Norman O. Brown. They espouse a philosophy of untrammeled individualism, one that insists on "an elaborate and sometimes quite artistic manner of presenting oneself," expressed "with hair, with clothes, with drugs and cosmetics, with genitalia, with round trips through evil, monstrosity, and orgy, with even God approached through obscenities" (229). This philosophy is Bellow's version of the adversary culture—a romantic cult of radical self-expression opposed to all of the institutions and customs that might restrict it. It fundamentally entails a revolt against the bourgeoisie and its traditional values of self-control, family affiliation, religiosity, and sexual continence. One of the novel's central conflicts thus pits Sammler's dying nephew, Elya, against Elya's two spoiled adult children, Wallace and Angela. Elya is the archetypal, self-made American man. Although born into poverty as an immigrant East European Jew, he established himself as a successful doctor and later became rich through real estate speculation. As Sammler reflects, Elya "was devoted to ideas of conduct which seemed discredited, which few people explicitly defended" (261). Elya's two children, in contrast, illustrate the collapse of the bourgeois work ethic that Sammler believes to be typical of the late 1960s. The son, Wallace, cannot settle down to a single profession. His excuse is his refusal to betray his essential inclinations. "I have to have my own necessities," he tells Sammler, "and I don't see them anywhere" (245). Wallace thus embodies the paradox of radical "authenticity" that Trilling explores in *Sincerity and Authenticity* (1972):[13] the impulse to be true to oneself, even when that self is conceived of as a bundle of incoherent, precivilized desires and emotions. Angela similarly embodies the collapse of her father's family-oriented sexual morals. She is a typically spoiled member of the new class, with a "bad education" (11) in literature from Sarah Lawrence College and a penchant for every new intellectual fashion. Her problem is at the core the same as Wallace's—a devotion to her authentic self that prevents her from respecting bourgeois sexual conventions. In the hospital, Sammler pleads with her to cave in to her father's values before his death; he chastises her, in particular, for showing up at his deathbed wearing "a microskirt, a band of green across her thighs" (295). The point, for Sammler, is for Angela at least to conform outwardly to the forms of bourgeois social life in order to please her conservative father. For Angela, however, catering to her father's values would be inauthentic, a form of playacting and a betrayal of the self. "As far as I can see," she tells Sammler, "if there is anything at all in what you say, you want an old-time deathbed scene. . . . But how could I—It goes against everything. You're talking to the wrong person" (306).

According to the novel's logic, this individualist philosophy is at once opposed to the rationalism of progressive liberals such as Wells yet also a natural outgrowth from it. In an early scene, Bellow stages a confrontation between these two philosophies when Sammler gives a lecture on "the British scene in the 1930s" to an audience of university students. Lapsing into nostalgia, Sammler evokes the original promise of the Cosmopolis project until he is interrupted and driven off the stage by a bearded New Left radical: "Why do you listen to this effete old shit? What has he got to tell you? His balls are dry. He's dead. He can't come" (42). The young man's rebut is typical, Sammler later reflects, of the ways in which the younger generation emphasizes the phallus over rational thought; unlike his own generation, this one "had no view of the nobility of being intellectuals and judges of the social order" (45). However, Bellow implies that the radical's sexualized mode of intellectual engagement is the inevitable consequence of Wells's utopianism. Wells, Sammler reflects, also wanted to liberate human sexuality from its Victorian constraints, believing that doing so would lead men and women toward a more rational and controlled enjoyment of sexuality; "utopian, he didn't even imagine that the hoped-for future would bring excess, pornography, sexual abnormality" (72). Rationalism, in other words, had dissolved the customs and traditions that keep human irrationality in check, thus paving the way toward new, postenlightenment theories that assault rationality itself. Through Sammler, Bellow thus prefigures the neoconservative equation between the counterculture and the progressive liberalism that it rebelled against.[14] Technocratic liberals created a permissive society that encouraged the sexual and political excesses of the counterculture and New Left.

What these two generations especially have in common, for Sammler, is a penchant for "explanations." As we have seen, throughout the novel Sammler distinguishes between explanations and the natural knowledge of the soul. This distinction derives in part from his idiosyncratic reading of Schopenhauer, who distinguished between the Will and Platonic Ideas: "only Ideas are not overpowered by the Will—the cosmic force, the Will, which drives all things. A blinding power. The inner creative fury of the world. What we see are only its manifestations. Like Hindu philosophy—Maya, the veil of appearances that hangs over all human experience" (209). The Will is the origin of the explanations that underlie and threaten human society, and its seat, for Schopenhauer, is the sexual organs. It is an erotic and intellectual will to power, an urge to reinvent the world in one's own image. Hence, Sammler looks on with particular dismay at the liberation of sexual energies that Wells had called for and that the younger generation in late-1960s New York actualized. This liberation goes hand in hand with an unchecked proliferation of explanations, which take the form of the sex philosophy advocated by the counterculture— sexualized theories breeding in turn more theories.

Sammler codes this liberation of sexuality and explanations in gender terms—as a release of feminine erotic energies normally kept in check by bourgeois conventions of courtship and marriage and by male moral seriousness. Women, in his view, are endlessly productive of sex and explanation—both of them detached from and destructive of the soul's innate knowledge.[15] This ostensibly feminine capacity for aimless explanation is exemplified by Margotte, Sammler's apartment mate and his dead wife's niece. Her former husband, who died in a plane crash, was a professor of political theory at a women's college (filled with "charming, idiotic, nonsensical girls" [16]), and now Margotte has taken over his métier. Trapped with her inside their apartment, Sammler is tortured by her endless parroting of fashionable ideas, a habit that parallels her sloppy housekeeping and undisciplined generative powers: "She talked junk, she gathered waste and junk in the flat, she bred junk. Look, for instance, at these plants she was trying to raise. She planted avocado pits, lemon seeds, peas, potatoes. Was there anything ever so mangy, trashy, as these potted objects?" (21). What Margotte needs, in Sammler's view, is a firm masculine presence to keep her in check, to direct her sexual energies, and to recall her explanations when they stray too far from the basic moral truths. This role used to be performed by her dead husband, who would interrupt her when her theorizing got out of control: "after she had gone on a while, he would say, 'Enough, enough of this Weimar *schmaltz*. Cut it, Margotte!' That big virile interruption would never be heard again in this cock-eyed living room" (17). In the novel, Margotte is particularly attracted to the ideas of Hannah Arendt—another unruly female intellectual detached from basic moral principles. Sammler objects in particular to Arendt's thesis about the banality of evil—the idea that the executioners at the death camps "were just ordinary lower-class people, administrators, small bureaucrats, or *Lumpenproletariat*. A mass society does not produce great criminals" (16). For Sammler, this theory obscures the fact that "everybody (except for certain bluestockings) knows what murder is. That is very old human knowledge. The best and purest human beings, from the beginning of time, have understood that life is sacred" (18). The banality of evil is another explanation, used by the Nazis themselves as "the adopted disguise of a very powerful will to abolish conscience." Arendt is thus complicit with the Nazis she describes; she, like them, is engaging in a cultural assault on "modern civilization itself" (18). Hence, Sammler sees in Margotte's repetition of Arendt a particularly noxious example of one female pseudo-intellectual's repetition of another, taking us farther and farther away from basic moral truths about the sanctity of life. Arendt's alleged moral obtuseness is compounded by Margotte, who repeats her ideas in front of a Holocaust survivor.

This critique of Arendt sets up what becomes Sammler's harshest condemnation of late 1960s New York—that it is repeating the same intellectual and cultural trends found in Weimar Germany before the rise of the Nazis; "like many people who had seen the world collapse once, Mr. Sammler entertained the possibility that it might collapse twice" (33). As we have seen, Sammler characterizes contemporary U.S. culture in terms of the prevalence of two philosophies—a technocratic rationalism that has culminated in the space program and the Great Society, on the one hand, and a radical individualism that has culminated in the counterculture, on the other. Both philosophies originated in the new class and its will to power and loosely delineate the class's division between the technical intelligentsia and humanistic intellectuals. Reflecting on this intraclass conflict, Sammler predicts that "an oligarchy of technicians, engineers, the men who ran the grand machines . . . would come to govern vast slums filled with bohemian adolescents, narcotized, beflowered, and 'whole'" (182). This same division, Sammler believes, also characterized Weimar Germany and contributed to the Nazi takeover. On the one hand, the Germans were masters of "Method," of industrial and social planning. On the other hand, "to relax from rationality and calculation, machinery, planning, technics, they had romance, mythomania, peculiar aesthetic fanaticism" (19). The result was that the technical intelligentsia pursued ever more soulless technologies for manipulating human beings and nature, and the humanistic intellectuals spun out radical ideologies that undermined the people's faith in the nation's traditions and institutions. The U.S. welfare state and adversary culture, Sammler believes, might therefore be the harbingers of a future totalitarian regime. The irony of this parallel is that it repeats the same "Weimar schmaltz" that Sammler criticizes in Arendt. Arendt's "banality of evil" thesis, like much of her work, suggests that many of the excesses of totalitarianism are latent within democratic states such as the United States—within the mentality of pencil-pushing bureaucrats who can just as easily orchestrate genocide as plan out a new housing project. Bellow's novel develops a parallel argument through its critique of the new class—that the same social impulses that culminated in Nazism are more generally present in Western civilization's educated elite.

Sammler thus struggles to distance himself from the intellectual tendencies that have led to this impasse, to reconstruct himself as a different, more serious kind of intellectual. One of the novel's ironies is that in spite of Sammler's repudiation of explanations, he himself is an endless explainer. The difference for him is that he, unlike women such as Margotte, tries to maintain a constant moral control over his theorizing, to police diligently the feminine tendency toward irresponsible talk. Sammler's model for intellectual discussion is his long dinner table talk with Dr. Govinda Lal—a Hindu scientist who has written a manuscript on moon colonization that figures prominently in the novel. The women—Margotte and Sammler's daughter, Shula—are shunted off to the kitchen to prepare the food and later sit silently at the table while Sammler holds forth on the irresponsibility of the younger generation and the need "to have some order within oneself" (228). It is a talk guided by Sammler's hard-won connections with essential moral truths—in particular, his "impressions of eternity," his "God adumbrations in the many daily forms" (237). Even then, he is afterward dissatisfied with his conversation, worried that he has become too much like the intellectuals he despises. His talk, he realizes, evaded the central moral truth of the situation—the impending death of his friend Elya, in whose house they were staying and whose food they enjoyed. "He had explained," he reflects, "he had taken positions, he had said things he hadn't meant, meant things he hadn't said. Indoors, there were activities, discussions, explanations, arrangements, rearrangements. In the house of a dying man" (247). The ideal intellectual, for Sammler, is the silent one who converses with his own soul and leaves idle talk to others.

BUSINESS ETHICS AND THE CONSERVATIVE INTELLECTUAL

Mr. Sammler's Planet thus echoes or prefigures many common themes of late 1960s–early 1970s neoconservatism: the too rapid expansion of the welfare state, the cultural effects of feminism and sexual liberation, the spread of campus radicalism, the antibourgeois ethos perpetuated by humanistic intellectuals within the new class. However, the novel also dramatizes some of the central contradictions of neoconservative thought—especially about the possibility of conservative counterintellectuals and the desirability of an alliance between them and the U.S. business elite. The neoconservatives devoted themselves to defending existing institutions—the free-market system, bourgeois values, liberal education, the nuclear family, organized religion, and so forth—on the Burkean principle that the institutions that have shown their worth over a long period of time are better than new ones invented by utopian intellectuals. The potential problem with this Burkean conservatism is that it often seemed as if the neoconservatives defended existing institutions *only* because they were established, not because the values they were based on were inherently good. As Kristol put it, the responsible conservative should give only "two cheers" for capitalism; it was the best possible social system, far better than any socialist alternative, but it was still deeply flawed. Conservatives should defend capitalism against its detractors because the system works, not because of any utopian promise inherent within it; "a capitalist society does not want more than two cheers for itself. Indeed, it regards the impulse to give three cheers for any social, economic, or political system as expressing a dangerous—because it is misplaced—enthusiasm."[16] At the same time, Kristol and other neoconservatives affirmed the need for capitalism to be rooted in a supportive value system, especially in religious beliefs that reinforce rather than undermine the bourgeois order. This desire to root capitalism in religion was not a problem for all neoconservatives, some of whom, like the Catholic Michael Novak, saw little distinction between politics and theology; in *The Spirit of Democratic Capitalism* (1982), Novak argued that capitalism was the social system most congruent with Christian ethics.[17] However, it was a problem for others, such as Kristol, who were essentially secular Jews. In the well-known essay "Christianity, Judaism, and Socialism" (1978), Kristol distinguished between "gnostic" and "orthodox" religions. The former rebel against the world; "the gnostic tends to say that the proper and truly authentic human response to a world of multiplicity, division, conflict, suffering and death is some kind of indignant metaphysical rebellion, a rebellion that will liberate us from the prison of this world." The latter urge us to live in the world as it is; "the function of orthodoxy in all religions is to sanctify daily life and to urge us to achieve our fullest human potential through virtuous practice in our daily life, whether it be the fulfillment of the law in Judaism or Islam or *imitatio Christi* in Christianity."[18] Kristol, needless to say, was in favor of orthodoxy; every stable society must have an established religion to guide its citizens and provide them with stable values. However, it did not matter much to Kristol *which* orthodoxy was in power. For this reason, he urged his fellow neoconservatives, many of them Jewish, to make alliances with fundamentalist Christians in the Republican Party.[19] He referred to himself as a "neo-orthodox Jew": "That is, I am nonpracticing—or nonobservant as we say—but in principle, very sympathetic to the spirit of orthodoxy."[20] Paleoconservatives such as William F. Buckley Jr. and Pat Buchanan therefore complained that Kristol's defense of religion often veered into instrumentalism.[21] The question raised by Kristol's writing on religion and capitalism was, "How do conservative counterintellectuals defend an orthodoxy that they do not believe is absolute?"

Sammler faces this problem throughout Bellow's novel. One of Sammler's basic complaints about the counterculture is that it rejects the established forms of life as inauthentic. The counterculture refuses to accept any form of orthodoxy and instead embraces a secular gnosticism that would sweep away all existing traditions and institutions, leaving nothing in their place. Wallace Gruner, for instance, exemplifies this disdain for tradition in his attitude toward the house that he grew up in. In the midst of Dr. Lal and Sammler's long discussion about space travel and individualism, Wallace breaks into some pipes in his father's attic, searching for money he thinks his father has hidden there. Later, standing outside the flooded house, he explains that roots mean nothing to him: "Roots? Roots are not modern. That's a peasant conception, soil and roots. Peasantry is going to disappear. That's the real meaning of the modern revolution, to prepare world peasantry for a new state of existence" (245–46).

This same rootlessness, the novel suggests, is also characteristic of the technical intelligentsia who have inherited the rationalism of the Western tradition. Dr. Lal, the Hindu scientist, literally wants to disconnect humankind from its ancestral home—by propelling the species into outer space. This, he believes, will resolve much of the cultural chaos that he, like Sammler, observes in contemporary New York. Humankind will now have a new frontier into which it can direct its boundless destructive energies: "Not to accept the opportunity would make this earth seem more and more a prison. If we could soar out and did not, we would condemn ourselves" (219). Like Wallace, Dr. Lal depicts this project as a personal revolt against an established, traditional culture—in his case, the close-knit Hindu household of his childhood. "As a child," Lal reflects, "I could not bear to be separated from Mother. Nor, for that matter, father. . . . I see now that I had set myself a task of distance from objects of closest attachment. In which, Mr. Sammler, outer space is an opposite—personally, an emotional pole" (221–22).

However, Sammler himself lacks roots. As we have seen, he has developed a personal belief system based on his rejection of his earlier utopian progressivism. He now believes that the soul has an essential understanding of its moral obligations, based on an original contract with God. Hence, his final prayer over Elya's body praises Elya for being "aware that he must meet, and he did meet—through all the confusion and degrading clowning of this life through which we are speeding—he did meet the terms of his contract. The terms which, in his inmost heart, each man knows" (313). Alan Berger argues in his discussion of the novel's Jewish influences that this prayer is a kaddish and that Sammler's notion of the contract is a modified version of the Jewish covenant.[22] However, Sammler seems distant from any existing version of Judaism; he was raised in a secular home, was named after an anti-Semitic philosopher, and today lives in exile in New York. He mocks his daughter's obsession with attending rabbinical lectures, and there is no evidence that he practices Jewish dietary restrictions; his dinner with Dr. Lal includes a very nonkosher lobster salad. Instead, he too has embraced a gnostic faith—albeit one that seeks to flee from the world without actually changing it. In his old age, he has embraced the mysticism of Meister Eckhart, which holds that true contact with God comes only after we have stripped ourselves of all this-worldly distractions. "'See to it that you are stripped of all creatures, of all consolation from creatures,'" Sammler quotes. "'For certainly as long as creatures comfort and are able to comfort you, you will never find true comfort. But if nothing can comfort you save God, truly God will console you'" (253). Sammler, like Lal, fantasizes about leaving this world behind. Indeed, his chief objection to Lal's technological proposal is that it does not go far enough. "This is not the way to get out of spatial–temporal prison," he reflects. "Distant is still finite. Finite is still feeling through the veil, examining the naked inner reality with a gloved hand" (53).

Sammler, like Kristol, thus seems torn between a personal, skeptical gnosticism and a belief that the rest of the world needs some sort of orthodoxy. This opposition between a freethinking elite and an orthodox populace runs throughout much neoconservative thought. It was central to the work of Leo Strauss, the Jewish émigré political philosopher who taught in Bellow's department at the University of Chicago from 1949 to 1968. In Kristol's terms, Strauss was "an intellectual aristocrat who thought that the truth could make *some* minds free, but he was convinced that there was an inherent conflict between philosophic truth and the political order, and that the popularization and vulgarization of these truths might import unease, turmoil, and the release of popular passions hitherto held in check by tradition and religion."[23] Hence, the cornerstone of political thought, Strauss believed, should be Plato's *Republic*, which imagines a philosophical elite disseminating to the nonphilosophical populace useful myths that are conducive to social order. This kind of elitism had its attractions for Bellow, as it did for the rest of the neoconservatives. Bellow's most unalloyed presentation of it was his portrait of Allan Bloom, Strauss's most famous disciple, as Ravel-

stein in the novel of the same name published in 2000. Many neoconservatives read this novel as a betrayal of their creed, in particular for its focus on Bloom's homosexuality. However, the novel was
in fact the apotheosis of Bellow's interest in the possibility of creating a conservative counterelite. On the one hand, Ravelstein is a gay
man dying of AIDS who disregards the lifestyle restrictions of the
Moral Majority in order to devote himself to a life of philosophical
inquiry and hedonistic pleasure. On the other hand, he excoriates
the moral laxness of the society he lives in and has trained a generation of neoconservative disciples who work in the Reagan and elder
Bush administrations.[24] The novel's point is not that Ravelstein is a
hypocrite; rather, it is that he belongs to the worthy few who can embody the adversary culture in a spirit of philosophical free play. In
the novel's opening scene, Chick (the Bellovian double) and Ravelstein are breakfasting in a penthouse of Paris's most expensive hotel,
relishing the money earned from Ravelstein's best-selling book
(Bloom's *The Closing of the American Mind*). Meanwhile, Michael Jackson (whom Ravelstein dismisses as a "glamour monkey"[25]) and his
retinue occupy the entire floor below them. The novel juxtaposes the
deserving intellectual elite (the Nobel Prize–winning novelist,
the learned philosopher) with the undeserving, black popular enter-
tainer. Ravelstein's lifestyle, like Bellow's, is licensed by his Platonic
search for the True and the Good; Jackson's lifestyle supposedly exemplifies the culture of immorality disseminated through his music.

Something similar is at work in the case of Artur Sammler's
search for the soul's essential knowledge. The novel's young intellectuals, women, and ethnic minorities lack the moral fortitude necessary for this search. They need the useful myths, and their lives
need to be constrained in ways appropriate to them. However, these
myths, if they are to maintain the social order, must in some way
conform to the soul's knowledge—just as in Plato's *Republic* the myth
of the three classes of human beings conforms to the philosopher's
notion of justice. Hence, throughout the novel Sammler searches for
an individual or institution that might be a this-wordly translation

of the soul's truth, a model for how order might be restored in America. This embodiment, as we have seen, is not present in any of the novel's other intellectuals and scientists. Nor does it inhere in the nation of Israel, which Sammler visits during the Six Day War and writes about for a Polish newspaper. Israel, at first glance, seems like an ideal example of a society that combines religious orthodoxy (in Kristol's sense) with secular statehood; Israel is a self-conscious effort to rediscover Jewish roots, to re-create a lost homeland. For this reason, it occupies a special place in neoconservative thought. Sammler, however, like his creator, is ambivalent about Zionism.[26] On the one hand, he cares for Israel's survival and visits it fearing that "for the second time in twenty-five years the same people were threatened by extermination" (142). On the other hand, Israel's attempt to embody Jewish tradition is exemplified by Eisen, Shula's abusive and estranged husband, who migrated to Israel after World War II. Eisen is in some ways Sammler's double; he too survived the Holocaust and was partially crippled by it, losing his toes to frostbite. However, as Sander Gilman puts it, he is someone who, "like Israel, has strengthened himself, has become a 'muscle Jew.'"[27] An ironworker by trade, Eisen forges artistic medallions that try to reinvent a more violent, triumphant Judaism. One of them is shaped like a Sherman tank; another's inscription reads "Hazak," or "strengthen thyself," the order that God gives to Joshua before the battle of Jericho (170). In a grotesque image of interethnic conflict, during a visit to New York Eisen uses a bag full of these medallions to brain the black pickpocket who had been troubling Sammler, leaving him unconscious and bleeding on the pavement. This scene evokes Sammler's memory of the dead and dying Arabs from the Six Day War, killed by napalm contravened by international law (250). The implication is that Zionism is a deformed version of Judaism, one that translates the desire to protect one's tradition into a violent intolerance toward others. It is a case of orthodoxy transformed into ideological extremism.

Instead, Sammler believes that his desired synthesis of tradition and this-worldly virtue might be found in his successful nephew, Elya. For him, Elya is the model of a good man, one who has fulfilled his contract with God; as Sammler explains to Angela, "your father has had his assignments. Husband, medical man—he was a good doctor—family man, success, American, wealthy retirement with a Rolls Royce. We have our assignments. Feeling, outgoingness, expressiveness, kindness, heart—all these fine human things which by a peculiar turn of opinion strike people now as shady activities" (303). Elya embodies Kristol's ideal of orthodoxy; he has channeled his energies into material success, never rebelling against the status quo. As a former gynecologist, a specialist in the "female generative slime" (82), he is a figure for masculine control over female energies. He is akin to Margotte's deceased husband, with his "virile interruption" (17) of her unruly explanations. As a real estate mogul, he exemplifies the bourgeoisie's supposed investment in stability and roots—the aspects of social life dismissed by his adversarial son and daughter. Sammler's implication is that if more Americans were like Elya, the country would escape from its current cultural chaos; "if the earth deserves to be abandoned," Sammler silently addresses his nephew, "if we are now to be driven streaming into other worlds, starting with the moon, it is not because of the likes of you" (86). Most especially, Elya has a facility with interpersonal relations that Sammler lacks. Elya, Sammler reflects, "courted everyone, tried to make contact with people, winning their hearts, engaging their interest, getting personal even with waitresses, lab technicians, manicurists" (302). Sammler, in contrast, cannot even express affection for his neurotic daughter, a fellow Holocaust survivor. Hence, the novel's entire impulse is to reunite Sammler and Elya, to bring together the conservative humanist with the hard-working doctor and businessman. This union is mutually beneficial. For Sammler, Elya's largesse provides him with the material means to pursue his life as an independent humanist. Elya is Sammler's patron; he has freed him from the need to associate himself with the academy or to publish his ideas on the mass market. For Elya, Sammler's "knowledge of the soul" is essential in helping him prepare for death. Throughout his last days, Elya has been on the telephone with his lawyer, making final business arrangements, buying and selling stock and settling his will. However, "at the very end business would not do for Elya. Some, many, would go on with business to the last breath, but Elya was not like that, not so limited" (260). Sammler believes that if he can only return to Elya's deathbed, they will have a final conversation about "essentials": "Any degree of frankness might have been possible. In the going phase, a moment of truth" (260).

This desire for a union between conservative intellectuals and respectable businessmen was typical of neoconservative thought; the neoconservatives believed that civilization could be saved through a spirited defense of the business elite from its liberal detractors. The problem with capitalism is that the adversary culture has unmoored it from its ideological justification—the Protestant work ethic. Hence, Kristol looked back with nostalgia to the days when Horatio Alger was a popular writer. In Alger's work, he argues, "one finds a moral conception of business as an honorable vocation for honorable men."[28] The Alger hero combines worldly success with moral probity. This myth, however, has been undermined by decades of attacks on business civilization by the liberal-dominated mediacracy; humanistic intellectuals demonize the business executive as a selfish villain, guided by the profit motive and indifferent to society's well-being. This hatred of business, Kristol claims, has spread throughout society so that even the children of the business elite look on their parents' accomplishments with disdain. The solution is for the capitalists of today to fund conservative intellectuals who will reinvent the bourgeois myths. Kristol thus exhorts the business elite to take better care of their ideological interests—to direct their philanthropy, for instance, away from liberal universities toward conservative think tanks.

However, this proposed marriage of capital and ideological savvy is a problematic one. The problem—as neoconservatives of the 1960s and 1970s, including Kristol, well knew—is that capitalism is no longer what it was in the days of Ragged Dick. The entrepreneurial business class that Horatio Alger extolled no longer exists. Instead, corporations are administered by managers and executives who are themselves defined by their educationally acquired cultural capital rather than by their ownership of the means of production. By appealing to the business elite, neoconservatives were in fact appealing to one segment of the new class against another. These corporate managers themselves frequently lack the respect for tradition and existing institutions that, according to Kristol, should justify their existence; in Alvin Gouldner's terms, they too are dependent on the culture of critical discourse that erodes traditional forms of authority. Hence, Kristol often called attention to unscrupulous behavior on the part of corporations and exhorted his business readers to become conscious of their public image and ethical duty to the community; "in a liberal democracy, everyone's self-interest is best served if each of us is capable, when required, of temporarily rising above self-interest. *That* is the social responsibility of a corporation: to behave like a citizen when circumstances seem to require it, and regardless of whether or not the law demands it."[29] The corporate elite, in other words, should forestall the antibourgeois complaints of humanistic intellectuals by morally policing itself. Indeed, one of the reasons why the counterculture thrives and disseminates antibourgeois values is that so many corporations fund it; "how many businessmen refuse, as a matter of honor and of principle, to advertise in a publication such as *The Rolling Stone* [*sic*] or even *Playboy*, publications which make a mockery of their industry, their integrity, their fidelity, the very quality of their lives? The question answers itself."[30] At times, neoconservatives such as Kristol thus claimed to be opposed to corporate interests—especially when corporations disseminated products, such as pornography, that corroded public virtue.

Hence, Kristol's work uneasily combined two strands of neoconservative thought—a strand that blamed all of the alleged deprivations of late capitalist society on the cultural influence of left-wing humanistic intellectuals and a strand that saw these deprivations as effects of corporate capitalism itself. This later, more pessimistic reading of capitalism originated in the work of the economist and sociologist Joseph Schumpeter, another key influence for many neoconservatives. In *Capitalism, Socialism, and Democracy* (1940), Schumpeter prefigured both Trilling's account of the adversary culture and the neoconservative assault on the new class by arguing that capitalism would be undone by its petted intellectuals. However, Schumpeter's more basic points are that capitalism itself gives rise to a rationalist demystification of all traditions and values and that this demystification at once makes possible the expansion of the intellectual stratum and generates the social discontent to which intellectuals give voice. "Unlike any other type of society," he argues, "capitalism inevitably and by virtue of the very logic of its civilization creates, educates and subsidizes a vested interest in social unrest." The problem with capitalism, according to Schumpeter's analysis, is that it undermines all of the traditions, institutions, and values of the traditional societies out of which it emerged. However, it cannot generate any enthusiasm or collective belief to replace them and thus undermines the cultural conditions necessary for its own survival; "capitalism creates a critical frame of mind which, after having destroyed the moral authority of so many other institutions, in the end turns against its own; the bourgeois finds to his amazement that the rationalist attitude does not stop at the credentials of kings and popes but goes on to attack private property and the whole scheme of bourgeois values."[31] Indeed, according to Schumpeter, capitalism even erodes enthusiasm for itself on the part of its ruling business elite. With the transition from entrepreneurial capitalism to corporate capitalism, the system is increasingly run by individuals with no stake in its survival; stockholders have no emotional investment in a particular company or its products apart from the dividends it pays them, and the executives who make managerial decisions are merely salaried functionaries.

This pessimistic strand of neoconservative thought culminated in the work of sociologist Daniel Bell, who was approvingly cited by most of the neoconservatives but who maintained his distance from the movement. Like many neoconservatives, Bell echoed Trilling's critique of the adversary culture as an antinomian trend that would tear apart U.S. society. However, unlike Kristol, he did not imagine that liberal intellectuals created this culture. The neoconservative notion of the new class, he argues in a 1979 essay, is "a linguistic and sociological muddle. It mixes together two concepts: the emergence of a new social *stratum* [the professional-managerial class] and the stridency of a cultural *attitude*."[32] The former is a variegated array of professions with little ideological consistency. The latter is a product of changes that have occurred within capitalism itself. He describes these changes in *The Cultural Contradictions of Capitalism* (1976): "mass production on an assembly line, which made a cheap automobile possible; the development of marketing, which rationalized the art of identifying different kinds of buying groups and whetting consumer appetites; and the spread of installment buying, which, more than any other social device, broke down the old Protestant fear of debt."[33] Echoing Max Weber's analysis of the later stages of the Puritan ethic, Bell argues that capitalism gives rise to a hedonistic culture that is required by the demands of consumer capitalism but that also threatens to destroy it.

This account of the cultural contradictions of capitalism is a nagging undercurrent in *Mr. Sammler's Planet*, threatening to unravel Sammler's critique of intellectuals' corrosive impact on society. In particular, this strand comes to the fore in Bellow's depiction of Elya Gruner. It is telling that Bellow can only imagine an individual who conforms to the Horatio Alger myth by making him a doctor. As a poor immigrant, Elya can establish the economic capital necessary for his transformation into a real estate mogul only through the meritocratic route of professional accomplishment. In addition, he exemplifies all of the problems that would haunt Kristol's efforts to idealize the U.S. business elite. Like Kristol's executives, Elya is not above profiting from the counterculture; "youth is a big business," he explains to Sammler. "Schoolchildren spend fantastic amounts. If enough kids get radical, that's a new mass market, then it's a big operation" (80). He is more directly responsible for his children's lack of professional and sexual constancy; he has spoiled them and put them on a comfortable monthly stipend. As Sammler points out to Angela, "he's not stupid and giving a young woman like you a capital of half a million dollars to live in New York City, he would have to be very dumb to think you were not amusing yourself" (163). This corrosion of his children's values can be directly tied to his own entrepreneurial accomplishments. As Sammler discovers at the end of the novel, Elya, in his first career as a gynecologist, performed abortions for the mafia and hid the cash in his country estate. The moral uncertainty that plagues Elya's children thus originates in their conventional father. Sammler's concluding invocation of Elya's contract with God is as much a hopeful prayer as anything else; the myth of the virtuous bourgeois can be invoked only in that figure's absence.

Instead, the novel offers another, more cynical account of what a synthesis of humanistic learning and business sense might look like. This synthesis is embodied in Lionel Feffer, the graduate student in diplomatic history who arranges for Sammler's disastrous lecture on Wells's Cosmopolis project. On the one hand, Feffer is a typical, dissolute member of the new class as envisaged by the neoconservatives; he's up to date with the newest theoretical ideas and an avid seducer of young wives. His academic specialization exemplifies his new-class desire to refashion the world according to intellectual ideas; he belongs to a society called the Foreign Ministers' Club, whose members "took up a question like the Crimean War or the Boxer Rebellion and did it all again, writing one another letters as the foreign minister of France, England, Germany, Russia. They obtained very different results" (39). On the other hand, he is a budding entrepreneur, with money on the stock market and a controlling interest in a Guatemalan insurance company. He is a recurring figure in Bellow's fiction—the small-time, capitalist con artist who besets Bellow's humanist protagonist and tries to involve him in shady moneymaking schemes. This figure is at once repellant and attractive. He is repellant in that he accelerates the breakdown in traditions and values that Bellow laments. However, he also embodies a primal acquisitive energy that Bellow sees as fundamental to American society: "Sammler appreciated the degree of life in young Feffer, the marvelous rich color of his cheeks, the passion-sounds he made" (110). He functions, to a certain degree, as a figure for the artist himself. As Andrew Hoberek argues, one of the ways in which Bellow distanced himself from the university and other new-class institutions was by insisting on his dual success as a literary entrepreneur and an uncompromising artist; for him, Hoberek suggests, "the market of public taste comes to seem like not only a comparative refuge but indeed the very place where intellectual virtues per se can be realized."[34] Feffer is thus the character in *Mr. Sammler's Planet* who most approximates Bellow's own economic and institutional position. However, his market connections, which liberate him from the university, in fact exacerbate his new-class disregard for morals and traditions. Through Feffer, *Mr. Sammler's Planet* blames the corruption of American values on the entrepreneurial spirit itself; the Horatio Alger hero is just as oblivious to the soul's essential knowledge as the university-bred members of the adversary culture.

This pessimistic assessment of capitalism's cultural contradictions troubles Bellow's insistence, throughout his work, that societies are made and unmade by their ruling ideas. As I argued in the introduction, Bellow first established this theme in *The Adventures of Augie March*, which envisaged humanity as a horde of reality inventors making and remaking the world. This theme determined many of the formal innovations of Bellow's subsequent oeuvre; his loosely structured, verbose novels dramatize the dialectical conflict of ideas that Trilling and other New York intellectuals argued should be central to the novel in an era of new-class hegemony. In a world literally constructed out of ideas, the novelist's task is to play these ideas against each other in order to arrive at the basic certainties that they conceal. However, Bellow's suggestion in *Mr. Sammler's Planet* that the culture of late-1960s New York is a necessary product of capitalism's historical development hints at a more complicated account of the relation between ideas and social reality otherwise obscured in his work. It hints that the intellectuals that Bellow writes about in his fiction are not inventors of reality but rather figures giving voice to changes they did not create and cannot master. As Daniel Bell complains about the neoconservative notion of the new class, "in seeking to map the course of social change, one should not mistake the froth for the deeper currents that carry it along."[35] In adumbrating the cultural politics of the neoconservative movement, *Mr. Sammler's Planet* also traces out the consequences of this mistake.

Moreover, the novel at once prefigures the right-wing coalition that would emerge in the 1970s and highlights potential fissures within it. This coalition was one that would bring together new-class dissidents with the business elite, who together would appeal to a populist constituency of conservative-value voters. It was a coalition that culminated in the Reagan Revolution and later in Newt Gingrich's "Contract with America." However, it was also one that Bellow never felt entirely comfortable with. In novels after *Mr. Sammler's Planet*, Bellow increasingly represented the moneyed elite as a corrupting influence on his intellectual heroes. For instance, *More Die of Heartbreak* (1987), written at the height of the Reagan era, revisits many of the themes and relationships of *Mr. Sammler's Planet*. Like the earlier novel, it exemplifies the moneyed elite through a gynecologist, Dr. Layamon, who also dabbles in real estate. And like *Mr. Sammler's Planet*, it revolves around a failed relationship between Dr. Layamon and a conservative scholar—Benn Crader, a botanist who marries Layamon's socialite daughter.[36] This time, however, it is the moneyed elite who consume a dissolute popular culture; conversations at Layamon family dinners typically focus on recent Hollywood horror films. And it is the moneyed elite who disregard tradition and family affections; Dr. Layamon pressures Benn into suing his elderly uncle—an action that precipitates the uncle's death. The intellectual, in this rewriting of the Sammler/Gruner relationship, finally flees from the bourgeois' embrace; at the end of the novel,

Benn abandons his wife and her family in order to study arctic lichens. Benn in the arctic wilderness exemplifies Bellow's new sense of the incompatibility between intellect and established wealth. The moneyed elite, in Bellow's later account, has been thoroughly corrupted by the adversary culture. Conservative intellectuals, concerned with the pursuit of the True and the Good, stand alone in a society hostile toward them.

5

EXPERTS WITHOUT INSTITUTIONS

NEW LEFT PROFESSIONALISM IN MARGE PIERCY AND URSULA K. LE GUIN

For Alvin Gouldner, one of the clearest examples of the new class's growing restiveness was the dramatic emergence of the New Left in the 1960s. This movement, he noted, attracted students from disciplines most closely associated with the culture of critical discourse: the humanities, the liberal arts, and the social and theoretical sciences. It also attracted activists who grew up within professional households; their parents "commonly taught that authority was not right just because it was authority, that people had to be given reasons for their actions and policies."[1] This ingrained sense of professional autonomy, in Gouldner's account, ran up against the bureaucratic structure of the postwar university and other U.S. institutions. The New Left was thus a movement of young professionals who hoped to disseminate their version of the culture of critical discourse throughout the welfare state. Tom Hayden described the New Left's class consciousness as follows: "Most of the active student radicals today come from middle to upper-middle class professional homes. They were born with status and affluence as facts of life, not goals to be striven for. In their upbringing, their parents stressed the right of children to question and make judgments, producing perhaps the first generation of young people both affluent and independent of mind. And then these students so often encountered social institutions that denied them their independence and betrayed the democratic ideals they were taught."[2] Amplifying the new-class fantasies of the postwar era, the New Left envisaged themselves as the saving remnant of the educated middle class, attuned to anti-instrumental values in an era dominated by technical rationality.

However, this new-class politics pulled the New Left in at least two different directions. As Gouldner and Hayden's comments suggest, the student movement was in part an expression of the educated middle class's newfound sense of independence, which chafed at any restrictions placed on professional autonomy. In order to become "part of the system," Mario Savio complained in 1964, university students "must suppress the most creative impulses that they have" and conform to a "depersonalized, unresponsive bureaucracy."[3] As several intellectual historians have suggested, this individualist tendency was not really at odds with the changing dynamics of postindustrial society, which tended to pit the entrepreneurial creativity of individual knowledge workers against the rigidity of established institutions. George Vickers argues that the New Left objectively represented "a force for the rationalization of social relationships and cultural values *within* capitalist economic organization, rather than a force for the abolishment of that economic form."[4] Sean McCann and Michael Szalay similarly argue that the student radicals were unknowing harbingers of expert professionalism—the newer model of professionalism that conceived of experts as independent entrepreneurs who sell their knowledge and abilities to the highest bidder. They point out that, as Hayden and other activists recognized, "[A] little noticed but important battle was shaping up between young professionals and the very organizational structures that had shielded their disciplines but that increasingly seemed hidebound and outmoded." This conflict, McCann and Szalay argue, contributed to the "increasing doubtfulness about public institutions" that helped erode the welfare state.[5]

However, if the New Left was the vanguard of expert professionalism, it was also a movement of young professionals who distrusted the very notion of expert privilege and wanted to subject it to community controls. Hence, many of the New Left's most influential political initiatives consisted of efforts to dissolve the boundaries between professionals and nonprofessionals so as to give nonexperts a greater say in the application of expert knowledge. These efforts were spearheaded by Students for a Democratic Society's (SDS) community-development projects of the mid-1960s, which coincided with the federal government's emphasis on community action in the War on Poverty. They culminated in various movements to reform social work, psychiatry, and other helping professions through the creation of community centers and free clinics, often staffed by volunteer workers disenchanted with established institutions.[6] A key strand of New Left thinking, in other words, was oriented toward fashioning an antiauthoritarian version of social trustee professionalism, counteracting its paternalism but reinforcing its emphasis on social responsibility. In contrast to the libertarian strand described by Vickers, McCann, and Szalay, this opposing strand gave free play to the New Left's communitarian ideology; New Left activists envisaged professionals as catalysts for the creation of local communities that would counter the anomie of postindustrial society. This version of professionalism, which influenced many of the progressive social movements that survived the 1960s, such as second-wave feminism, consumer advocacy, and environmentalism, was the New Left's most important positive contribution to American political life.

As I argue in this chapter, this contradiction in the New Left's orientation toward the new class was central to one of the movement's most lasting literary legacies—the new utopian science fiction of the 1970s. The two most famous works in this genre are Marge Piercy's *Woman on the Edge of Time* (1976) and Ursula K. Le Guin's *The Dispossessed* (1974),[7] both by writers generationally removed from the student movement but sympathetic to its aims.[8] Both novels enact the historical vision held by Gouldner and other new-class theorists, attempting to imagine what it might mean for professional expertise to displace economic capital entirely as society's ruling impulse.[9] In so doing, the two works dramatize the New Left's conflicted class identity as movement intellectuals alternately demanded absolute autonomy for professional work and attempted to subordinate that work to community controls. Both Piercy and Le Guin try to resolve this conflict by imagining their utopians as at once professionals and nonprofessionals, as self-directed new-class experts and communalistic outsiders. Both construct high-tech, agrarian utopias in which small communities of skilled professionals till the land in the manner of premodern peasants. However, in both cases the contradiction at the heart of New Left professionalism reasserts itself, and this synthesis falls apart. Hence, *Woman on the Edge of Time*'s new-class utopia finally depends on the total eradication of professional autonomy. *The Dispossessed*, in contrast, recoils at the prospect of this loss and instead moves toward a libertarian conception of professional autonomy that approaches the emergent expert professionalism of the 1960s and 1970s.

By this point, these efforts to work through the ideology of professionalism were not unprecedented within the utopian tradition. As Frederic Jameson argues, utopian fiction is typically circumscribed by its authors' class position—generally, some segment of the intellectual stratum. Sir Thomas More's foundational text, for instance, reflects "that public sphere that is in reality and in history unable to come into being: that situation of mandarin governmental power and authority that the humanist intellectuals are unable to achieve."[10]

In America, the utopian tradition, beginning with Edward Bellamy's *Looking Backward* (1887),[11] similarly embodied a managerial vision of enlightened technocrats rationally planning society for the benefit of all. Conversely, in the dystopian tradition popularized by George Orwell's *Nineteen Eighty-Four* (1949), managerial idealism becomes synonymous with totalitarian nightmare.[12] What is distinctive about the new utopian fiction of the 1970s is the way that its conflicted attitude toward the new class leads to an amalgamation of these two perspectives. In attempting to balance the New Left's demands for professional autonomy and public responsibility, this literature ends up developing an incisive critique of the very class that supposedly brings utopia into being—but without, for all that, relinquishing the hope that it might do so. *Woman on the Edge of Time* and *The Dispossessed* thus reflect the simultaneous idealization and distrust of the new class that runs throughout postwar fiction and social theory and reaches its sharpest articulation in the 1960s and 1970s.

PEASANT TECHNICIANS

The political destiny of the professional stratum was a particularly vexing problem for Marge Piercy, who was one of the founders of Movement for a Democratic Society (MDS), an adult chapter of SDS that was oriented toward mobilizing disgruntled professionals. With Robert Gottlieb, she coauthored MDS's central working paper (1968), one of the key statements of new-class theory within the New Left.[13] Lower-rank professionals, she argued, were an ideal constituency for the radical movement. On the one hand, professional work embodied the promise of autonomous, nonalienated labor: "People in the service professions, the arts and sciences often do strongly identify with their work. What are you? I am a physicist. I am a doctor. I am a sculptor in welded steel."[14] On the other hand, this sense of vocation clashed with the bureaucratic structure and private-sector funding of most middle-class workplaces, which pushed professionals into projects at odds with their personal ethics. MDS's function, Piercy and Gottlieb argued, was twofold. First, members should change from within the institutions they inhabit so that the institutions are based on "human rather than profit needs." Second, they should question the notion and practice of professionalism itself, paring away the artificial barriers that separate experts from nonexperts. Every radical professional should learn "to sort out what is truly creative in his field, the red meat of it, from the part that is merely professional obfuscation."[15] Revolutionary professionalism, for Piercy, would eschew the rhetoric and symbols of authority with which experts surround themselves. However, it would maintain the creative aspects of professionalism, which offer the best hope for instituting a better social system.

At the same time, Piercy saw professionalism as an insidious force, one that threatened to corrupt political movements aimed at the transformation of U.S. society, including the New Left itself. Hence, after her involvement with MDS, Piercy became one of many feminists to break with the New Left on the basis that it perpetuated the sexism and authoritarianism of the society it wanted to escape. The problem with many movement men, she argued in "The Grand Coolie Damn" (1969), one of the most influential feminist essays to emerge from this period, was that they arrogated a pseudo-professional authority that mimicked typical workplace patterns: "To be a professional anything in the United States is to think of oneself as an expert and one's ideas as semi-sacred, and to treat others in a certain way—professionally. Do you question your doctor when he prescribes in dog Latin what you should gulp down?" The New Left, for her, had become the ultimate other-directed workplace, in which male leaders "use all the forms of workers' control and collective decision making to persuade others that they are involved in a 'we' that is never out of [the male leaders'] control."[16] Indeed, this tendency was worse within the New Left than in the bureaucratic institutions of the welfare state; the latter at least were governed by formal rules and a self-evident hierarchy that checked the professional will-to-power. The New Left, in contrast, gave free reign to a charismatic authoritarianism that was a direct consequence of its male members' demands for absolute individual autonomy. The problem, for Piercy, was to discover new, communalistic models of professionalism that avoided the twin dangers of bureaucracy and charisma.

Much of Piercy's subsequent fiction can be read as an attempt to respond to this challenge: how to transform professionalism into a radical social practice while avoiding the authoritarianism of the later New Left. As Heather Hicks observes, the central characters in Piercy's various novels are often professional workaholics—typically computer programmers and scientists—who identify absolutely with their work and find pleasure and meaning in it; at the heart of her aesthetic is a "liberal feminist faith that women can be empowered by lives wholly committed to paid, public work."[17] At the same time, her novels offer a programmatic critique of the institutions within which this work takes place—the corporate workplace, public institutions, and the university. In the case of *Woman on the Edge of Time*, this critique is directed against medicine, psychiatry, and social work—disciplines that most dramatically lend themselves to the complaint that professionals are no more than agents of social control, charged with disciplining lower-class populations. The novel focuses on the plight of Consuela ("Connie") Ramos, a Chicana woman involuntarily committed to a New York state mental hospital after she violently attacks her niece's abusive pimp. Here, she discovers that she can project herself into various possible futures, including a future utopia that remedies all of the flaws of the present-day welfare state. Drawing on the antipsychiatry movement of the period and echoing Ken Kesey's *One Flew Over the Cuckoo's Nest* (1962),[18] the novel anatomizes the techniques that mental health professionals use to demean and dominate their clients—rigid rules about when patients can eat, who they can talk to, and so on. In addition, it portrays these professionals as motivated by a desire to further their careers, even at their patients' expense; for example, Connie is a test subject in a project that involves implanting electrodes inside patients' brains in order to regulate their behavior. Like Kesey, Piercy views this impetus toward social control as typical of welfare-state professionals and thus uses the asylum as a figure for the U.S. social system.[19] Inverting the usual metaphor of the welfare system as a safety net, Connie instead thinks of it as an entrapping net of discourse cast over her by welfare professionals who presume to control the lives of the city's underclass: "All those experts lined up against her in a jury dressed in medical white and judicial black—social workers, caseworkers, child guidance counselors, psychiatrists, doctors, nurses, clinical psychologists, probation officers—all those cool knowing faces had caught her and bound her in their nets of jargon hung all with tiny barbed hooks that stuck in her flesh and leaked a slow weakening poison" (52). The conclusion toward which the novel moves is that members of this underclass must fight back against this professional control using any means necessary. Hence, in the concluding chapter Connie kills her doctors and nurses by poisoning their coffee.

As in the case of many New Left and second-wave feminist attacks on the welfare state, this imagined retaliation against the helping professions seemingly dovetails with contemporaneous right-wing arguments for dismantling public services. This attack seems particularly misguided in the context of Piercy's representation of the public mental health system, which had already been decimated by the time Piercy wrote her novel. In the early 1970s, long-term involuntary patients such as Connie were increasingly rare; more commonly, after decades of deinstitutionalization and cutbacks, mental patients were living on the streets or in run-down welfare hotels.[20] As Maria Farland notes, by the 1970s, "paradoxically, even though [the] widespread expulsion of the mentally ill had already become a *fait accompli*, public outcry against involuntary incarceration began to gain momentum."[21] In conceiving of the damage done to mental patients as endemic to public institutions, Farland argues, antipsychiatric literature contributed to a shift in the treatment of mental patients toward the private sphere.[22] In spite of the anticorporate communitarianism of Piercy's novel, it too exemplifies this shift. Connie spends most of her time in the hospital longing to return to her bug-ridden apartment in the Latino ghetto: "Around her kitchen she would sing and dance, she would sing love songs to the cucarachas and the chinces, her chinces! Her life that had felt so threadbare now spread out like a full velvet rose. . . . Her ordinary penny-pinching life appeared to her full beyond the possibility of savoring every moment" (20–21). The correlative to this return to the private sphere is Connie's recurring fantasy about taking revenge on her captors. In one of her hallucinations/future projections, she imagines herself as the gunner in an aerial battle against enemy cyborgs. As Connie watches, the pilots of the airships morph into the various welfare-state professionals who have dominated her life:

> As she stared to left and right she saw that [the airships] were piloted and manned by Judge Kerrigan, who had taken her daughter, by the social worker Miss Kronenberg, by Mrs. Polcari, by Acker and Miss Moynihan, by all the caseworkers and doctors and landlords and cops, the psychiatrists and judges and child guidance counselors, the informants and attendants and orderlies, the legal aid lawyers copping pleas, the matrons and EEG technicians, and all of the other flacks of power who had pushed her back and turned her off and locked her up and medicated her and tranquilized her and punished her and condemned her. They were all closing in, guns blazing. (330)

Connie takes aim with her laser cannon and vaporizes her tormentors. This massacre of the public sector parallels the gutting of the welfare state that began in the 1970s.

However, Piercy's attitude toward welfare-state professionalism in the novel, as in the case of her MDS writings, is much more complex; at the heart of *Woman on the Edge of Time* is an idealistic effort to imagine a new, antiauthoritarian version of the social trustee ideology.

This complexity can be glimpsed in the irony of Connie's position in the hospital; as a young woman, after escaping from her Mexican immigrant family, she too aspired to be a public-sector professional and even took courses in psychology at a community college. Years later she again tried to enter the professional class, vicariously this time by becoming the "secretary–mistress–errand girl–laundress–maid–research assistant" (42) to a professor of romance languages at the City University of New York. Her downward trajectory—from would-be professional to sexual adjunct to object of professional scrutiny—reflects the perils that surround those who try to rise from the working class into the lower-prestige professions. The novel's goal is not so much to destroy professionalism as to transform it into a social practice available to all. This is the point of the utopian future that Connie discovers—a decentralized, agrarian society in the year 2137, established after a worldwide anticorporate revolution by various minority groups. The part that Connie visits—a village in Mattapoisett, Massachusetts—incorporates some high-tech machinery but overall looks more like the kind of rural village from which Connie escaped as a child: "Most buildings were small and randomly scattered among trees and shrubbery and gardens, put together of scavenged old wood, old bricks and stones and cement blocks. . . . In the distance beyond a blue dome cows were grazing, ordinary black-and-white and brown-and-white cows chewing ordinary grass past a stone fence" (60–61). On one level, this society represents the destruction of the ideology of professionalism embodied in the doctors and nurses at the state mental hospital; it is a radically egalitarian society, without divisions of status and bureaucratic institutions. On another level, Mattapoisett represents the culmination of this ideology. It is a society in which everyone is a professional, occupying a technically specialized, self-chosen vocation. Routine seasonal work still exists in the form of agricultural labor, a task deemed necessary in order to foster a healthy relationship between people and the land. However, most of the routine white-collar jobs have been eliminated entirely: "after we dumped the jobs telling people what to do," one of the utopians explains, "counting money and moving it about, making people do what they don't want or bashing them for doing what they want, we have lots of people to work" (120–21). With these jobs out of the way, everyone is free to specialize; there is no need for a particular class to carry out the menial labor necessary for society's survival. Mattapoisett is the kind of society in which, Connie imagines, her professional ambitions could have been fulfilled: "everybody studied as long as they wanted to," she reflects. "They took courses all the time in fours and fives and sixes" (228). Indeed, Connie's future double, the woman she might have become had she lived in Mattapoisett, is a brown-skinned plant geneticist. The central promise of Piercy's utopia is that professional obfuscation will disappear, and the creative aspects of expert labor will be made available to all.

This fantasy was, in a sense, a central part of postwar theories of the new class. Indeed, one of the striking aspects of *Woman on the Edge of Time* is the extent to which it literalizes idealistic notions of professionalism that run through the liberal social science of the 1950s and 1960s. For instance, the novel's dissolution of the distinction between professionals and nonprofessionals reflects the basic impulse behind the Johnson-era Community Action Programs, with their vision of eliciting the "maximum feasible participation" of welfare clients.[23] While attending a political meeting between utopian villages, Connie remembers that she was once involved in a Community Action Program: "it was just the same political machine," she reflects, "and us stupid poor people, us . . . idiots who thought we were running things for a change. We ended up right back where we were" (147). Piercy implies that Mattapoisett realizes the unfulfilled promises of the War on Poverty, which had been stymied by the bureaucracy and power politics of the welfare state.

Mattapoisett similarly literalizes a Durkheimian idea that runs through many postwar theories of the new class: the notion that professional communities synthesize the best of modern, technological and traditional, agrarian societies. In Talcott Parsons's terms, discussed in chapter 1, professional organizations are societal communities—associations of skilled and differentiated individuals who nevertheless experience the feeling of social integration typical of premodern communities. Piercy's utopians thus resemble premodern peasants. They till the land, share property in common, and have adopted many premodern cultural traditions. "We learned a lot from societies that people used to call primitive," Luciente explains. "Primitive technically. But socially sophisticated. . . . We tried to learn from cultures that dealt well with handling conflict, promoting cooperation, coming of age, growing a sense of community, getting sick, aging, going mad, dying" (117). At the same time, the utopians' lifestyle is more typical of late-twentieth-century professionals; each maintains a personal living space and pursues a series of casual sexual relationships subordinate to the imperatives of his or her career. Indeed, the premodern traditions they have adopted (in Mattapoisett's case, those of the Wamponaug Indians) seem like a superficial veneer on an essentially modern cultural system. In the gemeinschaft tradition exemplified by the U.S. New Critics and by Mary McCarthy's description of North Vietnam, agrarian cultures are imagined as direct outgrowths of their natural environment; the tribe's identity comes from the land it cultivates, the local resources out of which it builds its homes and tools. This notion of culture implies an essentialist conception of race—a vision of generations of women and men living and interbreeding on the same land. In Mattapoisett, in contrast, all children are test-tube babies with no genetic link to the women and men who raise them, and culture is something selected from the historical record and freely altered or discarded. Each member of the tribe, Luciente explains, is free to move to another tribe and adopt its cultural ways: "When you grow up, you can stick to the culture you were raised with or you can fuse into another. But the one we were raised in usually has a . . . sweet meaning to us" (96). In addition, every culture has been adapted to fit with the egalitarian ideology shared by the tribes—the product of their revolution; like Gouldner's new class, Piercy's utopians have subjected all customary folkways to the antiauthoritarianism of the culture of critical discourse. Traditions having to do with lineage, descent, and sexual relations—the core elements of most cultures—have been discarded. In other words, in spite of the utopians' desire to retain cultural diversity, to avoid "the melting pot where everybody ends up with thin gruel" (96), the cultural differences they have maintained are superficial practices used to flavor an essentially rationalized, middle-class lifestyle.

Hence, Mattapoisett seems to represent an ideal synthesis of the two contrary tendencies that mark New Left thinking about the professional stratum. On the one hand, the novel depicts a community of highly educated, self-directed experts; on the other hand, those experts have dissolved the social space between themselves and the various class and ethnic groups usually excluded from the 1960s and 1970s new class. However, this synthesis hinges on the destruction of the very component of professionalism that made it attractive to many New Left activists—namely, professional autonomy. Connie is startled to learn that scientists such as Luciente must have all of their projects ratified by community consent; nonspecialists judge the ethical and aesthetic consequences of specialist work. "In our time science was kept . . . pure maybe," Connie complains. "Only scientists could judge other scientists" (272). In contrast, Luciente emphasizes scientists' accountability to their communities: "[W]hat we do comes down on everybody. We use up a confounded lot of resources. Scarce resources. Energy. We have to account" (272). This argument also extends to artists and other humanistic intellectuals, who must subordinate their work to their community's ethical standards. One of Luciente's lovers, Jackrabbit, is a designer of "holies"—holographic installations involving sight, sound, and smell that interpret world history from the perspective of the triumphant, anticorporate revolution. The utopians perceive this work as identical to that carried out by Mattapoisett's other experts. "We think art *is* production," Luciente explains. "We think making a painting is as real as growing a peach or making diving gear. No more real, no less real. It's useful and good on a different level, but it's production" (261). As such, art is subject to the same community scrutiny. "If we don't crit you, how will you grow?" (204), one of the utopians asks Jackrabbit at a community meeting that diagnoses the ideological failings of his most recent work of art. This aspect of Mattapoisett seems, on one level, like an extension of a problem endemic to all utopian fiction—that of imagining art in a society without social contradictions. On another level, it articulates one of Piercy's central aesthetic assumptions—her rejection of the high-modernist emphasis on cultivating style and form for their own sake.[24] Such an emphasis is, for Piercy, an illusionary and amoral form of professionalism akin to that practiced by Connie's doctors. One of the things that would be lost in Luciente's future, she explained in an interview published after *Woman on the Edge of Time*, would be highly technical forms of artistic genius: "For instance, the violin prodigy who starts at age two and practices seventeen hours a day, yes, I don't think there'd be any. Because I don't think anybody would be willing to have their life warped in that way."[25] This rejection of technical genius for its own sake does not exclude the need for expert writers skilled at their craft. This expert labor, however, must contribute to the red meat of literary enjoyment and ideological edification rather than perpetuate a version of new-class careerism.

Indeed, Piercy's novel suggests that the only alternative to public control of expert work is a free-market dystopia in which professionals become the paid servants of corporate enterprise. As Luciente points out, professional autonomy was always something of an illusion: "But Connie, in your day only huge corporations and the Pentagon had money enough to pay for big science. Don't you think that had an effect on what people worked on?" (272). The utopian world that Connie visits is only one possible future for the American welfare state. The dystopian alternative, which Connie briefly visits after some initial brain surgery, is one in which the world has been carved up by multinational corporations with cyborg CEOs who

have transformed professionals into proletarianized corporate servants. In this section of the novel, which prefigures the cyberpunk
fiction of the 1980s and 1990s, Piercy depicts a world of expert professionalism run amok.[26] The welfare state has been replaced by a
social order in which medical professionals feed on the underclass,
harvesting their organs to prolong the lives of the rich. Here, Connie's double is Gildina 547-921-45-822-KBJ, a surgically altered
courtesan contracted to a middle-level "flack" named Cash, whose
name reflects the total subordination of professional expertise to
economic capital in his society. Like all middle-level professionals,
Cash enjoys some of the perks of the technological civilization of
which he is a part; he gets to live in a high-rise tower above the pol-
luted streets. However, he is also a paid employee who identifies
absolutely with his corporate bosses. In both of the novel's future
worlds, the distinction between professionals and nonprofessionals
has disappeared. Either professionals are assimilated into an egalitarian democracy, or they are proletarianized, literally becoming corporate property. For Piercy, the same dynamic applies in the present
day; professionals (including artists) must choose their masters: corporations or the people.[27]

However, even the subordination of new-class expertise to community consensus may not be enough to check the dangerous effects
of professional self-direction. In "Grand Coolie Damn," Piercy diagnosed the ways in which the New Left was infected by a charismatic authoritarianism latent within many of its leaders' professional background. Her utopians in *Woman on the Edge of Time* solve this
problem through their perpetual vigilance against "power surges"
(220). When one of them must adopt a position of unique responsibility, he or she resigns after a year and pays penance, serving "in a
job usually done by young people waiting to begin an apprenticeship
or crossers atoning a crime" (246). More radically, the people of
Mattapoisett have reengineered human beings so as to eradicate the
original division of labor between women and men. Echoing Shulamith Firestone's proposal for eliminating gender difference in *The*

Dialectic of Sex (1970),[28] Piercy's utopians grow test-tube babies in "brooders" so as to liberate women from the burdens of childbirth (93). The novel thus outlines the conditions under which a revolutionary movement wholly free from professional obfuscation might exist: a society without the will to power, guaranteed by an as yet impossible technological transformation of human beings. However, the very technology that allows Piercy's utopians to eradicate the new class's will-to-power threatens to reintroduce it in an even more virulent form. When Connie visits the community, they are enmeshed in a debate between "shapers," who want to completely engineer the human race, developing superhuman traits such as heightened intelligence and strength, and "mixers," who want to maintain the status quo (220). The former, Luciente believes, are in thrall to a power surge similar to that which impels Connie's doctors to operate on her brain. Mattapoisett, in other words, is in danger of degenerating into a new-class dystopia, belatedly following the path toward Gildina's corporate future. It is threatened by the amoral fascination with expert accomplishment for its own sake that pervades the new class's culture of critical discourse. Professionalism, for Piercy, thus functions as the interface between utopia and dystopia, and the problem with this interface is that it is dangerously porous. The seeds of dystopia are sown in the professional ethos that makes utopia possible.

NEW-CLASS PROTESTANTS

This failed synthesis of New Left professionalism also characterizes Ursula K. Le Guin's *The Dispossessed*, published two years before *Woman on the Edge of Time*. Like Piercy, Le Guin was interested in creating agrarian utopias that embody the communalistic, antiauthoritarian tendencies of New Left social thought. Too much of the utopian tradition, she complained, "is trapped, like capitalism and industrialism and the human population, in a one-way future consisting only of growth."[29] In contrast, Le Guin hoped to expand this tradition by exploring "non-European, non-euclidian, non-masculinist" utopias,[30] ones modeled after the cultures of precon-quest Native Americans. She most fully realized this ambition in her experimental novel *Always Coming Home* (1985),[31] an imaginary eth-nography of a future society in which the surviving humans of a re-source-depleted Earth have reorganized into scattered, matriarchal tribes. This interest in the premodern dovetailed with Le Guin's political anarchism; her political ideal was the commune, governed by community consent and public opinion rather than by formal laws. However, unlike Piercy, Le Guin often placed a greater empha-sis on the other half of New Left professionalism: its valuation of creative individualism and antiorganizational autonomy. Much of her most celebrated science fiction focuses on heroic, self-directed intellectuals who rebel against their society through the disinter-ested pursuit of their professional calling. This theme is central to *The Dispossessed*, which develops the thesis that such work is anarchis-tic in a more profound way than the communitarian societies that Le Guin heralds in her nonfiction.

Hence, *The Dispossessed*, like *Woman on the Edge of Time*, depicts an agrarian society that embodies many of the ideals of the 1960s New Left: an arid moon named Anarres, colonized by anarchists who fled their home planet Urras in order to establish a stateless utopia based on the political philosophy of their founder, Laia Odo. As Le Guin explained, she based this society on her extensive readings in the anarchist tradition, "the most idealistic, and to me the most inter-esting, of all political theories."[32] The residents of Anarres have no currency and no laws; the planet's scarce resources are shared col-lectively, and criminals are punished by their victims' friends and neighbors. Marriage does not exist, although some individuals choose to form lifelong partnerships, and there are no restrictions on juve-nile or adult sexuality. All residents, who live in scattered small com-munities, participate in the labor-intensive agriculture necessary to prevent mass starvation. However, as many of Le Guin's critics have pointed out, the novel's unique contribution to the utopian tradition is that it depicts this world as a flawed, dynamic society with its own internal contradictions.[33] Indeed, when the novel begins, Anarres is in the process of transforming into a subtly repressive regime. Although it lacks a formal justice system, public opinion and gossip fulfill the same function, rigidly controlling what people say and do. "On Urras," a disgruntled anarchist complains, "they have government by minority. Here we have government by majority. But it is government! The social conscience isn't a living thing any more but a machine, a power machine!" (148–49). In addition, the Odonians have embraced a narrowly instrumental view of their founding philosophy that evaluates everything based on whether it contributes to their world's survival. According to Odo's theory, society is an organism, with all of the parts acting together for the whole. The Odonians interpret this theory to mean that anything nonfunctional is a social danger, including the arts and advanced sciences. "Excess is excrement," one of Odo's maxims states. "Excrement retained in the body is a poison" (87).

This calcification of Odonianism into utilitarianism has particularly severe effects on Anarres's scientists and artists, especially those with exceptional talents. *The Dispossessed* focuses on an Odonian temporal physicist named Shevek, who believes in the philosophical principles underlying his society but discovers that they leave little space for intellectuals such as himself. This problem is made clear in an early scene from Shevek's childhood in one of his planet's communal schools, when a school matron chastises him for claiming a patch of sunlight as his own. "Mine sun!" he exclaims when a fat child with a sagging diaper pushes him aside to share it with him. The matron, pulling Shevek away, explains Anarres's central ideological tenet: "Nothing is yours. It is to use. It is to share. If you will not share it, you cannot use it" (24). On one level, the matron's injunction highlights the absurdity of the propertarian creed that the Odonians have relinquished; no one can own the sun. On another level, the two children want the sun for different reasons.

The infant Shevek gazes at the sunbeam with a look of "blank rapture," gaining an aesthetic pleasure from it that transcends mere utilitarian considerations. Critics have therefore read this scene as the beginning of Shevek's intellectual awakening: "To him," Winter Eliott explains, "the sun represents ideas, knowledge, something brilliant and far away, to be reached after struggle and challenge."[34] In contrast, the fat baby is a grotesque figure for the conformist utilitarianism of the average Odonian; he approaches Shevek "out of boredom or sociability" (24) and covets the spot of sunshine for its warmth. Neither Shevek nor the fat infant can own the sun, but one gets a higher pleasure from it than the other. This higher pleasure is reminiscent of Kant's concept of the beautiful—an appreciation unsullied by considerations of utility or interest. Baby Shevek thus becomes an updated version of Trilling's John Laskell from *The Middle of the Journey*: an anti-ideological dissident attuned to the anti-instrumental. This excess aesthetic appreciation, dismissed as excremental by the Odonians, becomes central to the novel's account of creative professionals; the true intellectual, the novel suggests, is one who experiences disinterested pleasure in knowledge for its own sake.

A related problem is posed by the Odonians' rejection of "egoizing"—any effort at individual self-expression that threatens or disturbs the community. Le Guin dramatizes this problem in another vignette from Shevek's early education. While participating in a "Speaking-and-Listening" group at his school, he stumbles across a version of Zeno's paradox, which he tries to teach to the other children. "Speech is sharing," his teacher rebukes him, "a cooperative art. You're not sharing, merely egoizing" (26). The point of the lesson is for the children to repeat what each of them already knows, thereby reaffirming their collective ideology. The young Shevek, in contrast, wants to communicate a troubling paradox that might disrupt their commonsense understanding of the world. The resistance he encounters affects both scientists and exceptional artists on Anarres. One of Shevek's friends, Tirin, is publicly reprimanded for a play he writes that satirizes the Odonian way of life. "Tir's a born artist,"

Shevek explains years later. "Not a craftsman—a creator. An inventor-destroyer, the kind who's got to turn everything upside down and inside out. A satirist, a man who praises through rage" (289). The problem that Shevek and Tirin face is that the Odonians are in a sense right; true intellectual accomplishment is egoistic. "I am that book" (212), Shevek reflects when his major theoretical opus is turned down for publication; intellectual work means projecting oneself into books or works of art that become permanent testaments to their maker. For this reason, when Tirin's play is rejected, he goes insane and falls prey to a compulsive urge to rewrite it continually; he must fix the artifact that embodies himself but that is irremediably unacceptable to his fellow citizens. Unlike Piercy's Jackrabbit, he cannot relinquish his artistic autonomy in order to produce ideologically acceptable art.

Hence, Anarres at once embodies the New Left's communitarian ideals and its anxieties about lost student autonomy within the paternalistic university of the early 1960s. Indeed, the planet is in the midst of producing a conformist, bureaucratic elite, much like the university administrators against whom the New Left directed many of their protests. Anarres officially has no state apparatus. Nevertheless, because of the planet's scarce resources, some centralized system of transportation and distribution is necessary in order to prevent mass starvation. Odonian philosophy attempts to resolve this problem by distinguishing between "administering things and governing people" (149); Anarres's settlers have constructed a central computer, Divlab, responsible for distributing food and water to the various communities. In practice, however, this distinction cannot be maintained. As one of Shevek's fellow dissidents explains, several informal power groups have emerged around the various institutions responsible for administering things, and these groups make policy decisions that affect the entire populace: "Learning centers, institutes, mines, mills, fisheries, canneries, agricultural development and research stations, factories, one-product communities—anywhere that function demands expertise and a stable institution.

But that stability gives scope to the authoritarian impulse" (149). This bureaucracy spreads with every drought or famine that threatens the planet: "every emergency, every labor draft even, tends to leave behind it an increment of bureaucratic machinery . . . and a kind of rigidity: this is the way it was done, this is the way it is done, this is the way it *has* to be done" (290). Sabul, Shevek's academic advisor at the Central Institute of the Sciences, exemplifies this petty-minded attitude. Sabul has established his intellectual reputation by insinuating himself into the new bureaucracy, in particular those portions of it that oversee the exchange of information between Anarres and Urras; this position has enabled him to plagiarize Urrasti ideas and publish them under his name. Shevek's conflict with him concerns his efforts to publish his own work; Sabul edits everything that Shevek writes and insists on being listed as coauthor. Most problematically, Sabul shares the purely utilitarian mindset of the rest of the planet's expert class. "Every Odonian has to be a functions analyst," he tells Shevek during a final interview before he is fired. "[D]o you consider the work you've done here functional?" (234). The conflict between the two physicists thus replicates Shevek's primal encounter with the fat baby. Shevek is interested in physics in itself as a source of pure aesthetic pleasure for himself and for the handful of fellow scholars who understand his work. Sabul, in contrast, is interested in physics for what it gives him—his reputation on Anarres and petty control over others.

In contrast, the propertarian mother-planet, Urras, seemingly embodies a very different attitude toward its intellectuals. Le Guin modeled this planet after contemporary Earth; it is divided into a capitalist nation named A-Io, a repressive state Communist nation named Thu, and a variety of poorer nations over which the two world powers fight for ascendancy. A-Io, which Shevek visits through an exchange program, seems to facilitate the autonomous intellectual work restricted on Anarres. The nation lavishes resources on its physicists, housing them in opulent apartments and providing them with personal body servants. Here, Shevek finally encounters people who understand his work. Back on his home planet, "[h]e had had no equals. Here, in the realm of inequity, he met them at last" (64). A-Io thus seems like the newer, corporate university that was emerging in the 1970s—a place that encourages competitive entrepreneurship among its employees. It quickly becomes obvious, however, that Urras is just as utilitarian as its anarchist neighbor. During a visit to the Space Research Foundation, Shevek encounters an engineer who explains Shevek's function on Urras; they hope that his breakthrough in temporal physics will enable faster-than-light space travel and thus ensure Urras's ascendancy within the League of All Worlds—a kind of galactic United Nations. Moreover, the government of A-Io views Shevek's work as intellectual property that they have paid for by funding his visit. In terms of intellectuals' condition, the chief difference between A-Io and Anarres is that the former sees the instrumental value of Shevek's work, whereas the latter does not. "To be a physicist in A-Io," he reflects, "was to serve not society, not mankind, not the truth, but the State" (240). These conditions make genuine intellectual work impossible: "There is no way to act rightly," Shevek realizes, "with a clear heart, on Urras. There is nothing you can do that profit does not enter into, and fear of loss, and the wish for power" (305). Like Anarres, Urras conjures up many of the anxieties about intellectual labor that attended the student revolts of the 1960s, which revolved around the issue of to what extent intellectual knowledge should be paid for and influenced by government and industry—whether, for example, universities should willingly carry out military research.

Shevek's goal is to create an anti-instrumental model of intellectual work that conforms to neither Anarres's nor A-Io's model, one that is faithful to his society's anarchist ideology yet also leaves room for pure research. He accomplishes this through a critical reinterpretation of Odonianism. As we have seen, most Odonians derive a pettyminded pragmatism from Odo's central analogy between society and the human body; the individual is subordinate to the social organism and tailors her acts to ensure its survival. Shevek, in contrast, derives an absolute insistence on the individual's duty to pursue her professional calling. Theoretical physics, he realizes, is "the work he can do best, therefore his best contribution to his society. A healthy society would let him exercise that optimum function freely, in the coordination of all such functions finding its adaptability and strength" (293). The Anarrestis' error has been to think of the social organism as a kind of machine to which parts can be added or subtracted based on calculations about their utility. Shevek's revised interpretation makes such calculations meaningless. Every profession, no matter how eccentric, is already an integral part of the social organism; it is an end in itself and must not be compromised. Shevek's "radical and unqualified will to create," he reflects, "was, in Odonian terms, its own justification. His sense of primary responsibility toward his work did not cut him off from his fellows, from his society, as he had thought. It engaged him with them absolutely" (294). Autonomous professional work, in other words, may seem entirely selfish and irresponsible, much like the professional work for profit carried out on Urras. For Shevek, however, this work is inherently anarchist and communitarian. "The Odonian society was conceived as a permanent revolution," he reflects, "and revolution begins in the thinking mind" (293–94).

Unlike Odo's original creed, however, Shevek's reinterpreted anarchism does not entail the planned creation of a new society. Rather, it is an anarchism enacted through each individual's unconditional relationship with her work, a relationship that transcends all external political and social imperatives. This is the political vision that Shevek ultimately brings to the people of Urras after he escapes from his propertarian keepers at the university and joins a working-class resistance movement. Facing the crowd at a mass demonstration, he praises his home planet in conventional Anarresti terms: "We have no law but the single principle of mutual aid between individuals. We have no government but the single principle of free association." However, he also articulates his newfound understanding of Odonianism. "You cannot make the Revolution. You can only be the

Revolution. It is in your spirit, or it is nowhere" (265). What Shevek offers the unemployed and hungry crowd, who are soon massacred by government troops, is not a concrete plan for building a better society but rather his own vision of absolute intellectual freedom. Anarchist utopia, for him, is embodied in those who can "be" a revolution rather than just "make" a revolution. Shevek dramatizes this principle through his most important act on Urras; he smuggles the notes for his General Temporal Theory away from A-Io into the hands of the League of All Worlds. He thus ensures that his ideas do not become the instrument of A-Io foreign policy but are instead made available to scientists throughout the universe. As he explains to the Terran ambassador, his gift ensures "that one of you cannot use it, as A-Io wants to do, to get power over the others, to get richer or to win more wars. So that you cannot use the truth for your private profit, but only for the common good" (304). Indeed, his theory's function is to create a universal community of ideas that Shevek could find on neither Urras nor Anarres; it enables the construction of the "ansible," an instantaneous communications device that plays a central role in Le Guin's other Hainish novels.

The Dispossessed, ostensibly a utopian exposition of communitarian anarchism, thus becomes a vehicle for Le Guin to develop a model of absolute professional integrity opposed to the bureaucratism of the postwar welfare state. In so doing, the novel dramatizes the New Left's similar emphasis on unfettered professionalism as a revolutionary force. Le Guin's depiction of Shevek specifically owes much to Paul Goodman's writings on professionalism. Goodman, the author of *Growing Up Absurd* (1960),[35] was a formative influence on the New Left and 1960s counterculture. Le Guin frequently cited him as a key figure in the anarchist tradition that she drew on when writing *The Dispossessed*.[36] His basic political principle was that anarchism does not consist of trying to reform society according to some concrete model. Rather, to be an anarchist "is to live in present society as though it were a natural society."[37] In Shevek's terms, one must "be" a revolution rather than "make" a revolution. From this perspective,

Goodman concluded that authentic professionals—those who follow their calling irrespective of the pressures of the society they live in— are the most thorough anarchists. "Professionals," he argued, "become radicalized when they try to pursue their professions with integrity and courage—their professions are what they know and care about— and they find that many things must be changed."[38] However, as Goodman also recognized, the vast majority of professionals are not authentic in this way; they inhabit and perpetuate institutions that prostitute professional knowledge to pecuniary ends. He therefore called for a "new reformation," a revolt of professionals against their own class; "the closest analogy I can think of is the Protestant Reformation, liberation from the Whore of Babylon and return to the pure faith."[39] This reformation would distinguish between the true professionals and the false professionals of American society. The former are the "mandarins" or "monks" that control the school system. They breed a dangerous conformism, much like the deadening small-mindedness that Shevek encounters on Anarres. Like the clergy of the medieval church, they are bound to a centralized institutional system and to the orthodox beliefs that it embodies. In contrast, the true professionals are guided by an autonomous professional ethic independent of existing institutions; "scientists and inventors and other workmen are responsible for the uses of the work they do, and they ought to be competent to judge these uses and have a say in deciding them."[40] Goodman thus hoped to replace the "old" new class of scholastic Jesuits with a "new" new class of protestant ministers, one guided by an innate, spiritual understanding of its professional responsibilities.

Goodman, like Le Guin, arrived at an idealization of the nonconformist, self-directed professional in a manner that highlights the New Left and counterculture's proximity to the emergent expert professionalism of the postwar era. Crucially, however, both Le Guin and Goodman made this ideal attractive by reconciling it with the New Left's anticapitalist and communitarian ideology so that professional work, carried out within an institutional setting, could seem inherently antiestablishment. As we have seen, Shevek's disinterested interest in knowledge for its own sake differentiates him from the physicists on both Urras and Anarres and transforms him into an anarchist icon capable of throwing both planets into revolutionary chaos. More so than Piercy's imagined destruction of professional autonomy, this model prefigures the version of new-class fantasy that survived within the academic humanities throughout the 1980s and 1990s, long after it became evident that the reformist hopes of left-wing new-class theorists such as Alvin Gouldner had come to naught. This version of the fantasy still nods toward social trustee professionalism's ethos of responsibility and allows humanistic intellectuals to imagine that their work serves a political constituency outside of the academy. However, its primary function is to defend the absolute integrity of autonomous professional work, severed from its connections with the regulatory state or from any sort of political movement. With this fantasy, we move farther away than ever from the organizational idealism that animated segments of the professional stratum in the early twentieth century and toward a model of intellectual agency at once more grandiose and less ambitious.

6

DON DeLILLO'S ACADEMIA

Early in *White Noise* (1985), Don DeLillo's professor protagonist, Jack Gladney, comments that in contemporary America "there is a teacher for every person. Everyone I know is either a teacher or a student."[1] Jack echoes the sometimes optimistic, sometimes fatalistic account of the new class typical of post–World War II writers and social theorists—the sense that, in Alvin Gouldner's terms, the professional-managerial class had become the "universal class" of late-twentieth-century America.[2] Indeed, one of the objects of DeLillo's satire in *White Noise* is the fact that this class identity is so widely available; anyone can lay claim to some sort of specialized knowledge that can be transmitted to others, regardless of his or her educational accomplishments or actual income. Jack's comment, for instance, is a response to his discovery that his German teacher, a former chiropractor named Howard Dunlop, also offers courses in Greek, Latin, ocean sailing, and meteorology out of his dingy room in a local boarding house. Jack's purpose in taking lessons with Dunlop is to escape professional scrutiny. He is the world's preeminent specialist in Hitler studies, the head of a department devoted solely to that subject, and yet he cannot speak German. He must therefore step outside of the usual networks that determine professional reputation. However, once he does so, he only discovers further networks of sub- or lumpen professionals who mimic the aspirations and values of the new class. Jack's own wife, the earthy and nurturing Babette, inhabits this professional netherworld. While Jack teaches German history at an elite liberal arts college perched on top of the town's highest hill, she offers adult-education courses in posture, eating, and drinking to senior citizens in the basement of a local Congregational church. From top to bottom, DeLillo's college town is saturated with professional pedagogy. This saturation belies the town's name, "Blacksmith," which designates the traditional, artisanal knowledge long ago displaced by the new methods and attitudes of the professional-managerial class. The novel thus actualizes the post–World War II fantasy that American society would be reshaped in the image of its universities.

However, in *White Noise* this universal diffusion of professional expertise is not an especially welcome development. Indeed, as I argue in this chapter, DeLillo's novel offers a critical assessment of the simultaneous triumph and failure of new-class fantasy—the notion that the rapid increase in the number of Americans educated at the postsecondary level offered artists and intellectuals new opportunities for disseminating aesthetic attitudes and creating an enriched public sphere. This assessment is evident in the novel's fusion of two characteristically middle-class genres: campus satire and suburban domestic fiction.[3] DeLillo fuses these two genres in order to dramatize the extent to which the most corrosive features of American media culture have infiltrated the university and vise versa. On the one hand, *White Noise*'s campus satire focuses on the proliferation

of popular-culture studies in the 1970s and 1980s. This new discipline, DeLillo suggests, most fully embodies the university's impulse
to dissolve the boundary between itself and the surrounding culture.
For this reason, popular-culture studies also represents the humanities' abandonment of its traditional, Arnoldian imperative to dis-
turb and complicate the stock notions and habits of the middle class.
On the other hand, *White Noise* explores the ways in which pseudo-
professionals such as Babette and Howard, operating outside of the
academy, disseminate a quasi-religious belief in the value of professional expertise. This belief penetrates and reshapes the life of the
middle-class family, short-circuiting its ability to make sense of
an increasingly complex, technological society.

In exploring this interpenetration of the university and mass society, DeLillo reproduces the central assumptions of new-class fantasy but rejects the conclusions that postwar writers and sociologists
derived from them. In Gouldner's scenario, university-based intellectuals would disseminate the culture of critical discourse throughout the expanding middle class, thereby creating a self-aware and
critical citizenry. In *White Noise*, DeLillo echoes this portrait of the
new class's hegemony and, like Gouldner, interprets this hegemony
in cultural terms. In particular, *White Noise* examines how various
experts propagate their beliefs and opinions through the novel's
omnipresent mass media. For DeLillo, however, the culture of professionalism has done little to enliven the critical intelligence of the
American middle class. Rather, this culture has rendered this class
dependent on hyperspecialized forms of expertise that generally lie
beyond its ken. In place of the new class, DeLillo instead valorizes
the artisanal working class, which he imagines as having access to a
hands-on, practical know-how generally inaccessible to the professional-managerial class. In both *White Noise* and his later epic *Underworld* (1997),[4] DeLillo aligns his novelistic aesthetic with this practical knowledge, which he depicts as an endangered capacity soon to
be dismantled by the expanding expert class. *White Noise* thus exemplifies the waning of new-class idealism that took place in the late

1970s and early 1980s—a period when the idea that morally and aesthetically conscious professionals would create a transfigured welfare state seemed increasingly suspect. If there is an implicit argument in DeLillo's intensely self-ironic novel, it is that this idea has been accomplished all too well and that American society would have been better off if it had been left to its own devices.

THE OPEN UNIVERSITY

In the opening scene of *White Noise*, DeLillo offers a striking image of the class stratum that the post–World War II university was supposed to chasten. It is the beginning of the semester, and College-on-the-Hill is being invaded by its upper-middle-class students and their parents. Jack Gladney, narrating the scene, provides an exhaustive catalog of the consumer items that they unload from their station wagons: "the stereos, radios, personal computers; small refrigerators and table ranges; the cartons of phonograph records and cassettes; the hairdryers and styling irons; the tennis rackets, soccer balls, hockey and lacrosse sticks, bows and arrows; the controlled substances, the birth control pills and devices; the junk food still in shopping bags—onion-and-garlic chips, nacho thins, peanut creme patties, Waffelos and Kabooms, fruit chews and toffee popcorn; the Dum-Dum pops, the Mystic mints" (3). The scene evokes the philistine culture that Matthew Arnold hoped to remedy through humanist education—a culture entirely oriented toward the accumulation and consumption of material goods. Indeed, as Jack reflects, both the students and their parents have fashioned a sense of common identification around their objects. The assembly of station wagons "tells the parents they are a collection of the like-minded and the spiritually akin, a people, a nation" (4). The scene adumbrates one of *White Noise*'s central themes—the idea that consumerism generates social cohesion in a society otherwise bereft of lasting traditions. As Thomas Ferraro puts it, in *White Noise* "consumerism produces what we might call an aura of connectiveness among individuals: an illusion of kinship, transiently functional but without either sustaining or restraining power."[5] As imagined by DeLillo, the resulting collectivity is not especially attractive. The parents and students' sense of nationality does not derive from any shared values, traditions, myths, or beliefs. Rather, it derives from the fact that they share the same media-programmed impulses to buy similar things. As a result, they are a simultaneously atomized yet conformist nation—the kind diagnosed by post–World War II critics of American mass culture.

As the previous chapters have shown, throughout the postwar period writers and social critics hoped that the university would complicate or displace this materialist identity; the middle class would enter the institution resembling DeLillo's students but leave as more intelligent, aesthetically attuned people. They would enter the university as philistines but leave as the saving remnant that Matthew Arnold invoked in *Culture and Anarchy*. Something of this ambition to reform mass culture in the image of the university seems implicit in the name of DeLillo's institution, "College-on-the-Hill," which alludes to the Puritan conception of America as a model of public virtue. The College-on-the-Hill should function as a cultural model that the rest of society will learn to emulate. Indeed, there are signs that its students, under the influence of the postsecondary environment, are beginning to drift away from their parents' consumerist collectivism. Murray Siskind, an Elvis specialist and Jack Gladney's closest friend on campus, comments that his students "feel they ought to turn against the medium [television], exactly as an earlier generation turned against their parents and their country" (50). However, the point of DeLillo's satire is that the 1980s academy does little to encourage this change. Rather, the College-on-the-Hill reinforces the atomized conformism evoked by the massed station wagons in the novel's opening. Most of the humanities professors propagate the same culture that their students inhabit.

In satirizing popular-culture studies, DeLillo takes aim at the version of the discipline institutionalized in many U.S. universities in the 1970s and early 1980s. Centered at Bowling Green State University—the site of the nation's first popular-culture department—the discipline was founded by Americanists who felt that the American Studies Association focused too narrowly on canonical U.S. writers.[6] Although there was significant diversity in the field, its researchers often drew on a combination of archival research, myth–symbol criticism, and Lévi-Straussian structuralism to interpret popular culture. They read popular artifacts as expressions of collective myths, attitudes, and values embedded in U.S. culture. John Cawelti, for instance, in an often-cited methodological article, argued that popular formulas in literature and film exemplify "the Freudian insight that recurrent myths and stories embody a kind of collective dreaming process."[7] From the beginning, the discipline tapped into an antielitist defense of popular culture typical of 1960s critics such as Susan Sontag and Leslie Fiedler; popular-culture researchers viewed their work as the antithesis of the mass-culture argument propounded by cold war humanists such as Dwight MacDonald.[8] At times, this defense devolved into hyperbolic celebrations of popular institutions' ability to tap into deep-seated fantasies and desires. Gregory Hall, in his contribution to Bowling Green State University's 1978 popular-culture textbook, explained the attraction of American fast food as follows: "Like Faust before the Mater Gloriosa, an irresistible power draws us on and we find ourselves in the sanctum of a McDonald's kitchen. Although we may not genuflect after receiving the great beef cure, we may feel the urge to glance skyward, giving thanks that we do not need to leave a tip."[9] At such moments, popular-culture studies resembled a genteel, consensus-driven rewriting of Roland Barthes's *Mythologies*.[10]

At DeLillo's College-on-the-Hill, all of the popular-culture faculty work in this celebratory mode; their goal is "to decipher the natural language of the culture, to make a formal method of the shiny pleasures they'd known in their Europe-shadowed childhoods—an Aristotelianism of bubble gum wrappers and detergent jingles" (9). Murray's pedagogy, for example, is structured around the assumption that students must overcome their resistance to mass entertainment and instead fully immerse themselves within it in the manner of Hall's McDonald's customers. In order to understand television, they must recapture the common impulse to buy that they experienced as children. "Even as you sit here," he explains in his lectures, "you are spinning out from the core, becoming less recognizable as a group, less targetable by advertisers and mass-producers of culture. . . . Once you're out of school, it is only a matter of time before you experience the vast loneliness and dissatisfaction of consumers who have lost their group identity" (50). Only by shutting off their critical capacities will students reconnect with the primitive sense of wonder, the "sacred formulas" (51), embedded in media broadcasts. Murray therefore encourages them to "root out content" (50), to focus on the collective experience that mass media enables. His course on the cinema of car crashes asks students to "look past the violence," to see Hollywood car crashes instead as "a reaffirmation of traditional values and beliefs" connected to "holidays like Thanksgiving and the Fourth" (218–19). Mass culture, for Murray, is a series of myths and rituals that bind society together.

In order to underscore the potentially troubling implications of this pedagogy, DeLillo draws a series of parallels between Murray's courses and Jack's area of specialization—Hitler studies. As a historian who studies the twentieth century's darkest chapter, Jack has a responsibility to understand the ethical and political dimensions of the subject that he teaches. Instead, his pedagogy does more or less the same thing to Hitler as Murray's does to popular culture. Like Murray, Jack encourages his students to look past the violence of Hitler's Germany, past the moral questions that seem ineradicably attached to the regime. "It's not a question of good and evil" (63), he explains when discussing Hitler's mystique. He instead invites his students to experience fascism's underlying sacred formulas, the hypnotic appeal of its mass rallies. Each semester, in his class "Advanced Nazism," he screens an "impressionistic eighty-minute documentary" (25) consisting entirely of Nazi film footage, edited together without commentary. As Stacey Olster notes, the film is, in effect, an extended homage to Leni Riefenstahl, and it encourages the same affective response—a passive sense of collective identification resistant to critical consciousness.[11] This emphasis on collective identification allows Jack to link Hitler with Murray's area of specialization, Elvis Presley, in an effort to help Murray secure a returning position at the College-on-the-Hill. Once these figures are drained of their specific ideological content, they become more or less the same. "How familiar this all seems, how close to ordinary," Jack explains to Murray's students. "Crowds come, get worked up, touch and press—people eager to be transported" (73). Both Elvis and Hitler are the focal points of mass rituals that allow participants to feel that they belong to something bigger than themselves, and Jack and Murray invite their students to experience this same feeling.

The College-on-the-Hill thus inverts the humanities' traditional Arnoldian project. The latter project promised to direct "a stream of fresh and free thought" on students' stock notions and habits.[12] In so doing, it desired to fashion a higher, more self-conscious nationalism than that typically available to the economically minded bourgeoisie. It could do so because humanists had access to a somewhat different culture than their middle-class students: "the best which had been thought or said in the world,"[13] as embodied in the liberal arts curriculum. Something of the Arnoldian project survives in Murray's teaching, which, if nothing else, challenges the ways in which students think that they might dissent from the media. For the most part, however, Murray and other humanities professors reinforce their students' notions and habits in their basest form. Indeed, they cannot help but do so because there is no substantive difference between the students' Waffelos and Mystic Mints culture and their professors' culture. Discussing the annual influx of students, Jack and Babette note that they too own a station wagon, although "it's small, it's metallic gray, it has one whole rusted door" (6). Humanists such as Jack and Murray, in other words, have embraced the same consumerist culture as their more affluent students. Most of the popular-culture professors at the College-on-the-Hill are avid collectors of the cultural minutiae that they study. Jack describes them as "smart, thuggish, movie-mad, trivia-crazed" (9), and they keep a collection of prewar soda pop bottles on permanent display in their department.

DeLillo's problem with the College-on-the-Hill, in short, is that it is too open to its cultural outside, a fact dramatized by the name of its popular-culture department: American Environments. This complaint is unusual in a novel about the American university; indeed, one of the remarkable features of *White Noise* is the way that it marks a fundamental shift within the tradition of campus fiction. This genre proliferated in the post–World War II period with works such as Mary McCarthy's *The Groves of Academe* (1952), Randall Jarrell's *Pictures from an Institution* (1954), Vladimir Nabokov's *Pnin* (1957), and Bernard Malamud's *A New Life* (1961).[14] It responded to the emerging centrality of the university within postwar society and to writers' increasing institutional dependence on English departments.[15] Like *White Noise*, these works satirized the behavior of academics, portraying them as all-too-human schemers rarely engaged in the disinterested pursuit of knowledge. However, the basis of their satire lay in the fact that ivory tower academia was a world apart, an enclosed and self-referential system.

Mary McCarthy's book, one of the earliest campus novels, adumbrates the logic of this satire. Set in the early 1950s and based on McCarthy's experiences as an instructor at Bard and Sarah Lawrence colleges, the novel focuses on an unscrupulous English professor's efforts to gain reappointment at a progressive college. To achieve this goal, Henry Mulcahy pretends that he is a member of the Communist Party and that the administration has caved into anti-Communist pressures by allowing his contract to expire. In order to maintain its image as a bastion of liberal politics, Henry reasons, Jocelyn College will have no choice but to keep him on. Many of the novel's critics have singled out this premise as an index of McCarthy's inadequate response to the House Un-American Activities

175

Committee investigations, which were destroying many academic careers when she wrote the book. M. Keith Booker, for instance, argues that *The Groves of Academe* prefigures right-wing polemics against political correctness; the novel suggests that "some American universities were so careful to avoid persecuting leftist professors that a communist affiliation could even be an advantage."[16] This critique seems more or less accurate. However, McCarthy's inversion of cold war anticommunism also serves a different function; it highlights her sense that academic politics obeys an internal logic that seems inaccessible and perverse to most outsiders. For this reason, most of the conflicts that divide Jocelyn's professors are purely administrative matters: debates about modernizing the spelling of the academic catalog, about winter work-study sessions and student advising. These conflicts are crucial to participants because they entail competing, intrainstitutional efforts to establish the conditions under which knowledge is reproduced within the college. As a result, they are fought out as if their stakes extended beyond the university. In particular, professors at Jocelyn are divided along disciplinary lines, with each side claiming to embody the principles of the American Left. "An unresolved quarrel between the sciences and the humanities was at the bottom of every controversy," McCarthy's narrator reflects, "each claiming against the other the truer progressive orthodoxy."[17] Academic politics, McCarthy suggests, may occasionally resemble national politics, may draw on similar references and involve homologously similar contestants. However, each kind of politics is oriented toward fundamentally different goals.

At DeLillo's liberal arts college, in contrast, the self-enclosed institutional culture that McCarthy satirizes has mostly disappeared. There are still a few residual signs of it. The College-on-the-Hill is perched above the town of Blacksmith like a medieval monastery, and department heads such as Jack walk across its grounds wearing traditional academic robes. However, most members of the campus community continually deface these signs of their institutional difference. For instance, the head of American Environments, Alfonse

Stompanato, has sewn the Brooklyn Dodger's logo onto the front of his academic gown (214). Indeed, the entire university is engaged in practices of institutional effacement. Jack comments that in a small town such as Blacksmith, one might expect the university to inspire animosity as an "emblem of ruinous influence." The College-on-the-Hill, however, arouses no such resentment; it "occupies an ever serene edge of the townscape, semidetached, more or less scenic, suspended in political calm" (85). In order to emphasize this absence of a distinguishable, institutional inside, DeLillo eliminates all of the byzantine internal conflicts that create havoc in McCarthy's college. There are no funding disputes between the humanities and sciences. In spite of the controversy that surrounded the expansion of popular-culture studies and other humanistic subdisciplines in the 1980s, there are no turf wars over the respective cultural capital that the humanities and sciences offer. *White Noise* is an academic novel without academic politics. Instead, the debates that play out among Jack's colleagues take the form of interminable one-upmanship contests in which professors quiz each other about their personal hygiene and participation in collective media events: "Did you ever brush your teeth with your finger?" (67); "Where were you when James Dean died?" (68); "Did you ever spit in your soda bottle so you wouldn't have to share your drink with the other kids?" (215). DeLillo's academics fight over who most fully belongs to the culture they study. The novel's structure similarly emphasizes this permeability between the academy and its outside. *The Groves of Academe* claustrophobically encloses its reader within its institutional setting; the novel begins and ends with Mulcahy's political machinations within college offices. *White Noise*, in contrast, opens with Jack descending from his campus office into his media-saturated suburban home. The narrative shuttles back and forth between these two locations, a movement that parallels its rapid transitions between novelistic genres.

Between McCarthy and DeLillo's respective fictional representations of the university, then, a profound shift took place. DeLillo precisely dates the moment when, he believes, this shift occurred:

1968, the year in which Jack proposed the idea of Hitler studies to his chancellor and the year most frequently associated with the student rebellions that transformed campus culture throughout North America and Europe. At the core of many of these rebellions were students' twin demands that universities start offering courses that pertain to real-world concerns and stop doing research for the military–industrial complex. The first demand, in particular, was the product of students' and younger professors' dissatisfaction with cold war paradigms such as the New Criticism and structural functionalism. The student rebellions, in short, were concerned with regulating the boundaries of the university—the same concern that motivates the campus satire in *White Noise* and *The Groves of Academe*. As I argued in the previous chapter, this critique of the university mirrored a pair of sometimes contradictory changes that the New Left hoped to implement within the broader practice of professionalism. First, professionals should dissolve many of the conventional divisions between experts and nonexperts—hence, the various efforts to reform teaching, social work, medicine, psychiatry, and other professions by narrowing or eliminating the distance between professionals and their clients. Second, university-trained professionals should secure new kinds of autonomy; they should be free from institutional and bureaucratic interference. This second demand sometimes devolved into an entrepreneurial conception of professional agency that facilitated the ongoing privatization of the university and other public-sector workplaces.

At first glance, *White Noise*'s College-on-the-Hill bears few traces of this 1960s upheaval. Its students come from a homogeneous upper-middle-class background and are, for the most part, aggressively nonpolitical. Their professors similarly do not seem motivated by the political concerns that animated students and rebellious professors in the 1960s. Nevertheless, the novel's humanities departments—Hitler studies and American Environments—represent DeLillo's assessment of how the New Left's efforts to change professionalism were perverted within the postmodern academy. American Environments is a reductio ad absurdum of New Left demands for a more relevant curriculum, one directly attuned to major social events and current cultural trends. As Ray Browne notes in his institutional history of popular-culture studies, one of the reasons why the discipline flourished in the early 1970s was that there was an influx of newly politicized students disenchanted with the traditional literary studies.[18] American Environments is also a reductio of the 1960s turn against New Critical formalism; it inverts almost all of the New Critics' prescriptions for professionalizing literary criticism. Whereas the New Criticism defined literature against the simpler products of mass culture, American Environments does away with literature altogether; as Murray comments, "there are full professors in this place who read nothing but cereal boxes" (10). Whereas the New Critics worried about policing the boundary between literary studies and the social sciences, DeLillo's popular-culture scholars happily dismantle this opposition. Professors in the department imagine themselves as ethnographers; Murray spends much of his research time interviewing shoppers in the local supermarket.

Hitler studies and American Environments also embody the entrepreneurial spirit that some New Left intellectuals embraced as an alternative to the bureaucratic restrictions of the cold war university. Hitler studies is, above all else, a marketing coup for Gladney, "an immediate and electrifying success" (4). It is a product that Jack sells within the academic marketplace, using cheap gimmicks such as changing his name to J. A. K. Gladney and sporting a pair of dark sunglasses. In this, DeLillo prefigures the posturing and capacity for reinvention characteristic of the academic superstars of the 1980s and 1990s, many of whose careers similarly originated in the cultural upheavals of the 1960s.[19] Indeed, *White Noise* suggests that this entrepreneurial mode of careerism has become the special property of the humanities. When Jack discusses the novel's mystery drug—Dylar—with the campus's chief neurochemist, he comments on the disparity between reputations in science and reputations in the humanities. Everyone at College-on-the-Hill refers to Winnie Richards as a brilliant scientist. In contrast, nobody calls Jack brilliant. "They call me shrewd. They say I latched onto something big. I filled an opening that no one knew existed" (188). Shrewdness, unlike brilliance, implies an intelligence tainted by economic or political self-interest. These latter qualities are the very ones that humanistic learning, insofar as it remains committed to a notion of aesthetic education, is supposed to circumvent. However, when an entrepreneurial model of intellectual autonomy suffuses the academy, humanists become the most self-interested figures on campus. Unlike scientists, they have no specific discoveries to sell to private corporations or the government. Instead, they must aggressively sell themselves as fascinating commodities.

DISAPPEARING ARTISANS AND THE CULT OF EXPERTISE

The university's openness to its media-saturated environment is only part of the larger problem that DeLillo explores in *White Noise*. The larger problem concerns that environment itself, which has in turn become too open to the university—to the specialized knowledge the university produces and the professional ethos it engenders. As I have argued, once Jack leaves the College-on-the-Hill and descends into the town of Blacksmith, he encounters a series of figures who mimic his professional aspirations: his wife, Babette, and his German teacher, Howard Dunlop. They are the kind of pseudo-professionals who fascinated Lionel Trilling in the 1950s—those "people of the minor intellectual professions, whose stock in trade is ideas of some kind."[20] Other writers, such as C. Wright Mills, also found hope in this diffusion of professional expertise, lauding adult education as a solution to the problems of mass culture.[21] Echoing this new-class idealism, Babette and Howard envisage themselves as itinerant revivalists who will bring their professional wares directly to the people. "I've taught meteorology in church basements," Howard explains, "in trailer parks, in people's dens and living rooms. They came to hear me in Millers Creek, Lumberville, Watertown. Factory workers, housewives, merchants, members of the police and the fire. I saw something in their eyes. A hunger, a compelling need" (56).

DeLillo suggests, however, that like their university-based counterparts, Howard and Babette's courses do more harm than good. In their university courses, both Murray and Jack disable their students' critical faculties, inducing in them a childlike receptivity to the sacred formulas embedded in television advertising and fascist rallies. At first glance, Howard and Babette's courses activate these same faculties, albeit on a very limited scale. Each applies scientific methodologies to everyday activities. Howard teaches his students the science behind weather watching, and Babette teaches hers to analyze eating, drinking, and posture by breaking them down into their component actions. "Given the right attitude and the proper effort," she explains, "a person can change a harmful condition by reducing it to its simplest parts. You can make lists, invent categories, devise charts and graphs. This is how I am able to teach my students how to stand, sit, and walk. . . . We can analyze posture, we can analyze eating, drinking, and even breathing" (191–92). Their courses, in spite of the fact that they take place off campus, seem more in tune with the culture of critical discourse than do Jack and Murray's. In their own small way, Howard and Babette try to transform weather watching, posture, eating, and drinking into self-conscious activities.

However, these off-campus courses do not so much as activate their students' critical intelligence as instill in them a quasi-religious dependency on others' expert opinion. Babette, for instance, offers her courses as a modern-day substitute for the lost common sense once embedded in her culture's rituals of food consumption but later displaced by scientific discoveries about health and nutrition: "Knowledge changes every day. People like to have their beliefs reinforced. Don't lie down after eating a heavy meal. Don't drink liquor on an empty stomach. If you must swim, wait at least an hour after eating. The world is more sophisticated for adults than it is for children. We didn't grow up with all these shifting facts and attitudes. One day they just started appearing. So people need to be reassured by someone in a position of authority that a certain way to do something is the right way or the wrong way, at least for the time being" (172). However, her course reproduces the same epistemological uncertainty that it claims to dispel; she can only reassure her elderly students that she is teaching them the right way to eat and drink "for the time being," until the prescriptions change. She encourages her students to approach eating and drinking as mysterious activities, ones that can be fully understood only by the specialists who study them. Howard likewise teaches his students to approach weather watching as an erudite science, one for which it is best to rely on expert meteorologists. The reductio ad absurdum of this faith in meteorology occurs when Jack debates with his son, Heinrich, about whether it is raining or not. Heinrich tells Jack that the radio predicts rain that evening; Jack points out that the rain is pouring down on their car windshield as they speak. Heinrich's defense of the meteorologists' faulty prediction appeals to the skepticism that he has absorbed from his high school science classes: "Our senses? Our senses are wrong a lot more often than they're right. This has been proved in the laboratory. Don't you know about all those theorems that say nothing is what it seems?" (23). Faith in others' expert opinion, DeLillo suggests, culminates in a crippling distrust of one's own ability to perceive and reason about the phenomenal world.

DeLillo's subprofessionals are thus on the vanguard of an uncontrolled diffusion of expert opinion throughout American society that he sees as a primary feature of postmodern culture. This expert opinion is a crucial part of the "white noise" that suffuses the novel. One of the most basic observations that critics make about *White Noise* is the extent to which it transforms television and radio into members of the Gladney family. Television and radio voices interrupt the Gladneys' conversations, infiltrate their subconscious thoughts, and eventually insinuate their way into Jack's first-person narration. This media content includes a lot of low-caliber programming; the

Gladneys spend an evening watching disaster footage on the news, and their household is so saturated with advertising that their daughter Steffie murmurs "Toyota Celica" in her sleep (155). For the most part, however, the Gladneys watch more sophisticated programs, ones that befit their status as an academic family. For much of the day, their television is tuned to nature shows and PBS-style science documentaries: "Until Florida surgeons attached an artificial flipper" (29); "There are forms of vertigo that do not include spinning" (56); "A California think-tank says the next world war may be fought over salt" (226). Like Babette's courses, this expert knowledge presents itself as the answer to the family's questions about how they should live their lives, what foods they should eat, and so on. However, as in the case of Babette's students, this knowledge is only available to them in a fragmentary, ever-changing form. As a result, the family's worldview ends up being structured around half-digested technical facts, such as the garbled fragments of scientific knowledge that they weave into their family discussions.

This omnipresence of expert opinion within the mass media is not accidental; according to DeLillo, the two complement each other in terms of their effects on the public. As the novel's opening scene with the station wagons makes clear, advertising in *White Noise* fashions a fragile sense of collectivity grounded in the common impulse to buy. Faith in expert opinion works the same way. It teaches its devotees that the practical knowledge that used to be embedded in customs and traditions is now being cultivated by highly trained specialists. However, trust in experts does not give the public any secure or definite access to that knowledge. Even the experts themselves, such as neurochemist Winnie Richards, understand only their own, specialized fragment of the culture's warehouse of useful knowledge. As a result of this hyperfragmentation, expert knowledge never coheres into know-how, just as the media never coheres into a system of traditions and beliefs. Heinrich, discussing this problem with his father, pinpoints the fragility of new-class expertise: "[W]hat good is knowledge if it just floats in the air? It goes from computer to computer. It changes and grows every second of every day. But nobody actually knows anything" (148–49). As a result, the American public is actually less educated than most so-called primitive peoples. If flung back in time to the prehistoric era, the new-class expert would be helpless in comparison to the average caveman. "Name one thing you could make," Heinrich challenges his professor father. "Could you make a simple wooden match that you could strike on a rock to make a flame?" (147).

The disastrous effects of this combined dependence on yet alienation from expert knowledge become obvious in the airborne toxic event that dominates the central section of *White Noise*. DeLillo emphasizes the involvement of experts in all stages of the disaster. The Nyodene D compound that leaks out of the tank car is an insecticide by-product, "a whole new generation of toxic waste" (138) developed in private laboratories. Army technicians respond by seeding the cloud with microorganisms that consume its toxic agents. Media experts struggle to name the situation, eventually settling on the "state-created terminology" *airborne toxic event* (117). SIMUVAC experts subsequently manage the chaotic evacuation, determining which residents have been exposed to the toxin and guiding them to shelters. The residents of Blacksmith invest these experts with a mysterious authority. Jack, for instance, reflects that the SIMUVAC technician at the shelter "had access to data. I was prepared to be servile and fawning if it would keep him from dropping casually shattering remarks about my degree of exposure and chances for survival" (139). In one sense, this quasi-religious regard for professionals is well placed. As the airborne toxic event and its aftermath highlight, experts in *White Noise* wield a terrifying technological power capable of altering nature itself. In another sense, this regard for professionals is somewhat bizarre because the cult of expertise no longer recognizes any division between clergy and laity. Almost everyone in Blacksmith is an expert. Although in many cases they are acutely self-conscious that their claims to expertise are tenuous and fragile—Jack is a Hitler specialist who cannot speak German—they all nevertheless share the same sense of dread in the face of each other's expertise. Jack, who is intimidated by the SIMUVAC experts, wields that same authority over his students in his Hitler classes; he too surrounds himself with a "professional aura of power, madness and death" (72).

The prominence of expertise in *White Noise* thus helps clarify the novel's postsecularism, which John McClure, among others, has tried to understand. As McClure argues, *White Noise*, like much of DeLillo's fiction, depicts a world that appears to have been "rationalized" in Max Weber's sense of the term. Traditional forms of religious authority have vanished; in one of the novel's most frequently discussed scenes, Jack encounters a convent of atheist nuns who simulate faith as a service for nonbelievers. However, the spiritual needs that institutional religion once fulfilled have been displaced onto other outlets: tabloid magazines, bizarre cults, television advertising, and consumer spending. "The old gods thrive," McClure argues, "mostly in virulent forms, at the margins of the global capitalist system [DeLillo] so brilliantly maps."[22] DeLillo's professionals and subprofessionals, who claim to be agents of rational expertise, are the primary figures who perpetuate this displaced spirituality in *White Noise*. In particular, they help Americans deal with the most fundamental question addressed by religious faith: the question of human mortality. Much of the novel's plot concerns Jack and Babette's search for a miracle drug Dylar, which is supposed to cure their fear of mortality. This search becomes particularly urgent after Jack is exposed to Nyodene D, which may or may not shorten his lifespan. Dylar, which in fact does not work, represents science's ultimate effort to conquer areas of experience once entirely dominated by religious faith; the white, "flying-saucer-shaped" (184) tablet resembles a communion wafer. In general, however, science in *White Noise* cannot actually provide its devotees with the kind of reassurance in the face of death that religions offer their adherents. After his exposure, Jack turns to technical sources for help: the SIMUVAC technicians who feed his personal data into their computers. The computers, however, can offer only cryptic responses to their devotees:

lines of "bracketed numbers with pulsing stars" (140) that have little relation to the life-and-death questions that trouble the disaster victims. Like Babette's eating and drinking lessons, this information is subject to constant reinterpretation; Jack may or may not die within thirty years, the technicians tell him, "knowing what we know at this time" (141).

Countering this omnipresence of new-class culture, DeLillo turns to whatever is left of traditional know-how in contemporary society. This knowledge is embodied in the artisanal working class, exemplified by Babette's elderly father, Vernon Dickey, who visits the family in the midst of their domestic problems. Unlike *White Noise*'s other major adult characters, Vernon has no professional pretensions; he is an itinerant handyman most at ease when talking "about gaskets and washers, about grouting, caulking, spackling . . . the things that built the world" (245). Unlike the novel's scientists and humanists, he is not alienated from the world of objects around him; he has a hands-on knowledge of how to build and fix things. Also unlike them, he is not hyperspecialized. As a result, Vernon is one of the few characters in *White Noise* who passes the caveman test that Heinrich outlines for his father; he would thrive just as well in prehistoric times as in modern times. Especially crucial, for DeLillo, is the fact that Vernon knows the names of household tools—an arcane knowledge available only at the margins of new-class society. As Murray puts it, talking about his own handyman superintendent, there is a limited class of people who are "very good with all those little tools and fixtures and devices that people in cities never know the names of. The names of these things are only known in outlying communities, small towns and rural areas" (33). This linguistic ability distinguishes *White Noise*'s artisans from its professionals, whose speech is marked by specialized neologisms. As Jack reflects, speaking of the linguistic and technological transformation of the United States since his childhood, "new names and shapes had been given to just about everything in the decades since I first became aware of objects and their functions" (297). Artisans, DeLillo imagines, have access to an older,

plainer, more tactile language than the new class, one in which signi-
fiers more readily evoke their signifieds. This low-tech language ironically gives artisans' a firmer purchase on the contemporary, technological world. While visiting the Gladneys, Vernon spends much of
his time "hanging around outside the house, waiting for garbage-
men, telephone repairmen, the mail carrier, the afternoon newsboy.
Someone to talk to about techniques and procedures. Sets of special
methods. Routes, time spans, equipment. It tightened his grip on
things, learning how work was done in areas outside his range"
(248–49). Vernon thus connects with the remnants of the traditional,
small-town working class signposted by the town's name, "Blacksmith." Unlike the novel's professionals, these workers are able to
talk concretely about those portions of the technological systems
within which they operate. As such, Vernon functions as an unlikely
figure for DeLillo's own novelistic practice. Unlike other postmodern writers, DeLillo has always claimed that his work fits into a realist tradition that concretely evokes places and occupations; his novels, he explains in interviews, always "paint a kind of thick surface"
and have a "strong sense of place."[23]

Of course, DeLillo ironizes Vernon just as he ironizes all of the
redemptive figures in his fiction. Jack sees Vernon as "Death's dark
messenger" (253); Vernon brings Jack the antique gun that he will
use in his attempted murder of Babette's lover and Dylar dealer Wil-
lie Mink. Vernon is also prone to a kind of small-town racism purged
from the consciousness of the novel's new class. Referring to his
superintendent, Murray complains that "people who can fix things
are usually bigots" (33). This stereotype turns out to be true in the
case of Vernon. "Routine things can be deadly," Jack explains to his
father-in-law, citing Murray. "I have a friend who says that's why
people take vacations. Not to relax or find excitement or see new
places. To escape the death that exists in routine things." Vernon's response is, "What is he, a Jew?" (248). From DeLillo's perspective,
however, these questionable aspects of Vernon's character do not entirely undercut his status as an alternative to the new class. Vernon's

anti-Semitism, for instance, is a reaction against Murray's denigration of blue-collar workers, reflected in Murray's dismissive reference to "routine things"—the practical matters that define Vernon's occupational identity. Most important, Vernon is one of the few characters in *White Noise* who accepts his own mortality. "Don't worry about me," he tells Babette, and he goes on to list exhaustively all of the various bodily ailments and personal failings about which Babette worries. His point is that these ailments do not interfere with his life project, which consists of gaining as much pleasure out of his dying body as possible before he passes away. Vernon links this acceptance of dying to his class status as an itinerant worker. The fact that he has "zero pensions, zero savings, zero stocks and bonds" (255) means that he doesn't have to think about anything but the present.

If DeLillo valorizes any sort of pedagogy, it is a pedagogy that reanimates the practical knowledge embodied in trade workers such as Vernon. This practical knowledge is at the center of the most important pedagogical scene in DeLillo's fiction, in which he envisages an alternative to the postmodern college parodied in *White Noise*. This scene takes place in DeLillo's later historical novel *Underworld*.[24] It depicts the mid-1950s Jesuit education of DeLillo's Italian American protagonist Nick Shay, an adolescent who murders a neighborhood junkie in the Bronx. This crime is the culmination of a series of delinquent acts, all stemming from his father's abandonment of his family five years earlier. The crime ultimately threatens to cut Nick off from the human community; in the reformatory, reflecting on the murder, he feels stranded in an "unknown country" (509). The Jesuits' task is thus to reconstruct his relationship with the world. They do this at an isolated collegium in northern Minnesota named "Voyageur," into which Nick is released after he serves his sentence. Voyageur is the opposite of *White Noise*'s postmodern college. Whereas the College-on-the-Hill charges an annual tuition of fourteen thousand dollars, Voyageur caters to the disadvantaged: poor city kids, juvenile delinquents, farm children, and third world youth. Whereas the College-on-the-Hill invites its students to bring their consumerist ephemera onto campus, Voyageur enforces asceticism and sequesters its students in ramshackle barracks. Whereas the College-on-the-Hill's humanities curriculum is the absurd culmination of post-1960s progressive education reform, Voyageur reinstates the classical curriculum of the eighteenth and nineteenth centuries. Father Paulus, one of its founders, describes the school's pedagogy: "Closer contact, minimal structure. We may teach Latin as a spoken language. We may teach mathematics as an art form like poetry or music. We will teach subjects that people don't realize they need to know" (675).

This pedagogy is not oriented toward instilling Catholic dogma; the Jesuits are not interested in rescuing their students' flagging faith. Rather, it is oriented toward developing more disciplined habits of mind. In one of his regular sessions with Nick, Father Paulus is distressed to hear that Nick has been rote memorizing his lessons without understanding them. Voyageur's classical education, Paulus worries, focuses too much on "abstract ideas. Eternal verities left and right. You'd be better served looking at your shoe and naming the parts. You, in particular, Shay, coming from the place you come from" (540). The lesson that follows, focused on Nick's wet winter boots, evokes the Catholic sacramental tradition that John McClure identifies as central to DeLillo's fiction. This tradition emphasizes the importance of the quotidian, representing it as "quick with redemptive energies."[25] Father Paulus's purpose is to teach Nick to look more deeply into the everyday world. "You didn't see the thing because you don't know how to look," the Jesuit explains, "and you don't know how to look because you don't know the names" (540). He wants to provoke in Nick an epistemological and linguistic transformation, teaching him to notice and name the specific details that are the province of realist writers such as DeLillo.

More specifically, Father Paulus, as his reference to the place where Nick comes from indicates, hopes to reactivate the artisanal knowledge embodied in Nick's working-class, Italian American

background. DeLillo evokes this background in the lengthy, penultimate section of *Underworld*, entitled "Arrangement in Gray and
Black," which focuses on Nick's troubled adolescence in the Bronx—
DeLillo's own childhood milieu. DeLillo imagines the Bronx of the
early 1950s as a community of tradespeople similar to the one that
Vernon discovers on the streets of Blacksmith. In the Bronx, the
neighborhood schoolteacher reflects, "there were streets to revisit
and men doing interesting jobs, day labor, painters in drip coveralls
or men with sledgehammers he might pass the time with, Sicilians
busting up a sidewalk, faces grained with stone dust" (661). This is a
neighborhood in which the old cultural traditions are still intact—
exemplified by the children's games passed on from generation to generation and by the banter exchanged between shopkeepers and their
patrons. It is also a neighborhood in which words are concretely
attached to the object world, in which "language is webbed in the
senses" (683). Above all, it is a neighborhood in which artisanal
know-how of some kind is available to almost every resident regardless of his or her specific vocational training. Nick, for instance, remembers an incident in which his father helped two young, unsea-
soned men lay bricks for a pair of gateposts: "First he watched, then
he advised, speaking a studied broken English that the young men
might grasp, and then he moved decisively in, handing his jacket to
someone and redirecting the length of string and taking the trowel
and setting the bricks in courses and leveling the grout" (277). Nick's
father is a small-time bookie, a white collar worker of the petty
criminal underground. Nevertheless, he can still activate the pragmatic skills that pervade his community; the Bronx, Nick reflects, is
one of the few places where you can still see "a man in a white shirt
and tie do a skillful brickwork bond" (277).

This representation is not quite prelapsarian; here, DeLillo, as in
the case of his depiction of Vernon in *White Noise*, complicates any
effort to read any portion of his work as an exercise in pure nostalgia.
The Bronx is the environment from which the novel's principal artist figure, Klara Sax, must escape in order to discover her vocation as

a painter. DeLillo also juxtaposes the Italian American Bronx with the more economically disadvantaged Harlem, which prefigures the devastated inner city that plays a central role in the novel's present-day chapters. Finally, the sections of *Underworld* set in the early 1950s are overshadowed by the beginning of the cold war, dramatized by the October 3, 1951, Soviet bomb test with which the novel begins. Nevertheless, "Arrangement in Gray and Black" is the closest that DeLillo has ever come to describing a community not yet fully colonized by the new-class culture that he describes in *White Noise* and in those chapters of *Underworld* that describe Nick's later transformation into a waste-disposal expert. As Nick explains in the present-day epilogue that immediately follows "Arrangement," "Capital burns off the nuance in culture" (785). The Bronx in the 1950s is a culture with its nuance still intact.

In *White Noise* and again in *Underworld*, DeLillo thus articulates a thoroughgoing critique of the professional-managerial class's impact on American society. This account at times brings DeLillo close to the leftist traditionalist new-class theory associated with Christopher Lasch in the late 1970s and 1980s. Echoing Gouldner and other new-class fantasists, Lasch believed that over the course of the twentieth century, the new class had displaced the old bourgeoisie as the ruling strata of U.S. society. Although the old bourgeoisie "still represents the summit of wealth," it is a "dying class," which "no longer controls national and multinational corporations or plays a dominant role in national politics."[26] Also echoing Gouldner, Lasch interpreted this class's impact in cultural terms. Citing the example of early reformers such as Jane Addams and John Dewey, he argued that the "new radicals" who prefigured the politics of the new class instituted a series of educational reforms geared toward disseminating a therapeutic perspective throughout U.S society.[27] Unlike Gouldner, however, Lasch interpreted this project as a sinister imposition of social control that was far more intrusive than anything attempted by the old bourgeoisie. Through its reforms, the new class had expropriated the practical knowledge of the American populace, reorganizing it into "a body of esoteric lore accessible only to the initiated."[28] Prefiguring DeLillo's satire of Babette's adult-education courses, Lasch argued that this expropriation has extended into the most basic forms of cultural knowledge, such as childrearing. Expert knowledge has rendered Americans dependent on expert opinion throughout all stages of their lives, from birth to death. In response, Lasch called for the dismantling of the welfare state and the professional-managerial class that runs it. He appealed to readers to resurrect the "traditions of localism, self-help, and community action"[29] that these entities have tried to destroy.

Like Lasch, DeLillo imagines that the new class has damaged America's basic, artisanal culture—exemplified in *White Noise* by the working-class underground of his representative small town, Blacksmith. The novel explores the idea that the new-class revolution predicted by both liberals and radicals in the post–World War II period has taken place, but that its results are far from salutary. Rather than countering the atomist conformism of mass consumerism, the new class perpetuates it. Rather than forming the core of a more intelligent citizenry, the new class has itself become a passive public, alienated from the very knowledge that it produces and distributes. For DeLillo, it seems unlikely that any saving remnant will emerge from this class that might reform or improve on its projects of cultural education.[30] Rather, DeLillo's saving remnant consists of tradition-minded teachers such as Father Paulus, artisanal handymen such as Vernon, and detail-oriented artists such as himself. The best that this remnant can hope to achieve is the gradual rehabilitation of those fragments of practical knowledge and habits of precise observation not yet displaced by new-class expertise.

AFTERWORD

In *The University in Ruins* (1996),[1] Bill Readings highlights both the fragility and the ongoing resilience of new-class fantasy within the literary academy. On the one hand, Readings's book is one of several published in the 1990s that traces the decline of literature as a form of cultural capital and explodes the project of new-class education outlined in the previous pages.[2] On the other hand, in trying to imagine a new rationale for literary scholarship and pedagogy, Readings reinscribes this same project. His analysis of the postmodern university hinges on the eclipse of an older, humanistic model of education rooted in the German bildung tradition and in the British tradition of cultural critique represented by Matthew Arnold. According to this model, the university's purpose is to inculcate the national culture into the minds of its citizenry. This conception,

Readings argues, could not survive the challenges to national sovereignty brought about by the rise of the transnational corporation. Nevertheless, both leftist literary intellectuals within the academy and neoconservative challengers outside of it continue to act as though the purpose of literary pedagogy is to perpetuate or challenge this culture: "Cultural Studies attacks the cultural hegemony of the nation-state, and the question of its politics becomes troubled when global capital engages in the same attack" (102). The university has instead embraced an alternative logic of excellence—a bureaucratic paradigm that reduces all aspects of university education to quantitative performance indicators such as grades, amount of revenue generated, and numerical teaching evaluations. Intellectuals who hope to resist the excellent university cannot return to the nationalist academy of the nineteenth and early twentieth centuries. Rather, they must cultivate what Readings calls "Thought." In the context of the contemporary university, doing so entails "finding ways *to keep the criteria of evaluation open*, a matter for dispute" (130, italics in original). Thinking, in other words, defers the corporatist rush to reduce education to fixed numbers. It insists that questions about measuring education are more complicated than we have assumed, that they are always occasions for further debate. Privileging thought as the basis for education entails a new task for the university: "the task of rethinking the categories that have governed intellectual life for over two hundred years" (169).

Readings derives this notion of the academy as a site of "Thought" from Jacques Derrida's writings on the university, especially his 1983 essay "The Principle of Reason." For Derrida, thinking is synonymous with deconstruction. It is an activity "not reducible to technique, nor to science, nor to philosophy,"[3] an activity that precedes the division of intellectual labor into the various disciplines. Derrida unsurprisingly argues that the university should be reorganized to make room for more thinking; indeed, this recommendation forms the core of his report for the French government on the creation of the Collège international de philosophie. For Derrida, thinking is perpetually at risk of "being reappropriated by socio-political forces that could find it in their own interest in certain situations." Even the most apparently useless knowledge, such as literature and the arts, can be employed for ideological purposes by "multinational military–industrial complexes or techno-economic networks." Indeed, this risk is constitutive of thought, which at some level always becomes instrumental. Nevertheless, the intellectual's task is to maintain a perpetual vigilance against such reappropriations; thinking must "unmask—an infinite task—all the ruses of end-orienting research."[4] The thinking intellectual's ultimate goal is to cultivate an alternative economy of intellectual work at odds with the economic imperatives of the corporate university. In Readings's terms, thinking "belongs rather to an economy of waste than to a restricted economy of calculation. Thought is non-productive labor, and hence does not show up on balance sheets except as waste" (175). For both Readings and Derrida, the intellectual attempts to open fragile spaces where nonproductive thinking can flourish within the excellent university.

On one level, it is difficult to argue with such accounts, which come close to reiterating the cliché that postsecondary education promotes critical thinking. On another level, what is remarkable about Readings and Derrida's texts is the way they claim to embody a new way of thinking about the university, whereas in fact they are recapitulating many features of the traditional, humanistic model of education that they supposedly transcend. Readings's claim that thinking invites members of the university community to reflect on their evaluative criteria echoes Arnold's notion that literary education dissolves the stock notions and habits of the British bourgeoisie. It also echoes Trilling's cold war version of this argument—that the job of criticism is to reveal the complexity and difficulty obscured by the organizational impulse of the expanding, educated middle class. Readings, in other words, imagines himself and other like-minded intellectuals as a new-class saving remnant at odds with the technocratic tendencies of the institutions they inhabit. Moreover, although both Readings and Derrida emphasize the fact that thinking precedes disciplinarity, they recapitulate the basic conflict between humanistic reason and social scientific rationality that, I have argued, was characteristic of many post–World War II literary intellectuals' version of newclass fantasy. Hitherto, Derrida argues, most reflection on the university has come from the perspective of "the sociology of knowledge, from sociology or politology." The problem with these disciplines is that they "never touch upon that which, in themselves, continues to be based on the principle of reason and thus on the essential foundation of the modern university. They never question scientific normativity, beginning with the value of objectivity or of objectification, which governs and authorizes their discourse."[5] Both the sciences and the social sciences are too close to the economistic logic of excellence that governs the modern university.

With Readings and Derrida's deconstructive articulation of newclass fantasy, however, the saving remnant's imagined social agency becomes more and more tenuous. Readings, for instance, delineates everything that an intellectual vocation based on thinking cannot do. Thinking intellectuals must abandon all of the transcendental justifications for their work that once flourished in the national university. They cannot "make redemptive claims for the role of the University of Culture, be that culture humanistic, scientific, or sociological." For them, the university no longer has a mission; intellectuals cannot offer "new pious dreams of salvation, a new unifying idea, or a new meaning for the University" (129). At the same time, thinking intellectuals cannot move beyond the tradition within which these transcendental justifications once made sense. Rather, they inhabit the "ruins" of the university, and the work of thinking entails the endless meditation on those ruins. Readings calls for an institutional "pragmatism," based on "an awareness of the complexity and historically marked status of the spaces in which we are situated" and "a refusal to believe that some new rationale will allow us to reduce that complexity, to forget present complexity in the name of future simplicity" (129). This pragmatism, however, is literally useless; in remaining faithful to thought's "economy of waste," it cannot formulate any alternative educational purpose that transcends the logic of the marketplace. Readings, of course, offers some concrete suggestions for reforming the university, many of them admirable. He argues, for instance, that students should write "evaluative essays that can themselves be read and that require further interpretation, instead of ticking boxes and adding up point-scores" (133). The point of such exercises is not to provide another, more circuitous method for quantifying the institution. Rather, it is to involve students and administrators in the endless, "necessary and impossible" (133) task of thinking. Once again, the literary intellectual disseminates an aesthetic awareness of complexity at odds with the instrumental rationality of the institution.

Once the question of resisting the "technocratic" university is put in these terms—as an opposition between instrumental rationality and endless anti-instrumental critique—narrow instrumentalism inevitably wins out. New-class fantasy becomes the perverse double of expert professionalism: the compensatory justification for humanistic work in a society wholly given over to technique. Hence, the counterpart to Readings and Derrida's work on the university is Mark C. Taylor's *The Moment of Complexity*, primarily an application of contemporary systems theory to postmodern culture and aesthetics. In its final chapter, Taylor turns to questions of digital education and offers a critique of Readings and Derrida. Their work, he argues, exemplifies literary intellectuals' deluded belief that they should remain autonomous of the market forces that shape the corporate university. "Protests to the contrary notwithstanding," Taylor writes, "the university is not autonomous but is a thoroughly parasitic institution, which continuously depends on the generosity of the host so many academics claim to reject."[6] Taylor's alternative to Derrida and Readings's purely negativistic thinking is to accommodate literary study to the corporate market. Contemporary network culture, he argues, is beset by an unprecedented level of turbulence that forces institutions to adapt or die: "Those who are too rigid to fit into rapidly changing worlds become obsolete or are driven beyond the edge of chaos to destruction."[7] The humanities are no exception to this rule, and Taylor offers a model for turning literary studies into a for-profit business: corporate-sponsored online education. Taylor's account thus turns Derrida and Readings' anti-instrumentalism on its head. Deconstruction, Taylor argues, is typical of the politics of literary studies insofar as it articulates an empty critique that is capable only of saying "no" to all manifestations of corporate culture, but without offering constructive alternatives. "Instead of showing how totalizing structures can actually be changed, deconstruction demonstrates that the tendency to totalize can never be overcome and, thus, that repressive structures are inescapable. For Derrida and his followers, all we can do is to join in the Sisyphean struggle to undo what cannot be undone."[8] Taylor instead argues that literary critics should embrace instrumental thinking, turning their work into marketable wares. The irony here is that Derrida, Readings, and Taylor offer identical alternatives. Either the intellectual becomes an expert professional who subordinates everything she does to the logic of the marketplace, or she engages in a quixotic, doomed conflict with the corporate university.[9]

A more complicated articulation of this imagined conflict between a triumphant instrumentalism and imperiled anti-instrumentalism can be found in Alan Liu's *The Laws of Cool*. Liu's book is, without question, the most ambitious and compelling study ever attempted of the connections between literary scholarship and contemporary knowledge work. Its premise is that the "vital task for both literature and literary study in the age of advanced creative destruction . . . is to inquire into the aesthetic value—let us simply call it *the literary*—once managed by 'creative' literature but now busily seeking new management amid the ceaseless creation and re-creation of the forms, styles, media, and institutions of postindustrial knowledge work."[10] The dominant aesthetic of our age is itself the product of the technical intelligentsia—software designers and computer artists. Liu provides a detailed, quasi-anthropological account of this subclass's culture and identifies the basic principles of its aesthetic: what he calls the "laws of cool." He thus seems to presage the complete absorption of humanistic intellectuals into the technical intelligentsia; as in the case of Taylor's scenario, literary intellectuals must adapt to this situation or become obsolete. However, in envisaging what this adaptation might look like, Liu develops a strange synthesis of Taylor and Readings: "Many intellectuals and artists will become so like the icy 'New Class' of knowledge workers that there will be no difference; they will be subsumed wholly within their New Economy roles as symbolic analysts, consultants, and designers. But some, in league with everyday hackers in the technical, managerial, professional, and clerical mainstream of knowledge work itself, may break through the ice to launch the future literary."[11] Humanistic intellectuals will infiltrate the technical intelligentsia only to inject it with the anti-instrumental logic of the humanities—the historical consciousness effaced by the perpetual presentism of corporate knowledge work. Liu's metaphor for this process is the "Kuang" computer virus from William Gibson's *Neuromancer*, which "transforms its own substance into that of the database, draws nearer and nearer until there seems to be no difference, and then at last injects the one powerful difference it has treasured at its core."[12] In spite of the imagined destruction of literary cultural capital, Liu, like Readings and Derrida, still sees literary critics as a saving remnant charged with humanizing the technical segments of the new class.

This politics, which casts intellectuals as caretakers of noninstrumental attitudes under assault by a rationalistic society, is a losing proposition for the humanistic Left. In the United States, it is chiefly a legacy of the post–New Deal era, when the welfare state's complexity and bureaucratic structure seemed to cut off the possibility of principled intellectual engagement in liberal reform. Today, when the welfare state remains the only bulwark against unchecked corporatism, continuing to attack instrumental rationality as the primary evil of contemporary society is a fruitless endeavor. The task for left-wing intellectuals from all disciplines should instead be to create a new version of social trustee professionalism, one that conceives of

new-class expertise as a resource to be used for the benefit of an informed public and one that eschews the simplistic antistatism of the
1960s counterculture and the later New Left. Among literary researchers, this project has already reaped dividends in the work of
scholars such as Michael Szalay, Sean McCann, and Bruce Robbins,
who have reevaluated the relationship between U.S. literature and
welfare-state reformism.[13] The project also informs the work of scholars who self-reflexively study critics' relationship to the academy,
following the example of John Guillory's path-breaking *Cultural Capital*.[14] In C. Wright Mills's terms, it is harder to sustain fantasies
about either the exaggerated power or total impotence of humanistic
learning when one pays attention to the specific "sphere of strategy"
within which one acts.[15] In particular, one of the most salutary contributions to recent critical discourse has been the work carried out
by scholars such as Mark Bousquet who have drawn attention to the
politics surrounding the exploitation of part-time and student workers within the university.[16] This scholarship has drawn attention
to institutional inequalities that academics of all disciplines can
meaningfully address but have generally ignored. It also highlights
the broader political coalition within which literary critics and other
humanists might find a place: the movement to unionize white-
collar workplaces.

These projects raise the question of what it might mean for literary critics and other university-based humanists to think of themselves as social trustees, as professionals who combine specialized
expertise with a commitment to public service. One of the problems
facing literary critics is that their scholarship fits so poorly with
expert professionalism—an ideology that conceives of professional
work as a saleable resource. The high theoretical version of new-class
fantasy—perpetuated by Derrida, Readings, and others in the 1980s
and 1990s—was a reaction against this ideology. This version offered
critics the compensatory privilege of viewing their work as an anti-
instrumental antidote to the triumph of instrumentalism. Social

trustee professionalism, in my view, provides a better rationale for literary pedagogy and scholarship. Among other things, it allows the critic to distinguish between instrumentalism in the service of private-sector profit and instrumentalism in the service of broader social goals. Possibly the best example of a twentieth-century theorist who tried to construct a model of literary scholarship along these lines was Kenneth Burke, who famously conceived of literature as "equipment for living."[17] Burke coined this phrase in the 1930s in a series of essays in which he constructed a sociology of literature, one that would disregard traditional distinctions between humanistic and social scientific inquiry. Engaging with and attempting to complicate the emerging New Critical consensus, Burke conceived of literary works as ritualistic strategies for naming and readying oneself for situations that recur in human societies. The aim of literary criticism is to codify these strategies, to draw connections between "strategies for selecting enemies and allies, for socializing losses, for warding off evil eye, for purification, propitiation, and desanctification, consolation and vengeance, admonition and exhortation, implicit commands or instructions of one sort or another" as they exist within literary and other texts.[18] Literature is above all else a warehouse of both useful and debilitating cultural attitudes that the critic organizes, evaluates, and applies to new situations. This conception of criticism guided the preceding pages, which tried to evaluate and compare the strategies that post–World War II writers and sociologists developed in response to the expanding new class.

The task of reconstructing social trustee professionalism seems especially necessary now, when the federal government, under the administration of former Harvard law professor Barack Obama, is tentatively reenlivening practices of expert governance and smart diplomacy to deal with the complex problems that face the United States and the world during a major recession and impending environmental crisis. After the disastrous right-wing populism of George W. Bush, the neoconservative critique of liberal elitism seems less persuasive than at any time since the Great Society. It remains to be seen whether the United States will produce a corresponding literary and intellectual culture eager to push the government toward more comprehensive economic and institutional reforms, such as existed during the Progressive and New Deal eras.

NOTES

INTRODUCTION: FANTASIES OF THE NEW CLASS

1. William Phillips and Philip Rahv, "Editorial Statement," *Partisan Review* 19, no. 3 (May 1952), 284.
2. Lionel Trilling, "Our Country and Our Culture," *Partisan Review* 19, no. 3 (May 1952), 319, 321–22.
3. The term *new class* is a subject of much debate among sociologists and is often used interchangeably with the terms *professional-managerial class* and *new middle classes*. There is much confusion about whether this group constitutes an actual class in any meaningful sense and, if so, how to draw its boundaries; depending on the writer, each of these terms encompasses everything from routine white-collar workers to upper-level managers. This book uses the term *new class* in a broad sense to designate a variegated stratum of professionals dependent on educationally acquired cultural capital. John Frow helpfully glosses the vast literature on the new class in *Cultural Studies and Cultural Capital* (Oxford, U.K.: Oxford University Press, 1995), 89–130, as does Alan Liu in *The Laws of Cool: Knowledge Work and the Culture of Information* (Chicago: University of Chicago Press, 2004), 31–35. Some of the major post–World War II works on the new class include Daniel Bell, *The Coming of Post-industrial Society: A Venture in Social Forecasting* (New York: Basic Books, 1973); Ralf Dahrendorf, *Class and Class Conflict in Industrial Society* (Stanford, Calif.: Stanford University Press, 1959); Barbara Ehrenreich and John Ehrenreich, "The Professional-Managerial Class," in *Between Labour and Capital*, ed. Pat Walker, 5–45 (Hassocks, U.K.: Harvester Press, 1979); John Kenneth Galbraith, *The New Industrial State*, 2d. rev. ed. (Boston: Houghton Mifflin, 1971); Alvin Gouldner, *The Future of Intellectuals and the Rise of the New Class: A Frame of Reference,*

Theses, Conjectures, Arguments, and an Historical Perspective on the Role of Intellectuals and Intelligentsia in the International Class Contest of the Modern Era (New York: Seabury Press, 1979); and Erik Olin Wright, *Class Structure and Income Determination* (New York: Academic, 1979), and *Classes* (London: Verso, 1985). The term *new class* itself originated in the work of early-twentieth-century Soviet dissidents such as Waclaw Machajski and Nicolai Bukharin, who used the concept to characterize the Soviet Union's bureaucratic elite. See Milovan Djilas, *The New Class: An Analysis of the Communist System* (New York: Praeger, 1957), which first introduced Soviet new-class theory to an American audience.

4. According to the U.S. Census, the percentage of Americans working in "professional and technical" occupations has been rising steadily since World War II, from 6.37 percent of the employed workforce in 1940 to 11.35 percent in 1960 to 16.06 percent in 1980 to 20.20 percent in 2000. These numbers may be somewhat misleading; it is unclear whether the Census Bureau used the terms *professional* and *technical* to refer to the same range of occupations over the course of the various decennial censuses. For instance, the 1940 census distinguishes between professional and semiprofessional vocations, whereas the others do not. The 1940 data are taken from Inter-University Consortium for Political and Social Research, "Census Data for the Year 1940," available at http://fisher.lib.virginia.edu/cgi-local/censusbin/census/cen.pl?year =940. The rest of the data is taken from the U.S. Census Bureau's Web site. See U.S. Census Bureau, "No. 673: Occupation of Employed Workers, by Sex, 1960 to 1980," in *1981 Statistical Abstract*, available at http://www2.census.gov/prod2/statcomp/documents/1981–07.pdf; and U.S. Census Bureau, "QT-P27: Occupation by Sex," in *Census 2000 Summary File 3, Matrix P50*, available at http://factfinder.census.gov/servlet/ QTTable?_bm=y&-geo_id=0100US&-qr_name=DEC_2000_ SF3_U_QTP27&-ds_name=DEC_2000_SF3_U&-redoLog=false.

5. For a recent account of middle-class reformism within the U.S. left-liberal tradition, see Doug Rossinow, *Visions of Progress: The Left-Liberal Tradition in America* (Philadelphia: University of Pennsylvania Press, 2008). See also Richard Hofstadter, *The Age of Reform: From Bryan to F. D. R.* (New York: Knopf, 1955); and Robert Wiebe, *The Search for Order, 1877–1920* (New York: Hill and Wang, 1967), for two classic studies of Progressive Era politics. See Alan Brinkley, *The End of Reform: New Deal Liberalism in Recession and War* (New York: Alfred A. Knopf, 1995), for an account of the various strands of managerial ideology during the

New Deal. In *The Revolt of the Engineers: Social Responsibility and the American Engineering Profession* (Baltimore: John Hopkins University Press, 1986), Edwin Layton highlights the existence of technocratic professionalism among early-twentieth-century engineers, an ideology that sometimes led to conflict with their corporate employers.

6. Steven Brint, *In an Age of Experts: The Changing Role of Professionals in Politics and Public Life* (Princeton, N.J.: Princeton University Press, 1994), 2.

7. Howard Brick, *Transcending Capitalism: Visions of a New Society in Modern American Thought* (Ithaca, N.Y.: Cornell University Press, 2006), 2.

8. Lionel Trilling, *The Liberal Imagination: Essays on Literature and Society* (1950; reprint, Garden City, N.Y.: Doubleday, 1957), xii.

9. Ibid.

10. Trilling also wrote an unfinished second novel, recently edited by Geraldine Murphy under the title *The Journey Abandoned* (New York: Columbia University Press, 2008). In many ways, this novel offers a more complex exploration of American intellectuals than any of Trilling's other criticism or fiction. In particular, *The Journey Abandoned* explores literary intellectuals' anxious relationship with the moneyed bourgeoisie in a society in which, as one of the novel's businessmen puts it, "even spiritual values are for sale, like everything else" (112).

11. Lionel Trilling, *The Middle of the Journey* (1947; reprint, New York: New York Review of Books, 2002), 31, 52, 19.

12. Immanuel Kant, *Critique of Judgment*, trans. Werner S. Pluhar (Indianapolis, Ind.: Hackett, 1987), 76, 62.

13. Trilling, *Middle of the Journey*, 31, 162.

14. Donald Pease outlined this reading of cold war literary culture in *Visionary Compacts: American Renaissance Writings in Cultural Context* (Madison: University of Wisconsin Press, 1987), which argues that the postwar critics who established the Americanist canon (F. O. Mathiessen, Richard Chase, Leslie Fiedler, and so on) read classic nineteenth-century literature through the lens of their era's binary opposition between collectivism and individual freedom. They therefore ignored an important dimension of the American Renaissance—U.S. writers' search for a postrevolutionary public culture that could overcome the purely negative freedom celebrated by cold war critics. Pease established a critical narrative whereby postwar intellectuals discredited the organizational and collectivist politics of the 1930s in order to reclaim an ostensibly benighted individualism. The impact of this narrative is evident in many subsequent accounts of the postwar period, which

focus on popular and intellectual anxieties about individuals being absorbed into collectivist entities—in particular the bureaucratic organizations described in David Riesman's *The Lonely Crowd: A Study of the Changing American Character* (1950; reprint, New Haven, Conn.: Yale University Press, 2001), and William H. Whyte's *The Organization Man* (New York: Simon and Schuster, 1956). In Timothy Melley's terms, the period was marked by a discourse of "agency panic" that opposed an "all-or-nothing conception of agency" against a "monolithic conception of 'society' (or 'system,' or 'organization')" (*The Empire of Conspiracy: The Culture of Paranoia in Postwar America* [Ithaca, N.Y.: Cornell University Press, 2000], 10).

15. Trilling complicated this view in *Beyond Culture: Essays on Literature and Learning* (1965; reprint, London: Secker & Warburg, 1966), which I discuss in greater detail in chapter 4. He argued that the negative capability that he described in his early criticism had itself rigidified into a new orthodoxy among the educated middle class—in part through the efforts of literary intellectuals such as himself.

16. Matthew Arnold, *Culture and Anarchy*, edited by Samuel Lipman (New Haven, Conn.: Yale University Press, 1994), 5, 73, italics in original.

17. Brick makes Parsons the central, post–World War II figure of the postcapitalist tradition that he explores in *Transcending Capitalism*.

18. Herbert Croly, *The Promise of American Life* (1909; reprint, Hamden, Conn.: Archon Books, 1963).

19. In his review of *The Lonely Crowd*, Trilling argued that Riesman explored American "morals and manners" in a fashion that put most contemporary novelists to shame. The last effective social novel was Sinclair Lewis's *Babbitt*; since then, Trilling stated, "few novelists have added anything new to our knowledge of American life. But the sociologists have, and Mr. Reisman [*sic*], writing with a sense of social actuality which Scott Fitzgerald might have envied, does literature a service by suggesting to the novelists that there are new and wonderfully arable social fields for them to till" (*A Gathering of Fugitives* [1956; reprint, London: Secker & Warburg, 1957], 86).

20. Trilling, *Middle of the Journey*, 348.

21. Trilling, *Liberal Imagination*, 219.

22. Wolf Lepenies, *Between Literature and Science: The Rise of Sociology*, trans. R. J. Hollingdale (Cambridge, U.K.: Cambridge University Press, 1988), 13.

23. See Carla Cappetti, *Writing Chicago: Modernism, Ethnography, and the Novel* (New York: Columbia University Press, 1993), for an account of the

Chicago School of Sociology's impact on literary naturalism in the 1930s.

24. Trilling, *Liberal Imagination*, 1–2.

25. Ibid., 7.

26. As Catherine Gallagher notes, this position became the consensus understanding of literature for a broad variety of critical paradigms that emerged after World War II: "one can find no more generally agreed-upon proposition in all sectors of literary criticism than the proposition that literature shakes us up and disturbs our moral equilibrium (liberal humanism), destabilizes the subject (deconstruction), and self-distantiates ideological formations (Marxism)" ("Marxism and the New Historicism," in *The New Historicism*, ed. H. Aram Veeser [New York: Routledge, 1989], 45).

27. Russell Reising remarks on post–World War II literary critics' abandonment of sociological determinism. Postwar critics opposed "crudely materialistic notions of reality, but they did so by swinging to the opposite extreme and defining the life of the mind as the very stuff of reality" (*The Unusable Past: Theory and the Study of American Literature* [New York: Methuen, 1986], 55).

28. In a typically hyperbolic statement from *The Armies of the Night: History as a Novel, the Novel as History* (New York: Penguin, 1994), published in 1968, Norman Mailer castigates the "liberal academic intelligentsia" for their role in establishing the technocratic welfare state: "Liberal academics had no root of a real war with technology land itself, no, in all likelihood, they were the natural managers of that future air-conditioned vault where the last of human life would still exist" (15).

29. Edward Shils, *Center and Periphery: Essays in Macrosociology* (Chicago: University of Chicago Press, 1975), 3.

30. C. Wright Mills, *Power, Politics and People: The Collected Essays of C. Wright Mills*, edited by Irving Louis Horowitz (New York: Oxford University Press, 1963), 607. As Irving Horowitz documents in his biography of Mills, this critique of Trilling led to an angry exchange of letters between the two Columbia University professors (*C. Wright Mills: An American Utopian* [New York: Free Press, 1983], 84–89).

31. Mills's most extensive critique of Parsons can be found in *The Sociological Imagination* (1959; reprint, Oxford, U.K.: Oxford University Press, 2000).

32. Ibid., 92.

33. C. Wright Mills, *The New Men of Power: America's Labor Leaders* (1948; reprint, Urbana: University of Illinois Press, 2001), *White Collar: The*

American Middle Classes (Oxford, U.K.: Oxford University Press, 1951), and *The Power Elite* (London: Oxford University Press, 1956).

34. C. Wright Mills, *The Causes of World War Three* (1958; reprint, London: Secker & Warburg, 1959).

35. Mills, *Power, Politics, and People*, 406.

36. Mills, *Sociological Imagination*, 16.

37. Mills, *Power, Politics, and People*, 226.

38. Mills, *Sociological Imagination*, 181.

39. The distinctiveness of Mills's sociology on this point can be seen by comparing *The Sociological Imagination* to Robert Lynd's *Knowledge for What? The Place of Social Science in American Culture* (Princeton, N.J.: Princeton University Press, 1939). Lynd's book, written from a progressive liberal perspective, assesses how social science might be restructured so as to play a leading role in welfare-state reform. Like Mills, Lynd criticizes the bureaucratic and narrowly disciplinary tendencies of social scientific research. Unlike Mills, he assumes that the purpose of this research is to be of use within government: "There is no way in which our culture can grow in continual serviceability to its people without a large and pervasive extension of planning and control to many areas now left to casual individual initiative. . . . It should be a major concern of social science to discover where and how such large-scale planning and control need to be extended throughout the culture so as to facilitate the human ends of living" (209).

40. See "Mass Society and Liberal Education" in Mills, *Power, Politics, and People*, 353–73.

41. Mills, *Power, Politics, and People*, 605.

42. Ibid., 604–5.

43. Kevin Mattson emphasizes Mills's ties to the liberal tradition. Mills, he argues, "performed an 'in-house' or friendly critique of liberals, one that pushed them on their self-professed ideals" (*Intellectuals in Action: The Origins of the New Left and Radical Liberalism, 1945–1970* [University Park: University of Pennsylvania Press, 2002], 67).

44. Robert Seguin, *Around Quitting Time: Middle-Class Fantasy in American Fiction* (Durham, N.C.: Duke University Press, 2001), 126.

45. Ann Douglas, in particular, articulates the harsh reassessment of the New York intellectuals made by many contemporary critics: "Who have the New York intellectuals converted lately? To what? A significant portion of what they wrote, particularly in the post–WWII years, has, in Hemingway's phrase, 'gone bad,' rancid with self-important eva-

sion" ("The Failure of the New York Intellectuals," *Raritan* 17, no. 4 [Spring 1998], 6).

46. Terry Cooney, *The Rise of the New York Intellectuals:* Partisan Review *and Its Circle* (Madison: University of Wisconsin Press, 1986), 38–119.

47. William Phillips and Philip Rahv, "Problems and Perspectives in Revolutionary Literature," *Partisan Review* 1, no. 3 (June–July 1934), 5.

48. As Alan Wald argues, Philips and Rahv were part of a broader movement of American and European Marxist intellectuals who challenged the strict economic determinism of the Second and Third International. In America, this movement included theorists such as Max Eastman and Sidney Hook; in Europe, its most famous proponent was Georg Lukács (*The New York Intellectuals: The Rise and Decline of the Anti-Stalinist Left from the 1930s to the 1980s* [Chapel Hill: University of North Carolina Press, 1987], 124–25).

49. William Phillips (a.k.a. "Wallace Phelps") articulated this argument in "Three Generations," *Partisan Review* 1, no. 4 (September–October 1934): 49–55. This notion of a formally experimental radical art influenced many 1930s writers, notably James Farrell, who had close ties with the *Partisan Review* in its early years.

50. Phillips and Rahv, "Problems and Perspectives," 5, italics in original.

51. In *The New York Intellectuals: From Vanguard to Institution* (Manchester, U.K.: Manchester University Press, 1995), Hugh Wilford argues that most of the New York intellectuals conceived of themselves as a Marxist–Leninist intellectual vanguard long after their break from any form of party politics. In effect, they shifted their class allegiances, viewing themselves as the vanguard of the educated middle class rather than of the proletariat.

52. William Phillips and Philip Rahv, "Literature in a Political Decade," in *New Letters in America*, ed. Horace Gregory (New York: W. W. Norton, 1937), 176, 177.

53. Saul Bellow, *Conversations with Saul Bellow*, ed. Gloria Cronin and Ben Siegel (Jackson: University of Mississippi Press, 1994), 94.

54. Thomas Strychacz, *Modernism, Mass Culture, and Professionalism* (New York: Cambridge University Press, 1993); Louis Menand, *Discovering Modernism: T. S. Eliot and His Context* (New York: Oxford University Press, 1987); Mark McGurl, *The Novel Art: Elevations of American Fiction After Henry James* (Princeton, N.J.: Princeton University Press, 2001). See also Jonathan Freedman, *Professions of Taste: Henry James, British Aestheticism, and Commodity Culture* (Stanford, Calif.: Stanford University

Press, 1990); and Christopher Wilson, *The Labor of Words: Literary Professionalism in the Progressive Era* (Athens: University of Georgia Press, 1985), and *White Collar Fictions: Class and Social Representation in American Literature, 1885–1925* (Athens: University of Georgia Press, 1992).

55. McGurl, *The Novel Art*, 11, italics in original.

56. Ibid., 7.

57. Andrew Hoberek, *The Twilight of the Middle Class: Post–World War II American Fiction and White Collar Work* (Princeton, N.J.: Princeton University Press, 2005), 21.

58. Philip Rahv, "Our Country and Our Culture," *Partisan Review* 19, no. 3 (May 1952), 306.

59. Edward Brunner describes a similar shift in post–World War II poetics. The absorption of poets into the academy led them to cultivate a "populist formalism" designed to appeal to an expanded, educated middle-class audience: "Formal poetry lent itself to presentation as an array of professional devices each of which was designed to foster communication. The packaging of formalist devices openly displayed the poem as labor-intensive, an exquisitely balanced verbal machine crafted by specialists in the language arts" (*Cold War Poetry* [Urbana: University of Illinois Press, 2001], 6).

60. Hoberek, *Twilight of the Middle Class*, 89.

61. James Farrell, *Studs Lonigan: Young Lonigan, The Young Manhood of Studs Lonigan, Judgment Day* (New York: Avon Books, 1977), 388–89.

62. Ibid., 389.

63. Saul Bellow, *The Adventures of Augie March* (New York: Penguin, 1953), 43.

64. Donald Pizer, *Twentieth-Century American Literary Naturalism: An Interpretation* (Carbondale: Southern Illinois University Press, 1982), 134.

65. Bellow, *Adventures of Augie March*, 117, italics in original.

66. Ibid., 402.

67. Sean McCann, writing about this passage, similarly remarks on Bellow's cultural determinism: "Bellow's novel dramatizes a simultaneous indulgence in and suspicion of rhetorical power, where the ability to invent and entice seems at once a valuable means to resist the rule of law and custom and, at the same time, a dangerous form of imperial overreach" (*A Pinnacle of Feeling: American Literature and Presidential Government* [Princeton, N.J.: Princeton University Press, 2008], 105).

68. Bellow, *Adventures of Augie March*, 454.

69. According to Janis Bellow's memoir, Bellow claimed that in Louis Wirth's courses, he encountered his "first highly cultivated German Jew,

who pronounced each exquisite syllable of every difficult word" ("Saul Bellow," in *An Unsentimental Education: Writers and Chicago*, ed. Molly McQuade, 1–12 [Chicago: University of Chicago Press, 1995], 2–3).

70. See James Atlas, *Bellow: A Biography* (New York: Random House, 2000), 476–78, for an account of Bellow's friendship with Shils. Shils also helped edit the manuscript of Bellow's 1970 novel *Mr. Sammler's Planet*, discussed in chapter 4.

71. Saul Bellow, *It All Adds Up: From the Dim Past to the Uncertain Future, a Nonfiction Collection* (New York: Viking, 1994), 96.

72. Ibid.

73. Gouldner, *Future of Intellectuals*, 48, 29.

74. Ibid., 92.

75. Hoberek similarly remarks on the datedness of celebratory theories about the new class: "The postwar middle class did well, but the fate of the middle class since the seventies suggests that this had more to do with the postwar boom and the redistributive polices of the mid-century welfare state than with the inherent nature of the postwar economy" (*Twilight of the Middle Class*, 6).

76. Brint, *In an Age of Experts*, 15.

77. As Christopher Newfield documents, this shift was necessitated by the 1970s recession, which decreased government funding for public institutions. More broadly, it was necessitated by the accelerated globalization of the world economy, which weakened the bond between the academy and the nation-state. This transformation of the university was reflected in changes to U.S. patent law, such as the Bayh–Dole Act (1982), which made it increasingly easy for university researchers to patent the results their work and sell them directly to the private sector. As a result, "it became harder to image how the university could serve society *without* serving the corporate sector to which society apparently owed its wealth, knowledge, and way of life" (*Ivy and Industry: Business and the Making of the American University, 1880–1980* [Durham, N.C.: Duke University Press, 2003], 177, italics in original).

78. Bill Readings, *The University in Ruins* (Cambridge, Mass.: Harvard University Press, 1996), 103.

79. Bourdieu's sociology of intellectuals is a pervasive feature of his work, but see especially *Homo Academicus* (trans. Peter Collier [Stanford, Calif.: Stanford University Press, 1988]), his study of the French academic field.

1. THE REPUBLIC OF LETTERS: THE NEW CRITICISM, HARVARD SOCIOLOGY, AND THE IDEA OF THE UNIVERSITY

An earlier version of this chapter appeared as "Fantasies of the New Class: The New Criticism, Harvard Sociology, and the Idea of the University," *PMLA* 122, no. 3 (May 2007): 663–78.

1. Terry Eagleton comments on some of the affinities between the New Criticism and structural functionalism, albeit in very different terms than I do here: "The literary text, for American New Criticism as for I. A. Richards, was therefore grasped in what might be called 'functionalist' terms; just as American functionalist sociology developed a 'conflict-free' model of society, in which every element 'adapted' to every other, so the poem abolished all friction, irregularity and contradiction in the symmetrical cooperation of its various features" (*Literary Theory: An Introduction* [Oxford, U.K.: Blackwell, 1983], 47).

2. John Guillory, *Cultural Capital: The Problem of Literary Canon Formation* (Chicago: University of Chicago Press, 1993), 168, italics in original.

3. Gerald Graff, *Professing Literature: An Institutional History* (Chicago: University of Chicago Press, 1987), 173.

4. Geoffrey Hawthorn remarks on structural functionalism's impact on sociology: "in exactly the way in which the instruments of survey analysis served to constitute a professional technique, functionalism served to constitute a professional value. This was most apparent in introductory textbooks and on those occasions when the profession explained itself to the laity" (*Enlightenment and Despair: A History of Sociology* [New York: Cambridge University Press, 1976], 214).

5. John Guillory, "The Sokal Hoax and the History of Criticism," *Critical Inquiry* 28, no. 2 (2002), 498.

6. Allan Tate, "The Present Function of Criticism," *Southern Review* 6 (1940–1941), 240.

7. Included in John Crowe Ransom, *Selected Essays of John Crowe Ransom*, ed. Thomas Daniel Young and John Hindle, 93–106 (Baton Rouge: Louisiana State University Press, 1984).

8. Barbara Ehrenreich and John Ehrenreich, "Professional-Managerial Class," in *Between Labour and Capital*, ed. Pat Walker (Hassocks, U.K.: Harvester Press, 1979), 27.

9. Carla Cappetti, *Writing Chicago: Modernism, Ethnography, and the Novel* (New York: Columbia University Press, 1993), 199.

10. James Farrell, *Studs Lonigan: Young Lonigan, The Young Manhood of Studs Lonigan, Judgment Day* (New York: Avon Books, 1977), 429.

11. See Henrika Kuklick, "A 'Scientific Revolution': Sociological Theory in the United States, 1930–1945," *Sociological Inquiry* 43, no. 1 (1973): 3–22, for a detailed account of how this backlash unfolded in the 1930s and 1940s.

12. According to Albert Biderman and Elizabeth Crawford, the total number of social scientists engaged in government work was about 680 in 1931. Most of them were economists. The figure rose to 2,150 over the next six years as New Deal programs were implemented (*The Political Economics of Social Research: The Case of Sociology* [Washington, D.C.: Bureau of Social Science Research, 1968], 41). Industrial sociology began with the Hawthorne experiments, which were conducted by Harvard researchers and extended from the late 1920s through the mid-1930s. The management innovations that came from these experiments became common practice during and after World War II. For more on the emergence of industrial sociology, see Loren Baritz, *Servants of Power: A History of the Use of Social Science in American Industry* (Middletown, Conn.: Wesleyan University Press, 1960).

13. For an account of the formation of the Harvard Department of Social Relations, see Nils Gilman, *Mandarins of the Future: Modernization Theory in Cold War America* (Baltimore: Johns Hopkins University Press, 2003), 76–79.

14. Talcott Parsons, *The Social System* (Glencoe, Ill.: Free Press, 1951). For an empirical account of the influence of structural functionalism in the 1950s and 1960s, see Seymour Martin Lipset and Everett Carll Ladd Jr., "Politics of American Sociologists," *American Journal of Sociology* 78 (1972): 67–104. These researchers review surveys of the frequency with which authors are cited in the literature of sociology, which show that Parsons and his student Robert Merton are the two most referenced figures. See also George Huaco, "Ideology and General Theory: The Case of Sociological Functionalism," *Comparative Studies in Society and History* 28 (1996): 34–54. Even in the 1950s, sociology was a diverse discipline; many quantitative sociologists remained untouched by Parsonian functionalism. In addition, popular sociologists such as David Riesman, Daniel Bell, and C. Wright Mills did not rely on a Parsonian framework.

15. Talcott Parsons, *The Structure of Social Action: A Study in Social Theory with Special Reference to a Group of Recent European Writers* (1937; reprint, New York: Free Press, 1968).

16. Robert Park and Ernest Burgess, *Introduction to the Science of Sociology* (1921; reprint, Chicago: University of Chicago Press, 1924).

17. Parsons, *Structure of Social Action*, 6.

18. Parsons quoted in C. Wright Mills, *The Sociological Imagination* (1959; reprint, Oxford, U.K.: Oxford University Press, 2000), 39. Mills's book initiated the backlash in sociology against Parsons's work that culminated in Alvin Gouldner's *The Coming Crisis of Western Sociology* (New York: Basic, 1970), essentially a book-length critique of Parsons.

19. Parsons, *Structure of Social Action*, 424.

20. Gouldner, commenting on this aspect of Parsons's work, notes that "Talcott Parsons's vast *oeuvre* can best be understood as a complex ideology of the New Class, expressed by and through his flattering conception of *professionalism*" (*The Future of Intellectuals and the Rise of the New Class: A Frame of Reference, Theses, Conjectures, Arguments, and an Historical Perspective on the Role of Intellectuals and Intelligentsia in the International Class Contest of the Modern Era* [New York: Seabury Press, 1979], 37, italics in original).

21. Howard Brick, *Transcending Capitalism: Visions of a New Society in Modern American Thought* (Ithaca, N.Y.: Cornell University Press, 2006), 131. For a more extensive account of Parsons's reformism in the 1930s, see also Howard Brick, "The Reformist Dimension of Talcott Parsons's Early Social Theory," in *The Culture of the Market: Historical Essays*, ed. Thomas Haskell and Richard Teichgraeber III, 357–96 (Cambridge, U.K.: Cambridge University Press, 1993).

22. Brick, *Transcending Capitalism*, 144.

23. Durkheim first introduced the idea that professional associations and other corporative organizations can play many of the same functions as families and other premodern institutions in his 1902 preface to the second edition of *The Division of Labor in Society*, trans. George Simpson (Glencoe, Ill.: Free Press, 1933).

24. See Parsons, *The Social System*, 428–79.

25. Talcott Parsons, *The System of Modern Societies* (Englewood Cliffs, N.J.: Prentice-Hall, 1971), 105.

26. Ibid.

27. Jamie Cohen-Cole describes how a broad swath of post–World War II intellectuals similarly viewed the academy as a potential model for U.S. society as a whole. Referring to the Macy conferences on cybernetics, which involved Margaret Mead, Marshall McLuhan, Gregory Bateson, and many others, Cohen-Cole notes, "[H]umanists and phys-

ical scientists joined social scientists in using academic culture to think about national and international issues. At the center of their diagnosis of society's ills and of the cure was a casual treatment of the social world of the academy as a microcosm of, and ideal type for, American society" ("The Creative American: Cold War Salons, Social Science, and the Cure for Modern Society," *Isis* 100 [2009], 248).

28. Graff, *Professing Literature*, 148.

29. Both John Fekete (*The Critical Twilight: Explorations in the Ideology of Anglo-American Literary Theory from Eliot to McLuhan* [London: Routledge, 1977]) and Terry Eagleton (*Literary Theory*) emphasize the discontinuities between the Agrarians and New Critics, arguing that the New Critics dropped their socioeconomic critique of northern industrialism with their transition into the academy. Other critics who echo Graff and Guillory and highlight the continuities between agrarianism and the New Criticism include Mark Jancovich, *The Cultural Politics of the New Criticism* (Cambridge, U.K.: Cambridge University Press, 1993); Paul A. Bové, *Mastering Discourse: The Politics of Intellectual Culture* (Durham, N.C.: Duke University Press, 1992); and Karen O'Kane, "Before the New Criticism: Modernism and the Nashville Group," *Mississippi Quarterly* 51, no. 4 (Fall 1998): 683–97.

30. Two excellent accounts of the Fugitives' evolution into Agrarians and subsequently into New Critics are John Stewart, *The Burden of Time: The Fugitives and the Agrarians* (Princeton, N.J.: Princeton University Press, 1965), and Thomas Daniel Young, *Gentleman in a Dustcoat: A Biography of John Crowe Ransom* (Baton Rouge: Louisiana State University Press, 1976). The three groups do not overlap exactly. Brooks, for instance, was an Agrarian and New Critic but never a Fugitive. In contrast, Donald Davidson was a Fugitive and Agrarian but never a New Critic.

31. The Agrarians' attitude toward race relations was predictable for conservative southern intellectuals of their era. They nostalgically recollected the plantation economy of the Old South and in so doing elided the problem of slavery and race discrimination; "slavery," Ransom argues in one of his contributions to the Agrarian essay collection *I'll Take My Stand*, "was a feature monstrous enough in theory, but, more often than not, humane in practice" ("Reconstructed but Unregenerate," in *I'll Take My Stand: The South and the Agrarian Tradition*, by Twelve Southerners [John Crowe Ransom and others] [1930; reprint, New York: Harper, 1962], 14). Other contributors, such as Frank Lawrence Owsley ("Irrepressible Conflict," 61–91) and Robert Penn Warren

("Briar Patch," 246–64), offered qualified defenses of the South's post–Civil War rejection of black suffrage.

32. John Crowe Ransom, *God Without Thunder: An Unorthodox Defense of Orthodoxy* (1930; reprint, Hamden, Conn.: Archon, 1965), 59.

33. Ransom developed this argument in "A Poem Nearly Anonymous" (1933), later reprinted as "Forms and Citizens" in *Selected Essays*, 59–73.

34. In Ransom, *Selected Essays*, 46.

35. Ransom, "Statement of Principles," in *I'll Take My Stand*, xliv. This introduction is by Ransom alone, although it is not attributed to him in the text (Young, *Gentleman in a Dustcoat*, 208–10).

36. In Ransom, *Selected Essays*, 57.

37. Although the Agrarians were hostile toward the New Deal, their nostalgic regionalism was not entirely at odds with the conception of culture developed by many federalist intellectuals associated with the Roosevelt administration. In particular, Ransom's regionalism prefigured the underlying philosophy that guided the most ambitious government foray into U.S. literary culture: the Federal Writers' Project. As Jerrold Hirsch details, the intellectuals and bureaucrats who administrated the project embraced a pluralist vision of the United States that emphasized the particularity of regional cultures. Many writers involved in the American Guide series articulated an organicist perspective that echoed the Agrarians' essays on southern culture. The Louisiana guidebook, published in 1941, describes how the region's buildings "evolved out of the material on hand, the exigencies of the climate, and the needs of the colonists" (cited in Jerrold Hirsch, *Portrait of America: A Cultural History of the Federal Writers' Project* [Chapel Hill: University of North Carolina Press, 2003], 72).

38. In Ransom, *Selected Essays*, 57.

39. The buildings constructed in the 1920s and 1930s were initially designed by the noted landscape architect company Olmsted Brothers, which also designed the campus layout for Stanford University in 1888. Another architect, Theodore Link, scrapped parts of their original plans to design Louisiana State University's well-known quadrangle.

40. John Crowe Ransom, *Selected Letters of John Crowe Ransom*, ed. Thomas Daniel Young and George Core (Baton Rouge: Louisiana State University Press, 1985), 217.

41. Samuel Taylor Coleridge, *On the Constitution of Church and State According to the Idea of Each*, ed. John Barrell (London: Dent, 1972), 36.

42. Ransom, *Selected Letters*, 219.
43. Ibid., 223.
44. In Ransom, *Selected Essays*, 94.
45. In ibid., 148.
46. Ibid., 105.
47. Ibid., 189, italics in original.
48. Cleanth Brooks also expressed this anxiety about disciplinary boundaries in *The Well-Wrought Urn: Studies in the Structure of Poetry* (New York: Harcourt, 1947). If the proponents of the humanities "are to be merely cultural historians, they must not be surprised if they are quietly relegated to a comparatively obscure corner of the history division. If one man's taste is really as good as another's, and they can pretend to offer nothing more than a neutral and objective commentary on tastes, they must expect to be treated as sociologists, though perhaps not as a very important kind of sociologist" (235).
49. Ransom, *Poems and Essays* (New York: Vintage, 1955), 116–17.
50. Ibid., 117.
51. Louis Kampf and Paul Lauter, "Introduction," in *The Politics of Literature: Dissenting Essays on the Teaching of English*, ed. Louis Kampf and Paul Lauter (New York: Pantheon, 1972), 44.
52. Donald Levine, *Visions of the Sociological Tradition* (Chicago: University of Chicago Press, 1995), 289. For other accounts of the crisis in sociology, especially as related to the use of sociology in public policy, see the essays collected in Terence Halliday and Morris Janowitz, eds., *Sociology and Its Publics: The Forms and Fates of Disciplinary Organization* (Chicago: University of Chicago Press, 1992).
53. Guillory, *Cultural Capital*, 45.

2. "LIFE UPON THE HORNS OF THE WHITE MAN'S DILEMMA": RALPH ELLISON, GUNNAR MYRDAL, AND THE PROJECT OF NATIONAL THERAPY

1. The review was turned down for publication by the *Antioch Review*. It appeared twenty years later in *Shadow and Act*, which is reprinted in Ralph Ellison, *The Collected Essays of Ralph Ellison*, ed. John F. Callahan, 47–340 (New York: Modern Library, 2003). Subsequent citations to the *Collected Essays* are noted parenthetically in the text as *CE*. See also Gunnar Myrdal, *An American Dilemma: The Negro Problem and Modern Democracy* (1944; reprint, New York: Pantheon Books, 1972).

2. Thomas Schaub details some of the affinities between Ellison's postwar essays and the work of New York intellectuals such as Trilling: "In Ellison's writing of this time, as in literary culture generally, one notes the characteristic rejection of naturalism and social realism as adequate forms of representation, and a redefinition of personal identity and social history as tragic, complex, ambivalent, and ironic" (*American Fiction in the Cold War* [Madison: University of Wisconsin Press, 1991], 91).

3. Ralph Ellison, *Invisible Man* (1952; reprint, New York: Vintage Books, 1995). All page references are to the 1995 Vintage edition and are hereafter noted parenthetically in the text as *IM*.

4. Kenneth Warren, *So Black and Blue: Ralph Ellison and the Occasion of Criticism* (Chicago: University of Chicago Press, 2003), 63. Other studies that address Ellison's critique of damage theory include Jerry Gafio Watts, *Heroism and the Black Intellectual: Ralph Ellison, Politics, and Afro-American Intellectual Life* (Chapel Hill: University of North Carolina Press, 1994); Roderick Ferguson, *Aberrations in Black: Toward a Queer of Color Critique* (Minneapolis: University of Minnesota Press, 2004); and Daryl Michael Scott, *Contempt and Pity: Social Policy and the Image of the Damaged Black Psyche, 1880–1996* (Chapel Hill: University of North Carolina Press, 1997). Watts focuses exclusively on Ellison's nonfiction and, like Warren, identifies moments when Ellison qualifies his opposition to sociological determinism. Ferguson explores Ellison's incorporation of his antisociological argument into a deleted chapter from *Invisible Man*. Scott discusses Ellison's review of Myrdal in the context of the Daniel P. Moynihan controversy of the mid-1960s (see note 16).

5. Andrew Hoberek, *The Twilight of the Middle Class: Post–World War II American Fiction and White Collar Work* (Princeton, N.J.: Princeton University Press, 2005), 55.

6. Myrdal, *American Dilemma*, lxix.

7. Michel Fabre, "From *Native Son* to *Invisible Man*: Some Notes on Ralph Ellison's Evolution in the 1950s," in *Speaking for You: The Vision of Ralph Ellison*, ed. Kimberly Benston (Washington, D.C.: Howard University Press, 1987), 206.

8. Richard Wright, *Native Son* (1940; reprint, New York: Perennial Classics, 1998) and *Black Boy* (1945; reprint, New York: Harper Perennial, 2007). As discussed in chapter 1, Wright had close connections with the Chicago School of Sociology; indeed, he wrote the introduction to St. Clair Drake and Horace Cayton's *Black Metropolis: A Study of Negro Life in a Northern City* (New York: Harcourt Brace, 1945), a landmark

study of Chicago's South Side. For more on this connection, see Carla Cappetti, *Writing Chicago: Modernism, Ethnography, and the Novel* (New York: Columbia University Press, 1993), 182–210, and Catherine Jurca, *White Diaspora: The Suburb and the Twentieth-Century American Novel* (Princeton, N.J.: Princeton University Press, 2001), 99–132.

9. Warren, *So Black and Blue*, 70. In *Slavery: A Problem in American Institutional and Intellectual Life* (1959; reprint, Chicago: University of Chicago Press, 1964), Stanley Elkins compares the psychological effects of slavery on African Americans to the effects of concentration camps on Holocaust survivors.

10. Barbara Foley, "Ralph Ellison as Proletarian Journalist," *Science and Society* 62, no. 4 (Winter 1998–1999), 539.

11. Herbert Aptheker, *The Negro People in America: A Critique of Gunnar Myrdal's "An American Dilemma"* (New York: International, 1946).

12. There are two excellent studies of *An American Dilemma* that provide extensive background information on the project: Walter Jackson, *Gunnar Myrdal and America's Conscience: Social Engineering and Racial Liberalism, 1938–1987* (Chapel Hill: University of North Carolina Press, 1990); and David Southern, *Gunnar Myrdal and Black–White Relations: The Use and Abuse of "An American Dilemma," 1944–1969* (Baton Rouge: Louisiana State University Press, 1987).

13. This was the position articulated by many of the black Marxists who helped prepare the research for Myrdal's work, such as Ralph Bunche, the militant head of political science at Howard University. Bunche's conclusion in his memorandum on black political organization for the project was that the best strategy for American blacks was to forge alliances with the white working class, thus creating an interracial proletariat: "If there is an ideology which offers any hope to the Negro . . . it would seem to be that which identifies his interests with the white workers of the nation." For him, the African American's "future status here will largely depend upon the political and economic course of the nation. This will prove even more vital to the Negro than his ability to 'develop' himself and to change white attitudes toward him" (cited in Jackson, *Gunnar Myrdal and America's Conscience*, 127, 129).

14. Myrdal, *American Dilemma*, 75.

15. Ibid., 928, 929, italics in original.

16. Prior to Myrdal's study, from the 1920s to the 1940s, most enlightened U.S. sociologists were involved in polemics against biological theories of black racial inferiority. Influenced by cultural anthropologists such

as Franz Boas and by the urban sociologists of the Chicago School of Sociology, they instead focused on the determining effects of race prejudice and economic deprivation on black populations. For more on the transition in U.S. social science from biological racism to social determinism, see James McKee, *Sociology and the Race Problem: The Failure of a Perspective* (Urbana: University of Illinois Press, 1993). This sociological argument extended into the 1960s, long after the extinction of biological racism as a viable scientific theory. It culminated in Daniel P. Moynihan's notorious government report *The Negro Family* (1965), which argued that female-centered black families were a historical legacy of slavery and Jim Crow discrimination. The text of *The Negro Family*, along with other documents pertaining to the controversy it aroused, can be found in Lee Rainwater and William Yancey, eds., *The Moynihan Report and the Politics of Controversy: A Trans-action Social Science and Public Policy Report* (Cambridge, Mass.: MIT Press, 1967).

17. Myrdal, *American Dilemma*, lxix.

18. As Doug Rossinow notes, this educational approach to combating racism was broadly influential among liberal antiracists in the late 1940s. It helped propel the "human relations" movement, which set for government "the task of reforming negative 'attitudes' among the populace" (*Visions of Progress: The Left-Liberal Tradition in America* [Philadelphia: University of Pennsylvania Press, 2008], 178).

19. Myrdal, *American Dilemma*, 1029, italics in original.

20. This is only one of several occasions in which Ellison paraphrased Myrdal's dilemma thesis. Other occasions include "Beating That Boy" (*CE*, 148), "The Shadow and the Act" (*CE*, 304), and "Tell it Like It Is, Baby" (*CE*, 31).

21. Howard Zinn, *The Southern Mystique* (New York: Knopf, 1964).

22. William Graham Sumner, *Folkways: A Study of the Sociological Importance of Usages, Manners, Customs, Mores, and Morals* (1907; reprint, New York: Dover, 1959), 5.

23. Ralph Ellison, *Flying Home and Other Stories*, ed. John F. Callahan (New York: Vintage Books, 1998), 143, 145.

24. Cleanth Brooks, *The Well-Wrought Urn: Studies in the Structure of Poetry* (New York: Harcourt, 1947), 195.

25. For the Black Arts movement's response to Ellison, see the essays collected in *Black World* 20 (December 1970).

26. Irving Howe, for instance, complained about "the sudden, unprepared and implausible assertion of unconditioned freedom with which [*Invis-*

ible Man] ends," which "breaks the coherence of the novel and reveals Ellison's dependence on the post-war Zeitgeist" (*A World More Attractive: A View of Modern Literature and Politics* [New York: Horizon Press, 1963], 115).

27. Myrdal, *American Dilemma*, 1030.

28. "Legislators now take it for granted that teachers and social workers ought to have a college degree; *a college education should be even more urgently required for fulfilling the duties of a police officer. . . . Ideally the policeman should be something of an educator and a social worker at the same time that he is the arm of the law*" (Myrdal, *American Dilemma*, 544–45, italics in original).

29. Ibid., 1030.

30. Hoberek, *Twilight of the Middle Class*, 55.

31. C. Wright Mills, *White Collar: The American Middle Classes* (Oxford, U.K.: Oxford University Press, 1951), xvii; see also David Riesman, with Nathan Glazer and Reuel Denney, *The Lonely Crowd: A Study of the Changing American Character* (1950; reprint, New Haven, Conn.: Yale University Press, 2001).

32. E. Franklin Frazier, *Black Bourgeoisie* (Glencoe, Ill.: Free Press, 1957), 162.

33. Sigmund Freud, *On Metapsychology, The Theory of Psychoanalysis: Beyond the Pleasure Principle, The Ego and the Id, and Other Works*, ed. Angela Richards (New York: Penguin Books, 1991), 374, italics in original.

34. Frazier documents the evolution of black colleges in *Black Bourgeoisie* (60–85). See also Raymond Wolters, *The New Negro on Campus: Black College Rebellions of the 1920s* (Princeton, N.J.: Princeton University Press, 1975), for an account of black student rebellions against the missionary model in the 1920s.

35. As Roderick Ferguson notes, this disciplinary effort was embodied in black colleges' architecture and geographical location: "As 'the cultural products of a recently emancipated people,' HBCUs [historically black colleges and universities] attempted to mimic the canonical features of modern architecture and claim its ideals of normativity and humanity, but the racial specificity of African American oppression disrupted efforts to display canonical and normative status through architecture. For instance, instead of being located within the heart of rural towns, southern HBCUs were often built on marginalized property and could only be accessed through backways that were distant from main streets" (*Aberrations in Black*, 60).

36. Hoberek, *Twilight of the Middle Class*, 57.

37. Robert Park and Ernest Burgess, *Introduction to the Science of Sociology* (1921; reprint, Chicago: University of Chicago Press, 1924), 139.

38. Ferguson, *Aberrations in Black*, 56.

39. As Lawrence Jackson argues, the invisible man evolves from black square into literary hipster over the course of the novel: "By the novel's own chronology, during the Prologue, the Invisible Man has evolved into a sharpie, a reefer-smoking theoretician walking down the street with a knife, attacking whites over petty insults" ("Ralph Ellison, Sharpies, Rinehart, and Politics in *Invisible Man*," *Massachusetts Review* 49 [Spring 1999], 81).

40. Ann Douglas provides an excellent account of these divisions within the Harlem Renaissance in *Terrible Honesty: Mongrel Manhattan in the 1920s* (New York: Farrar, Straus and Giroux, 1995), 82–84.

41. Nella Larsen, *Quicksand and Passing*, ed. Deborah E. McDowell (New Brunswick, N.J.: Rutgers University Press, 1986).

42. Arnold Rampersad, *Ralph Ellison: A Biography* (New York: Alfred A. Knopf, 2007).

43. Houston A. Baker Jr., *Afro-American Literature: A Vernacular Theory* (Chicago: University of Chicago Press, 1984), 193.

3. MARY McCARTHY'S FIELD GUIDE TO U.S. INTELLECTUALS: TRADITION AND MODERNIZATION THEORY IN *BIRDS OF AMERICA*

An earlier version of this chapter previously appeared under the same title in *Modern Fiction Studies* 53, no. 4 (2007): 821–44. © 2007 by the Purdue Research Foundation. Reprinted with permission of the Johns Hopkins University Press.

1. Hannah Arendt and Mary McCarthy, *Between Friends: The Correspondence of Hannah Arendt and Mary McCarthy, 1949–1975*, ed. Carol Brightman (New York: Harcourt Brace, 1995), 178–79.

2. David Halberstam, *The Best and the Brightest* (New York: Random House, 1972).

3. Mary McCarthy, *Birds of America* (1971; reprint, New York: Harcourt Brace Jovanovich, 1992); all page references are to the 1992 edition and hereafter are noted parenthetically in the text.

4. All these works are collected in Mary McCarthy, *The Seventeenth Degree: How It Went, Vietnam, Hanoi, Medina, and Sons of the Morning* (New York: Harcourt Brace Jovanovich, 1974).

5. Cited in Mary McCarthy, *Conversations with Mary McCarthy*, ed. Carol Gelderman (Jackson: University of Mississippi Press, 1991), 304.

6. David Laskin, *Partisans: Marriage, Politics, and Betrayal Among the New York Intellectuals* (New York: Simon and Schuster, 2000), 19, italics in original.

7. Harvey Teres, *Renewing the Left: Politics, Imagination, and the New York Intellectuals* (New York: Oxford University Press, 1996), 15.

8. Apart from Trilling's "'Elements That Are Wanted,'" *Partisan Review 7*, no. 5 (September–October 1940): 367–79, two other *Partisan Review* essays that place T. S. Eliot's cultural politics in conversation with Marxism are William Phillips and Philip Rahv, "Criticism," *Partisan Review* 2, no. 7 (April–May 1935): 16–25, and Philip Rahv, "A Season in Heaven," *Partisan Review* 3 (June 1936): 11–14. All of the New York intellectuals were also influenced by Edmund Wilson's assessment of Eliot in *Axel's Castle: A Study in the Imaginative Literature of 1870–1930* (1931; reprint, London: Fontana, 1984). This influence was particularly obvious in McCarthy's case; she and Wilson endured a notoriously stormy marriage in the late 1930s and early 1940s.

9. Trilling, "'Elements That Are Wanted,'" 376.

10. Ibid., 368.

11. Sabrina Fuchs Abrams, *Mary McCarthy: Gender, Politics, and the Postwar Intellectual* (New York: Peter Lang, 2004), 91.

12. Mary McCarthy, *The Writing on the Wall and Other Literary Essays* (New York: Harcourt, Brace and World, 1970), 204.

13. McCarthy, *Conversations*, 115.

14. See in particular Gary Snyder's celebration of the tribal as opposed to the civilized in *Earth House Hold: Technical Notes and Queries to Fellow Dharma Revolutionaries* (New York: New Directions, 1969).

15. Michael Latham, *Modernization as Ideology: American Social Science and "Nation Building" in the Kennedy Era* (Chapel Hill: University of North Carolina Press, 2000), 4. Nils Gilman provides a similar intellectual history of modernization theory in *Mandarins of the Future: Modernization Theory in Cold War America* (Baltimore: Johns Hopkins University Press, 2003).

16. Talcott Parsons and Edward Shils, *Toward a General Theory of Action* (Cambridge, Mass.: Harvard University Press, 1951), 77. As we saw in chapter 2, something like this dichotomy was at the root of Gunnar Myrdal's distinction between lower and higher value systems, which he used to distinguish between the American Creed and premodern,

racist prejudices. Parsons's ideal-type distinction between traditional and modern societies was more complex than Myrdal's. The opposition between particularism and universalism was the first of five "pattern variables"—paired sets of terms that Parsons used to classify societies. The other four pattern variables were "ascription" versus "achievement-orientation," "role diffusion" versus "role specificity," "orientation to the collective" versus "orientation to the self," and "nonaffective relationships" versus "affective relationships."

17. Gilman, *Mandarins of the Future*, 19–20.

18. The two most influential works setting forth this thesis were Eugene Staley, *The Future of Underdeveloped Countries: Political Implications of Economic Development*, rev. ed. (New York: Harper and Brothers, 1961); and Walt Whitman Rostow, *The Stages of Economic Growth: A Non-Communist Manifesto* (London: Cambridge University Press, 1960). Both writers were involved in the Kennedy administration.

19. Cited in Latham, *Modernization as Ideology*, 178.

20. Cited in ibid., 151.

21. McCarthy, *Seventeenth Degree*, 138.

22. Ibid., 109.

23. Ibid., 307, italics in original.

24. Cited in Abrams, *Mary McCarthy*, 85.

25. McCarthy, *Seventeenth Degree*, 293.

26. Ibid., 315.

27. McCarthy may have loosely based this character on Edward Shils, with whom she sparred during a panel at the 1960 Congress for Cultural Freedom conference in Warsaw, Poland. Shils was well known for his defense of mass culture and had a profound impact on the modernization theorists who worked within the Kennedy and Johnson administrations. At the panel, entitled "Modernity and Tradition," McCarthy accused Shils of being "Dr. Pangloss reborn and without Dr. Pangloss' charm and innocence" (Arendt and McCarthy, *Between Friends*, 83), the same epithet that Peter attaches to Dr. Small in the novel.

28. Immanuel Kant, *Critique of Pure Reason*, trans. Norman Kemp Smith (New York: St. Martin's Press, 1965), 487.

29. This food purism is not as idiosyncratic an obsession as it may at first seem to be; when *Birds of America* was published in the early 1970s, the health foods movement was just beginning, and it embodied much of Rosamund's culinary philosophy. Alice Waters, for instance, opened Chez Panisse at Berkeley in 1971; she similarly emphasized the use of

fresh, local ingredients and highlighted the detrimental environmental and health effects of eating mass-produced foods.

30. McCarthy, *Seventeenth Degree*, 309–10, italics added.

31. Rosamund's own family also exemplifies the cultural heterogeneity she cannot expunge from her kitchen. Two of her husbands are émigré Jews, and her half-Jewish son is living evidence of this mongrelization of the American stock. Moreover, Rosamund's multiple husbands and nonconventional career as a musician and scholar demonstrate that she is in conflict with the feminine traditions for which she feels nostalgia.

32. Carol Brightman similarly glosses this passage in her biography of McCarthy: "It is only a matter of time before our *faith* in nature, McCarthy suggests, like our original belief in God, goes, too" (*Writing Dangerously: Mary McCarthy and Her World* [New York: Harcourt Brace, 1992], 530, italics in original).

33. Mary McCarthy, *Ideas and the Novel* (New York: Harcourt Brace Jovanovich, 1980), 116.

34. Ibid., 117.

35. Lionel Trilling, *The Liberal Imagination: Essays on Literature and Society* (1950; reprint, Garden City, N.Y.: Doubleday, 1957), xii. McCarthy's insistence that literature sacrifices the conceptual clarity of ideological discourse in order to "save the particulars at all costs" also brings her close to the New Critics; she echoes John Crowe Ransom's emphasis in *The World's Body* (1938; reprint, Baton Rouge: Louisiana State University Press, 1968) on the "texture" of literary style, which supposedly imitates the phenomenal complexity of the natural world.

36. In Mary McCarthy, *On the Contrary* (New York: Farrar, Straus and Cudahy, 1961), 265.

37. Ibid., 266.

38. McCarthy, *Ideas and the Novel*, 4.

39. Arendt and McCarthy, *Between Friends*, 174.

40. McCarthy, *On the Contrary*, 274.

4. SAUL BELLOW'S CLASS OF EXPLAINING CREATURES: *MR. SAMMLER'S PLANET* AND THE RISE OF NEOCONSERVATISM

1. Saul Bellow, *Mr. Sammler's Planet* (New York: Viking Press, 1970); all page references are to the 1970 edition and are hereafter noted parenthetically in the text.

2. Lionel Trilling, *The Liberal Imagination: Essays on Literature and Society* (1950; reprint, Garden City, N.Y.: Doubleday, 1957), xii.

3. Lionel Trilling, *Beyond Culture: Essays on Literature and Learning* (1965; reprint, London: Secker & Warburg, 1966), xiii, 215.

4. For more detailed accounts of the neoconservative movement by sympathetic historians and political theorists, see John Ehrman, *The Rise of Neoconservatism: Intellectuals and Foreign Affairs, 1945–1994* (New Haven, Conn.: Yale University Press, 1995); Murray Friedman, *The Neoconservative Revolution: Jewish Intellectuals and the Shaping of Public Policy* (New York: Cambridge University Press, 2005); and Mark Gerson, *The Neoconservative Vision: From the Cold War to the Culture Wars* (Lanham, Md.: Madison Books, 1996). For critical accounts, see Gary Dorrien, *The Neoconservative Mind: Politics, Culture, and the War of Ideology* (Philadelphia: Temple University Press, 1993); and Peter Steinfels, *The Neoconservatives* (New York: Simon and Schuster, 1979). Barbara Ehrenreich also has an excellent chapter on the neoconservatives in *Fear of Falling: The Inner Life of the Middle Class* (New York: Pantheon Books, 1989). The neoconservative theory of the new class is scattered throughout the neoconservatives' works. A representative collection of essays on the topic, mostly by neoconservatives, can be found in Barry Bruce-Briggs, ed., *The New Class?* (New Brunswick, N.J.: Transaction Books, 1979).

5. Ehrenreich, *Fear of Falling*, 145.

6. Included in Irving Kristol, *Two Cheers for Capitalism* (New York: Basic Books, 1978), 145.

7. Ibid., 169.

8. Ibid., 145.

9. Bellow's affinities with the neoconservative movement are well known, although no critic of his work has discussed them in depth. Throughout the 1970s and 1980s, he gave interviews that echoed the movement's views on the 1960s counterculture, race relations, foreign policy, and other topics. He also joined one major neoconservative organization—the Committee for the Free World, founded in 1981 to advance "the struggle for freedom" (James Atlas, *Bellow: A Biography* [New York: Random House, 2000], 513). For many contemporary readers, *Mr. Sammler's Planet* was the novel that marked Bellow's affinity with the emerging movement; Richard Poirier referred to it and its predecessor, *Herzog* (New York: Viking Press, 1964), as efforts "to test out, to substantiate, to vitalize, and ultimately to propagate a kind of cultural conservatism" ("*Herzog*, or Bellow in Trouble," in *Saul Bellow: A Collec-*

tion of Critical Essays, ed. Earl Rovit [Englewood Cliffs, N.J.: Prentice-Hall, 1975], 81). Bellow himself, however, never embraced the neoconservative label; as late as 1994, he still proclaimed himself a liberal, although simultaneously distancing himself from liberal opinions and attitudes: "I consider myself some sort of liberal, but I don't like where liberalism has gone in this country in the last twenty years. . . . It's become mindless—medallion-wearing and placard-bearing. I have very little use for it. It's a cover also for a great deal of resentment and hatred, these terrible outbursts from people whose principles are affronted when you disagree with them" (Saul Bellow, *Conversations with Saul Bellow*, ed. Gloria Cronin and Ben Siegel [Jackson: University of Mississippi Press, 1994], 294).

10. Assessments of the novel's racial politics are given in Emily Miller Budick, *Blacks and Jews in Literary Conversation* (Cambridge, U.K.: Cambridge University Press, 1998); Ethan Goffman, "Between Guilt and Affluence: The Jewish Gaze and the Black Thief in *Mr. Sammler's Planet*," *Contemporary Literature* 38, no. 4 (1997): 705–25; L. H. Goldman, *Saul Bellow's Moral Vision: A Critical Study of the Jewish Experience* (New York: Irvington, 1983); and Mariann Russell, "White Man's Black Man: Three Views," *CLA Journal* 17 (1973): 93–100. In 2001, the *Saul Bellow Journal* also devoted a double issue to Bellow's treatment of race throughout his work. Gloria Cronin offers the most thorough account of Bellow's sexual politics in *A Room of His Own: In Search of the Feminine in the Novels of Saul Bellow* (Syracuse, N.Y.: Syracuse University Press, 2001), which includes a chapter on *Mr. Sammler's Planet*.

11. Saul Bellow, "Foreword," in *The Closing of the American Mind: How Higher Education Has Failed Democracy and Impoverished the Souls of Today's Students*, by Harold Bloom (New York: Simon and Schuster, 1987), 18, 17.

12. Andrew Hoberek similarly describes Bellow as both "the first fiction writer of his stature to make his living within the academy *and* a bitter, life-long critic of the university" (*The Twilight of the Middle Class: Post–World War II American Fiction and White Collar Work* [Princeton, N.J.: Princeton University Press, 2005], 18, italics in original). For an overview of Bellow's comments on the university, see Ben Siegel, "Saul Bellow and the University as Villain," in *Saul Bellow in the 1980s: A Collection of Critical Essays*, ed. Gloria Cronin and L. H. Goldman, 137–59 (East Lansing: Michigan State University Press, 1989).

13. Lionel Trilling, *Sincerity and Authenticity: The Charles Eliot Norton Lectures, 1969–1970* (Cambridge, Mass.: Harvard University Press, 1972).

14. Norman Podhoretz described this imagined affinity between welfare-state liberals and the student movement as a political conspiracy: "The New Class was using its own young people as commandos, sending them out into the streets to clash with the enemy's troops (the police and the National Guard) while the 'elders' directed the grand strategy from behind the lines and engaged in less dangerous forms of political warfare against the established power" (*Breaking Ranks: A Political Memoir* [New York: Harper and Row, 1979], 288–89).

15. Commenting on the explicit antifeminism of *Mr. Sammler's Planet*, Cronin defends the novel as a "concerted study of misogyny and misogynists" and a "self-conscious ironic production" (*A Room of His Own*, 124, 134). Cronin correctly notes that Bellow should not be conflated with his elderly protagonist. However, the misogynistic reading of contemporary society that Sammler voices is a recurring feature of Bellow's novels and nonfiction. Moreover, much of the novel's irony, if it is indeed present, is qualified by the fact that Sammler is a Holocaust survivor—that is, a sympathetic victim and witness of history.

16. Kristol, *Two Cheers for Capitalism*, ix.

17. Michael Novak, *The Spirit of Democratic Capitalism* (New York: Simon and Schuster, 1982).

18. Reprinted in Irving Kristol, *Reflections of a Neoconservative: Looking Back, Looking Ahead* (New York: Basic Books, 1983), 317.

19. In addition, throughout the 1980s many Jewish neoconservatives supported evangelical Protestant organizations because these organizations were staunch defenders of Israel. It did not matter that these Christians did so for theological reasons—that is, because they believed that the second coming of Christ was linked to the return of Jews to the Holy Land. Kristol observes, "The fact that the Moral Majority is pro-Israel for theological reasons that flow from Christian belief is hardly a reason for Jews to distance themselves from it. Why would it be a problem for us? It is their theology, but it is our Israel" ("Irving Kristol Writes," *Commentary* 78, no. 4 [October 1984], 17).

20. Kristol, *Reflections of a Neoconservative*, 315.

21. George Weigel, for instance, noted of Kristol that he "has an instrumental view of religion here because he—as he would admit—is tone-deaf to religious sensibilities. This is not music that makes his heart sing. Yet he is smart enough an observer of the human condition to understand that he should not take a Kantian imperative here" (cited in Gerson, *Neoconservative Vision*, 284–85).

22. Alan Berger, *Crisis and Covenant: The Holocaust in American Jewish Fiction* (Albany: State University of New York Press, 1985), 101.

23. Irving Kristol, *Neoconservatism: The Autobiography of an Idea* (New York: Free Press, 1995), 8.

24. This same contradiction marks Bellow's critique of the sexual revolution as exemplary of the "private disorder and public bewilderment" that pervade contemporary culture (*It All Adds Up: From the Dim Past to the Uncertain Future, a Nonfiction Collection* [New York: Viking, 1994], 92). He himself was a notorious philanderer, married five times and involved with multiple mistresses.

25. Saul Bellow, *Ravelstein* (New York: Penguin Books, 2000), 4.

26. Bellow expressed his ambivalence toward Israel in his most extended work of literary journalism, *To Jerusalem and Back: A Personal Account* (New York: Viking Press, 1976). He supported Israel's right to exist, especially against pro-Arab, leftist intellectuals. However, he was also dismayed at anti-Arab sentiment on the part of many Zionists and argued for the negotiated creation of a Palestinian state on the West Bank.

27. Sander Gilman, *Jewish Self-Hatred: Anti-Semitism and the Hidden Language of the Jews* (Baltimore: John Hopkins University Press, 1986), 373.

28. Kristol, *Two Cheers for Capitalism*, 86.

29. Ibid., 95, italics in original.

30. Ibid., 88.

31. Joseph Schumpeter, *Capitalism, Socialism, and Democracy* (1940; reprint, London: Unwin University Books, 1943), 146, 143.

32. Daniel Bell, "The New Class: A Muddled Concept," in Briggs, ed., *The New Class?* 169, italics in original.

33. Daniel Bell, *The Cultural Contradictions of Capitalism* (New York: Basic Books, 1976), 66.

34. Hoberek, *Twilight of the Middle Class*, 19.

35. Bell, "The New Class," 189.

36. Like *Mr. Sammler's Planet*, Bellow's novel *More Die of Heartbreak* (New York: William Morrow, 1987) also revolves around a homosocial relationship between a humanist and scientist. The humanist in this case is Benn's nephew, Kenneth, a Russian literature specialist and the novel's first-person narrator. Through this figure, Bellow explores the obsolescence of humanistic learning in 1980s America. Aesthetes such as Kenneth were "assigned to the humanities, to poetry, philosophy, painting—the nursery games of humankind, which had to be left behind

when the age of science began. The humanities would be called upon to choose a wallpaper for the crypt, as the end drew near" (247).

5. EXPERTS WITHOUT INSTITUTIONS:
NEW LEFT PROFESSIONALISM IN MARGE PIERCY
AND URSULA K. LE GUIN

1. Alvin Gouldner, *The Future of Intellectuals and the Rise of the New Class: A Frame of Reference, Theses, Conjectures, Arguments, and an Historical Perspective on the Role of Intellectuals and Intelligentsia in the International Class Contest of the Modern Era* (New York: Seabury Press, 1979), 70.

2. Tom Hayden, "The Politics of the Movement," in *The New Left: A Documentary History*, ed. Massimo Teodori (Indianapolis, Ind.: Bobbs-Merrill, 1969), 207.

3. Mario Savio, "An End to History," in Teodori, ed., *The New Left*, 159, 161.

4. George R. Vickers, *The Formation of the New Left: The Early Years* (Lexington, Mass.: Lexington Books, 1975), 124, italics in original.

5. Sean McCann and Michael Szalay, "Do You Believe in Magic? Literary Thinking After the New Left," *Yale Journal of Criticism* 18, no. 2 (2005), 454.

6. The community-development projects began in 1964 in the form of the Economic Research and Action Projects that SDS established in various lower-class urban neighborhoods. These initiatives provoked a debate within SDS between, on the one hand, activists such as Hayden who believed that SDS should move into the ghettos and organize the poor and, on the other hand, activists such as Al Haber who argued that the New Left was first and foremost a movement of professionals and intellectuals who should radicalize the middle-class workplace. Haber complained about Hayden's "cult of the ghetto": "Is radicalism subsisting in a slum for a year or two, or is it developing your individual talents so you can function as a radical in your 'professional' field and throughout your adult life?" (cited in James Miller, *Democracy Is in the Streets: From Port Huron to the Siege of Chicago* [Cambridge, Mass.: Harvard University Press, 1994], 190). For an account of these projects' community activism, see Miller, 184–217. For a discussion of the free-clinic movement, see Robert Castel, Françoise Castel, and Anne Lovell, *The Psychiatric Society*, trans. Arthur Goldhammer (New York: Columbia University Press, 1982), 214–55.

7. Marge Piercy, *Woman on the Edge of Time* (New York: Fawcett Books,

1976); and Ursula K. Le Guin, *The Dispossessed: An Ambiguous Utopia* (New York: Harper and Row, 1974); all page references to these two books are to these editions and are hereafter given parenthetically in the text.

8. The other major works of new utopian science fiction from this period, frequently discussed alongside Piercy and Le Guin's work, are Joanna Russ's *The Female Man* (1975; reprint, Boston: Beacon Books, 1986) and Samuel Delany's *Triton* (New York: Bantam Books, 1976).

9. Although much has been published on the politics of *Woman on the Edge of Time* and *The Dispossessed*, very little work has been done on how these texts reflect 1960s and 1970s debates about the new class. With regards to Le Guin, both Victor Urbanowicz, ("Personal and Political in *The Dispossessed*," in *Ursula K. Le Guin*, ed. Harold Bloom, 145–54 [New York: Chelsea House, 1986]) and Laurence Davis ("The Dynamic and Revolutionary Utopia of Ursula K. Le Guin," in *The New Utopian Politics of Ursula K. Le Guin's "The Dispossessed,"* ed. Laurence Davis and Peter Stillman, 3–36 [Lanham, Md.: Lexington Books, 2005]) touch on Le Guin's appropriation of Paul Goodman's theory of professionalism in the context of a broader discussion of her political anarchism. The best discussion of Piercy's class politics can be found in Heather Hicks, "Striking Cyborgs: Reworking the 'Human' in Marge Piercy's *He, She, and It*," in *Reload: Rethinking Women and Cyberculture*, ed. Mary Flanagan and Austin Booth, 85–106 (Cambridge, Mass.: MIT Press, 2002), an essay on Piercy's later cyberpunk novel *He, She, and It* (New York: Fawcett Crest, 1991). Hicks argues that this novel's exploration of the posthuman registers Piercy's anxieties about the proletarianization of the white-collar workforce in the 1980s and 1990s.

10. Frederic Jameson, *Archaeologies of the Future: The Desire Called Utopia and Other Science Fictions* (London: Verso, 2005), 30–31.

11. Edward Bellamy, *Looking Backward* (1887; reprint, New York: Random House, 1951).

12. Echoing James Burnham's *The Managerial Revolution: What Is Happening in the World* (New York: John Day, 1941), Orwell imagines that the ruling group that established Oceania "was made up for the most part of bureaucrats, scientists, technicians, trade-union organizers, publicity experts, sociologists, teachers, journalists, and professional politicians" (*Nineteen Eighty-Four* [1949; reprint, Harmondsworth, U.K.: Penguin Books, 1954], 164).

13. Marge Piercy and Robert Gottlieb, "Movement for a Democratic Society: Beginning to Begin to Begin" (1968), in Teodori, ed., *The New*

Left, 403–10. The most extensive New Left articulation of new working-class social theory was the "Port Authority Statement" (1967), by David Gilbert, Robert Gottlieb, and Gerry Tenney. The title of this unpublished document echoes the better-known "Port Huron Statement." Greg Calvert and Carol Neiman elaborated on this theory a few years later in their retrospective account of the New Left, *A Disrupted History: The New Left and the New Capitalism* (New York: Random House, 1971). See Wini Breines, *Community and Organization in the New Left, 1962–1968: The Great Refusal* (New York: J. F. Bergin, 1982), especially chapter 6, for an account of New Left debates about the new class.

14. Piercy and Gottlieb, "Movement for a Democratic Society," 408.

15. Ibid., 407, 408.

16. Marge Piercy, "The Grand Coolie Damn" (1969), in *Sisterhood Is Powerful: An Anthology of Writings from the Women's Liberation Movement*, ed. Robin Morgan (New York: Random House, 1970), 425–26, 432.

17. Hicks, "Striking Cyborgs," 98.

18. Ken Kesey, *One Flew Over the Cuckoo's Nest* (New York: New American Library, 1962).

19. Maria Farland comments on the centrality of the asylum to feminist theory in the 1970s: "Many of the decade's representations of women's liberation came to be embedded under a surface narrative of women's entrapment within totalizing, all-powerful institutions— 'every woman loves a fascist'—whose tentacles of power were believed to imprison and enslave women. Psychiatric institutions make frequent appearances in women's writings of the period, with psychiatry viewed as a form of 'social control over women' emblematic of larger structures of control" ("Total System, Total Solution, Total Apocalypse: Sex Oppression, Systems of Property, and 1970s Women's Liberation Fiction," *Yale Journal of Criticism* 18, no. 2 [2005], 387). Robert Castel, Françoise Castel, and Anne Lovell more generally describe the prevalence of the asylum as a synecdoche for the welfare state within New Left social thought: "Mental institutions served as a kind of countermodel, exhibiting rigid hierarchy, authoritarian control, formalistic relationships between patients and staff, and an ideology of professionalism" (*Psychiatric Society*, 215).

20. The population of state mental hospitals in the United States declined from an all-time peak of 558,000 in 1955 to 193,000 in 1975 (Castel, Castel, and Lovell, *Psychiatric Society*, 79); the average period of hospitalization over the same period shrunk from twenty years to seven

months (Steven Gillon, *That's Not What We Meant to Do: Reform and Its Unintended Consequences in Twentieth-Century America* [New York: Norton, 2000], 97). New York was no exception to this trend; its patient population dropped from 93,000 in 1956 to 39,000 in 1974 (Castel, Castel, and Lovell, *Psychiatric Society*, 93).

21. Maria Farland, "Sylvia Plath's Anti-psychiatry," *Minnesota Review* 55–57 (2000–2001), 246.

22. See also Peter Sedgwick, *Psychopolitics* (London: Pluto Press, 1982), for a critique of conservative undercurrents in the antipsychiatry movement.

23. The Community Action Programs got under way in the early 1960s with various experimental pilot projects funded by the Ford Foundation and the President's Committee on Juvenile Delinquency. They later became a central component of the Economic Opportunity Act of 1964, which declared that all Community Action Programs, in order to be eligible for federal funding, had to incorporate the "maximum feasible participation" of the poor. For more on these programs, see Michael Katz, *The Undeserving Poor: From the War on Poverty to the War on Welfare* (New York: Pantheon Books, 1989); and Alice O'Connor, *Social Science, Social Policy, and the Poor in Twentieth-Century U.S. History* (Princeton, N.J.: Princeton University Press, 2001).

24. Piercy was particularly hostile toward the New Criticism, which she encountered as an undergraduate in the 1950s. She details this early education in her autobiographical novel *Braided Lives* (New York: Summit Books, 1982).

25. Marge Piercy, *Parti-colored Blocks for a Quilt* (Ann Arbor: University of Michigan Press, 1982), 105.

26. Piercy later contributed to the cyberpunk genre with her 1991 novel *He, She, and It*.

27. This concern with corporate control over professional work pervades Piercy's fiction. For instance, it is at the center of the novels that precede and follow *Woman on the Edge of Time*: *Small Changes* (New York: Fawcett Crest, 1973) and *The High Cost of Living* (New York: Harper and Row, 1978). Both of these realist fictions feature heroines who are torn between their early experiences in the 1960s New Left and counterculture and their desire to assimilate into the professional class in the 1970s. In *Small Changes*, Miriam Berg, a computer programmer, finds herself designing software for a military, antimissile defense project. In *The High Cost of Living*, Leslie, a Ph.D. candidate in history, is involved

in her advisor's research project on capital investment, whose purpose is to demonstrate that "the development of industry [in the United States] was always intelligent and efficient" (198). In both cases, the novels suggest that women's professional aspirations can be better fulfilled if they volunteer their time and experience to feminist collectives.

28. Shulamith Firestone, *The Dialectic of Sex: The Case for Feminist Revolution* (New York: Morrow, 1970).

29. Ursula K. Le Guin, *Dancing at the Edge of the World: Thoughts on Words, Women, Places* (New York: Grove Press, 1989), 85.

30. Ibid., 90.

31. Ursula K. Le Guin, *Always Coming Home* (New York: Harper and Row, 1985).

32. Ursula K. Le Guin, *The Wind's Twelve Quarters* (Toronto: Bantam Books, 1976), 260.

33. See Davis's "Dynamic and Revolutionary Utopia" for more on Le Guin's departure from the utopian tradition on this point.

34. Winter Eliott, "Breaching Invisible Walls: Individual Anarchy in *The Dispossessed,*" in Davis and Stillman, eds., *New Utopian Politics*, 153.

35. Paul Goodman, *Growing Up Absurd: Problems of Youth in the Organized System* (New York: Random House, 1960).

36. See, for instance, Le Guin's introductory comments to "The Day Before the Revolution" in *The Wind's Twelve Quarters*, 260.

37. Paul Goodman, *Drawing the Line: The Political Essays of Paul Goodman*, ed. Taylor Stoehr (New York: Free Life Editions, 1977), 3.

38. Cited in Urbanowicz, "Personal and Political," 149.

39. Paul Goodman, *New Reformation: Notes of a Neolithic Conservative* (New York: Random House, 1970), 21.

40. Ibid., 17.

6. DON DeLILLO'S ACADEMIA: REVISITING THE NEW CLASS IN *WHITE NOISE*

1. Don DeLillo, *White Noise* (New York: Penguin, 1985); all page references are to this edition and are hereafter noted parenthetically in the text.

2. Alvin Gouldner, *The Future of Intellectuals and the Rise of the New Class: A Frame of Reference, Theses, Conjectures, Arguments, and an Historical Perspective on the Role of Intellectuals and Intelligentsia in the International Class Contest of the Modern Era* (New York: Seabury Press, 1979), 83.

3. The novel also briefly assimilates other novelistic genres: the disaster novel (in the middle section entitled "The Airborne Toxic Event") and the noir crime novel (in the novel's penultimate chapter). See Douglas Keesey, *Don DeLillo* (New York: Twayne, 1993), and Tom LeClair, *In the Loop: Don DeLillo and the Systems Novel* (Urbana: University of Illinois Press, 1987), for accounts of DeLillo's experiments with genre in this and other novels.

4. Don DeLillo, *Underworld* (New York: Simon and Schuster, 1997).

5. Thomas Ferarro, "Whole Families Shopping at Night!" in *New Essays on White Noise*, ed. Frank Lentricchia (Cambridge, U.K.: Cambridge University Press, 1991), 20.

6. The Popular Culture Association branched off from the American Studies Association in 1969. Ray Browne founded the Department of Popular Culture at Bowling Green State University in 1973. For more on the early history of popular-culture studies, see Ray B. Browne, *Mission Underway: The History of the Popular Culture Association / American Culture Association and the Popular Culture Movement, 1967–2001* (Bowling Green, Ohio: Popular Culture Association/American Culture Association, 2002).

7. John G. Cawelti, "The Concept of Formula in the Study of Popular Literature," *Journal of Popular Culture* 3, no. 3 (Winter 1969), 390.

8. In his 1970 introduction to the popular-culture discipline, Russel Nye concluded with a salvo against Dwight MacDonald's critique of mass culture: "To a generation that found in The Beatles, Bogart movies, Marvel Group Comics, and Peanuts a new parameter of experience, the warnings of the older critics that popular culture was false and dangerous meant little" (*The Unembarrassed Muse: The Popular Arts in America* [New York: Dial Press, 1970], 419). For an account of how popular-culture studies was part of a broader, antielitist effort to redefine the concept of culture in the 1960s, see Mary Land, "Whatever Happened to 'the Ooze at the Bottom of the Mass Mind'?" *Journal of Popular Culture* 9, no. 2 (Fall 1975): 423–32. Land argues that this effort also encompassed new developments in anthropology, history, and media theory.

9. Gregory Hall, "The Psychology of Fast Food Happiness," in *The Popular Culture Reader*, ed. Jack Nachbar, Deborah Weiser, and John L. Wright (Bowling Green, Ohio: Bowling Green University Popular Press, 1978), 133.

10. Roland Barthes, *Mythologies*, trans. Annette Lavers (New York: Hill and Wang, 1972).

11. Stacey Olster, "*White Noise*," in *The Cambridge Companion to Don DeLillo*, ed. John N. Duvall (Cambridge, U.K.: Cambridge University Press, 2008), 84.

12. Matthew Arnold, *Culture and Anarchy*, ed. Samuel Lipman (New Haven, Conn.: Yale University Press, 1994), 5.

13. Ibid.

14. Mary McCarthy, *The Groves of Academe* (1952; reprint, New York: Harcourt Brace, 1992); Randall Jarrell, *Pictures from an Institution, a Comedy* (New York: Knopf, 1954); Vladimir Nabokov, *Pnin* (1957; reprint, New York: Vintage, 1989); and Bernard Malamud, *A New Life* (1961; reprint, New York: Avon, 1980).

15. See Mark McGurl, *The Program Era: Postwar Fiction and the Rise of Creative Writing* (Cambridge, Mass.: Harvard University Press, 2009), for an ambitious account of how creative-writing programs shaped American literature from the 1930s to the present.

16. M. Keith Booker, *The Post-utopian Imagination: American Culture in the Long 1950s* (Westport, Conn.: Greenwood Press, 2002), 94.

17. McCarthy, *Groves of Academe*, 69.

18. Browne recounts how, when he started to offer popular-culture courses at Bowling Green State University, "the frame of mind of the late 60s was still in the air, and many students wanted to continue their training in fields and methodologies that they thought 'relevant' and 'useful'" (*Mission Underway*, 18).

19. Sean McCann and Michael Szalay discuss the connection among New Left libertarianism, entrepreneurial professionalism, and the emergence of theory and cultural studies: "It was 'theory,'" they argue, "that presided over the intellectual marriage of professionalism and a newly fortified version of the ethos of the counterculture. And it was 'theory' as well that lent intellectual credibility to libertarian attitudes that would dominate the literary academy in the last decades of the twentieth century" ("Do You Believe in Magic? Literary Thinking After the New Left," *Yale Journal of Criticism* 18, no. 2 [2005], 455–56).

20. Lionel Trilling, "Our Country and Our Culture," *Partisan Review* 19, no. 3 (May 1952), 321–22.

21. C. Wright Mills, *Power, Politics, and People: The Collected Essays of C. Wright Mills*, ed. Irving Louis Horowitz (New York: Oxford University Press, 1963), 353–73.

22. John McClure, *Partial Faiths: Postsecular Fiction in the Age of Pynchon and Morrison* (Athens: University of Georgia Press, 2007), 63.

23. Don DeLillo, *Conversations with Don DeLillo*, ed. Thomas DePietro (Jackson: University Press of Mississippi, 2005), 70.
24. All page references are to the 1997 Simon and Schuster edition of *Underworld* cited in note 4 and are hereafter noted parenthetically in the text.
25. McClure, *Partial Faiths*, 77.
26. Christopher Lasch, *The Culture of Narcissism: American Life in an Age of Diminishing Expectations* (New York: W. W. Norton, 1978), 220.
27. See Christopher Lasch, *The New Radicalism in America, 1889–1963: The Intellectual as a Social Type* (New York: Vintage, 1967).
28. Lasch, *Culture of Narcissism*, 222.
29. Ibid., 235.
30. DeLillo's resistance to the idea of a new-class "saving remnant" dedicated to cultural education is the point of his novels about creative artists, especially *Great Jones Street* (1973; reprint, New York: Vintage, 1989) and *Mao II* (New York: Penguin, 1991). At first glance, *Mao II* seems like a dirge for the romantic idea that writers are the unacknowledged legislators of the world. DeLillo's protagonist, the reclusive novelist Bill Gray, articulates the novel's central thesis: "There's a curious knot that binds novelists and terrorists. In the West we become famous effigies as our books lose the power to shape and influence.... Years ago I used to think it was possible for a novelist to alter the inner life of the culture. Now bomb-makers and gunmen have taken over that territory" (41). Gray later explains that Samuel Beckett was the last writer "to shape the way we think and see. After him, the major work involves midair explosions and crumbled buildings" (157). However, as Mark Osteen argues, DeLillo systematically undercuts Bill Gray's thesis: "Were novelists ever so powerful? Was the notoriously reticent and difficult Beckett really a major influence on mass consciousness?" ("DeLillo's Dedalian Artists," in *The Cambridge Companion to Don DeLillo*, ed. John N. Duvall [Cambridge, U.K.: Cambridge University Press, 2008], 143). Instead, DeLillo's artist novels describe their protagonists' destruction at the hands of U.S. celebrity culture and subsequent regeneration through contact with the everyday. This trajectory is most obvious in the case of *Great Jones Street*, which tells the story of rock star Bucky Wunderlick's physical, social, and linguistic isolation after he leaves his band midtour. The novel ends as Wunderlick immerses himself in New York's European immigrant neighborhoods, preparing to reemerge with a rediscovered poetic voice drawn from this street culture.

AFTERWORD

1. Bill Readings, *The University in Ruins* (Cambridge, Mass.: Harvard University Press, 1996); all page references are to this edition and hereafter are noted parenthetically in the text.

2. Other studies that explore this problem include John Guillory, *Cultural Capital: The Problem of Literary Canon Formation* (Chicago: University of Chicago Press, 1993), and Alvin Kernan, *The Death of Literature* (New Haven, Conn.: Yale University Press, 1990).

3. Jacques Derrida, "The Principle of Reason: The University in the Eyes of Its Pupils," trans. Catherine Porter and Edward P. Morris, *Diacritics* 13, no. 3 (Fall 1983), 16.

4. Ibid., 16, 11, 16.

5. Ibid., 16.

6. Mark Taylor, *The Moment of Complexity: Emerging Network Culture* (Chicago: University of Chicago Press, 2001), 256.

7. Ibid., 202.

8. Ibid., 65.

9. Taylor's career trajectory exemplifies the fact that these alternatives can be complementary; before he became interested in complexity theory and for-profit education, he was a prominent deconstructive critic interested in the intersections between Derrida's work and Christian theology.

10. Alan Liu, *The Laws of Cool: Knowledge Work and the Culture of Information* (Chicago: University of Chicago Press, 2004), 2–3.

11. Ibid., 8.

12. Ibid., 7; see William Gibson's *Neuromancer* (New York: Ace, 1984).

13. See Sean McCann, *Gumshoe America: Hard-Boiled Crime Fiction and the Rise and Fall of New Deal Liberalism* (Durham, N.C.: Duke University Press, 2000); Sean McCann, *A Pinnacle of Feeling: American Literature and Presidential Government* (Princeton, N.J.: Princeton University Press, 2008); Michael Szalay, *New Deal Modernism: American Literature and the Invention of the Welfare State* (Durham, N.C.: Duke University Press, 2000); and Bruce Robbins, *Upward Mobility and the Common Good: Toward a Literary History of the Welfare State* (Princeton, N.J.: Princeton University Press, 2007).

14. John Guillory, *Cultural Capital: The Problem of Literary Canon Formation* (Chicago: University of Chicago Press, 1993). See, in particular, Christopher Newfield, *Ivy and Industry: Business and the Making of the American University, 1880–1980* (Durham, N.C.: Duke University Press, 2003),

and Mark McGurl, *The Program Era: Postwar Fiction and the Rise of Creative Writing* (Cambridge, Mass.: Harvard University Press, 2009).

15. C. Wright Mills, *Power, Politics, and People: The Collected Essays of C. Wright Mills*, ed. Irving Louis Horowitz (New York: Oxford University Press, 1963), 300.

16. Marc Bousquet, *How the University Works: Higher Education and the Low-Wage Nation* (New York: New York University Press, 2008).

17. Kenneth Burke, *The Philosophy of Literary Form: Studies in Symbolic Action* (1941; reprint, New York: Vintage Books, 1957), 253.

18. Ibid., 262.

BIBLIOGRAPHY

Abrams, Sabrina Fuchs. *Mary McCarthy: Gender, Politics, and the Postwar Intellectual*. New York: Peter Lang, 2004.

Aptheker, Herbert. *The Negro Problem in America: A Critique of Gunnar Myrdal's "An American Dilemma."* New York: International, 1946.

Arendt, Hannah and Mary McCarthy. *Between Friends: The Correspondence of Hannah Arendt and Mary McCarthy, 1949–1975*. Ed. Carol Brightman. New York: Harcourt Brace, 1995.

Arnold, Matthew. *Culture and Anarchy*. Ed. Samuel Lipman. New Haven, Conn.: Yale University Press, 1994.

Atlas, James. *Bellow: A Biography*. New York: Random House, 2000.

Baker, Houston A., Jr. *Blues, Ideology, and Afro-American Literature: A Vernacular Theory*. Chicago: University of Chicago Press, 1984.

Baritz, Loren. *Servants of Power: A History of the Use of Social Science in American Industry*. Middletown, Conn.: Wesleyan University Press, 1960.

Barthes, Roland. *Mythologies*. Trans. Annette Lavers. New York: Hill and Wang, 1972.

Bell, Daniel. *The Coming of Post-industrial Society: A Venture in Social Forecasting*. New York: Basic Books, 1973.

——. *The Cultural Contradictions of Capitalism*. New York: Basic Books, 1976.

——. "The New Class: A Muddled Concept." In *The New Class?* ed. Barry Bruce Briggs, 169–90. New Brunswick, N.J.: Transaction Books, 1979.

Bellamy, Edward. *Looking Backward*. 1887. Reprint. New York: Random House, 1951.

Bellow, Janis. "Saul Bellow." In *An Unsentimental Education: Writers and Chicago*, ed. Molly McQuade, 1–12. Chicago: University of Chicago Press, 1995.

Bellow, Saul. *The Adventures of Augie March*. New York: Penguin, 1953.

——. *Conversations with Saul Bellow*. Ed. Gloria Cronin and Ben Siegel. Jackson: University of Mississippi Press, 1994.

——. "Foreword." In *The Closing of the American Mind: How Higher Education Has Failed Democracy and Impoverished the Souls of Today's Students*, by Harold Bloom, 11–18. New York: Simon and Schuster, 1987.

——. *Herzog.* New York: Viking Press, 1964.

——. *It All Adds Up: From the Dim Past to the Uncertain Future, a Nonfiction Collection.* New York: Viking, 1994.

——. *More Die of Heartbreak.* New York: William Morrow, 1987.

——. *Mr. Sammler's Planet.* New York: Viking Press, 1970.

——. *Ravelstein.* New York: Penguin Books, 2000.

——. *To Jerusalem and Back: A Personal Account.* New York: Viking Press, 1976.

Berger, Alan. *Crisis and Covenant: The Holocaust in American Jewish Fiction.* Albany: State University of New York Press, 1985.

Biderman, Albert and Elizabeth Crawford. *The Political Economics of Social Research: The Case of Sociology.* Washington, D.C.: Bureau of Social Science Research, 1968.

Bloom, Allan. *The Closing of the American Mind: How Higher Education Has Failed Democracy and Impoverished the Souls of Today's Students.* New York: Simon and Schuster, 1987.

Booker, M. Keith. *The Post-utopian Imagination: American Culture in the Long 1950s.* Westport, Conn.: Greenwood Press, 2002.

Bourdieu, Pierre. *Homo Academicus.* Trans. Peter Collier. Stanford, Calif.: Stanford University Press, 1988.

Bousquet, Marc. *How the University Works: Higher Education and the Low-Wage Nation.* New York: New York University Press, 2008.

Bové, Paul A. *Mastering Discourse: The Politics of Intellectual Culture.* Durham, N.C.: Duke University Press, 1992.

Breines, Wini. *Community and Organization in the New Left, 1962–1968: The Great Refusal.* New York: J. F. Bergin, 1982.

Brick, Howard. "The Reformist Dimension of Talcott Parsons's Early Social Theory." In *The Culture of the Market: Historical Essays*, ed. Thomas Haskell and Richard Teichgraeber III, 357–96. Cambridge, U.K.: Cambridge University Press, 1993.

——. *Transcending Capitalism: Visions of a New Society in Modern American Thought.* Ithaca, N.Y.: Cornell University Press, 2006.

Brightman, Carol. *Writing Dangerously: Mary McCarthy and Her World.* New York: Harcourt Brace, 1992.

Brinkley, Alan. *The End of Reform: New Deal Liberalism in Recession and War.* New York: Alfred A. Knopf, 1995.

Brint, Steven. *In an Age of Experts: The Changing Role of Professionals in Politics and Public Life*. Princeton, N.J.: Princeton University Press, 1994.

Brooks, Cleanth. *The Well-Wrought Urn: Studies in the Structure of Poetry*. New York: Harcourt, 1947.

Browne, Ray B. *Mission Underway: The History of the Popular Culture Association / American Culture Association and the Popular Culture Movement, 1967–2001*. Bowling Green, Ohio: Popular Culture Association/American Culture Association, 2002.

Bruce-Briggs, Barry, ed. *The New Class?* New Brunswick, N.J.: Transaction Books, 1979.

Brunner, Edward. *Cold War Poetry*. Urbana: University of Illinois Press, 2001.

Budick, Emily Miller. *Blacks and Jews in Literary Conversation*. Cambridge, U.K.: Cambridge University Press, 1998.

Burke, Kenneth. *The Philosophy of Literary Form: Studies in Symbolic Action*. 1941. Reprint. New York: Vintage Books, 1957.

Burnham, James. *The Managerial Revolution: What Is Happening in the World*. New York: John Day, 1941.

Calvert, Greg and Carol Neiman. *A Disrupted History: The New Left and the New Capitalism*. New York: Random House, 1971.

Cappetti, Carla. *Writing Chicago: Modernism, Ethnography, and the Novel*. New York: Columbia University Press, 1993.

Castel, Robert, Françoise Castel, and Anne Lovell. *The Psychiatric Society*. Trans. Arthur Goldhammer. New York: Columbia University Press, 1982.

Cawelti, John G. "The Concept of Formula in the Study of Popular Literature." *Journal of Popular Culture* 3, no. 3 (Winter 1969): 381–90.

Cohen-Cole, Jamie. "The Creative American: Cold War Salons, Social Science, and the Cure for Modern Society." *Isis* 100 (2009): 219–62.

Coleridge, Samuel Taylor. *On the Constitution of Church and State According to the Idea of Each*. Ed. John Barrell. London: Dent, 1972.

Cooney, Terry. *The Rise of the New York Intellectuals: Partisan Review and Its Circle*. Madison: University of Wisconsin Press, 1986.

Croly, Herbert. *The Promise of American Life*. 1909. Reprint. Hamden, Conn.: Archon Books, 1963.

Cronin, Gloria. *A Room of His Own: In Search of the Feminine in the Novels of Saul Bellow*. Syracuse, N.Y.: Syracuse University Press, 2001.

Dahrendorf, Ralf. *Class and Class Conflict in Industrial Society*. Stanford, Calif.: Stanford University Press, 1959.

Davis, Laurence. "The Dynamic and Revolutionary Utopia of Ursula K. Le Guin." In *The New Utopian Politics of Ursula K. Le Guin's "The Dispossessed,"* ed. Laurence Davis and Peter Stillman, 3–36. Lanham, Md.: Lexington Books, 2005.

Delany, Samuel. *Triton.* New York: Bantam Books, 1976.

DeLillo, Don. *Conversations with Don DeLillo.* Ed. Thomas DePietro. Jackson: University Press of Mississippi, 2005.

——. *Great Jones Street.* 1973. Reprint. New York: Vintage, 1989.

——. *Mao II.* New York: Penguin, 1991.

——. *Underworld.* New York: Simon and Schuster, 1997.

——. *White Noise.* New York: Penguin, 1985.

Derrida, Jacques. "The Principle of Reason: The University in the Eyes of Its Pupils." Trans. Catherine Porter and Edward P. Morris. *Diacritics* 13, no. 3 (Fall 1983): 2–20.

Djilas, Milovan. *The New Class: An Analysis of the Communist System.* New York: Praeger, 1957.

Dorrien, Gary. *The Neoconservative Mind: Politics, Culture, and the War of Ideology.* Philadelphia: Temple University Press, 1993.

Douglas, Ann. "The Failure of the New York Intellectuals." *Raritan* 17, no. 4 (Spring 1998): 1–23.

——. *Terrible Honesty: Mongrel Manhattan in the 1920s.* New York: Farrar, Straus and Giroux, 1995.

Drake, St. Clair and Horace Cayton. *Black Metropolis: A Study of Negro Life in a Northern City.* New York: Harcourt Brace, 1945.

Durkheim, Émile. *The Division of Labor in Society.* Trans. George Simpson. Glencoe, Ill.: Free Press, 1933.

Eagleton, Terry. *Literary Theory: An Introduction.* Oxford, U.K.: Blackwell, 1983.

Ehrenreich, Barbara. *Fear of Falling: The Inner Life of the Middle Class.* New York: Pantheon Books, 1989.

Ehrenreich, Barbara and John Ehrenreich. "The Professional-Managerial Class." In *Between Labour and Capital,* ed. Pat Walker, 5–45. Hassocks, U.K.: Harvester Press, 1979.

Ehrman, John. *The Rise of Neoconservatism: Intellectuals and Foreign Affairs, 1945–1994.* New Haven, Conn.: Yale University Press, 1995.

Eliott, Winter. "Breaching Invisible Walls: Individual Anarchy in *The Dispossessed.*" In *The New Utopian Politics of Ursula K. Le Guin's "The Dispossessed,"* ed. Laurence Davis and Peter Stillman, 149–64. Lanham, Md.: Lexington Books, 2005.

Elkins, Stanley. *Slavery: A Problem in American Institutional and Intellectual Life.* 1959. Reprint. Chicago: University of Chicago Press, 1964.

Ellison, Ralph. *The Collected Essays of Ralph Ellison.* Ed. John F. Callahan. New York: Modern Library, 2003.

———. *Flying Home and Other Stories.* Ed. John F. Callahan. New York: Vintage Books, 1998.

———. *Invisible Man.* 1952. Reprint. New York: Vintage Books, 1995.

Fabre, Michel. "From *Native Son* to *Invisible Man*: Some Notes on Ralph Ellison's Evolution in the 1950s." In *Speaking for You: The Vision of Ralph Ellison,* ed. Kimberly Benston, 199–216. Washington, D.C.: Howard University Press, 1987.

Farland, Maria. "Sylvia Plath's Anti-psychiatry." *Minnesota Review* 55–57 (2000–2001): 245–56.

———. "Total System, Total Solution, Total Apocalypse: Sex Oppression, Systems of Property, and 1970s Women's Liberation Fiction." *Yale Journal of Criticism* 18, no. 2 (2005): 381–407.

Farrell, James. *Studs Lonigan: Young Lonigan, The Young Manhood of Studs Lonigan, Judgment Day.* New York: Avon Books, 1977.

Fekete, John. *The Critical Twilight: Explorations in the Ideology of Anglo-American Literary Theory from Eliot to McLuhan.* London: Routledge, 1977.

Ferarro, Thomas. "Whole Families Shopping at Night!" In *New Essays on White Noise,* ed. Frank Lentricchia, 15–38. Cambridge, U.K.: Cambridge University Press, 1991.

Ferguson, Roderick. *Aberrations in Black: Toward a Queer of Color Critique.* Minneapolis: University of Minnesota Press, 2004.

Firestone, Shulamith. *The Dialectic of Sex: The Case for Feminist Revolution.* New York: Morrow, 1970.

Foley, Barbara. "Ralph Ellison as Proletarian Journalist." *Science and Society* 62, no. 4 (Winter 1998–1999): 537–56.

Frazier, E. Franklin. *Black Bourgeoisie.* Glencoe, Ill.: Free Press, 1957.

Freedman, Jonathan. *Professions of Taste: Henry James, British Aestheticism, and Commodity Culture.* Stanford, Calif.: Stanford University Press, 1990.

Freud, Sigmund. *On Metapsychology, The Theory of Psychoanalysis: Beyond the Pleasure Principle, The Ego and the Id, and Other Works.* Ed. Angela Richards. New York: Penguin Books, 1991.

Friedman, Murray. *The Neoconservative Revolution: Jewish Intellectuals and the Shaping of Public Policy.* New York: Cambridge University Press, 2005.

Frow, John. *Cultural Studies and Cultural Capital.* Oxford, U.K.: Oxford University Press, 1995.

Galbraith, John Kenneth. *The New Industrial State*. 2d. rev. ed. Boston: Houghton Mifflin, 1971.

Gallagher, Catherine. "Marxism and the New Historicism." In *The New Historicism*, ed. H. Aram Veeser, 37–48. New York: Routledge, 1989.

Gerson, Mark. *The Neoconservative Vision: From the Cold War to the Culture Wars*. Lanham, Md.: Madison Books, 1996.

Gibson, William. *Neuromancer*. New York: Ace, 1984.

Gillon, Steven. *That's Not What We Meant to Do: Reform and Its Unintended Consequences in Twentieth-Century America*. New York: Norton, 2000.

Gilman, Nils. *Mandarins of the Future: Modernization Theory in Cold War America*. Baltimore: Johns Hopkins University Press, 2003.

Gilman, Sander. *Jewish Self-Hatred: Anti-Semitism and the Hidden Language of the Jews*. Baltimore: John Hopkins University Press, 1986.

Goffman, Ethan. "Between Guilt and Affluence: The Jewish Gaze and the Black Thief in *Mr. Sammler's Planet*." *Contemporary Literature* 38, no. 4 (1997): 705–25.

Goldman, L. H. *Saul Bellow's Moral Vision: A Critical Study of the Jewish Experience*. New York: Irvington, 1983.

Goodman, Paul. *Drawing the Line: The Political Essays of Paul Goodman*. Ed. Taylor Stoehr. New York: Free Life Editions, 1977.

——. *Growing Up Absurd: Problems of Youth in the Organized System*. New York: Random House, 1960.

——. *New Reformation: Notes of a Neolithic Conservative*. New York: Random House, 1970.

Gouldner, Alvin. *The Coming Crisis of Western Sociology*. New York: Basic, 1970.

——. *The Future of Intellectuals and the Rise of the New Class: A Frame of Reference, Theses, Conjectures, Arguments, and an Historical Perspective on the Role of Intellectuals and Intelligentsia in the International Class Contest of the Modern Era*. New York: Seabury Press, 1979.

Graff, Gerald. *Professing Literature: An Institutional History*. Chicago: University of Chicago Press, 1987.

Guillory, John. *Cultural Capital: The Problem of Literary Canon Formation*. Chicago: University of Chicago Press, 1993.

——. "The Sokal Hoax and the History of Criticism." *Critical Inquiry* 28, no. 2 (2002): 470–509.

Halberstam, David. *The Best and the Brightest*. New York: Random House, 1972.

Hall, Gregory. "The Psychology of Fast Food Happiness." In *The Popular Culture Reader*, ed. Jack Nachbar, Deborah Weiser, and John L. Wright,

126–33. Bowling Green, Ohio: Bowling Green University Popular Press, 1978.

Halliday, Terence and Morris Janowitz, eds. *Sociology and Its Publics: The Forms and Fates of Disciplinary Organization*. Chicago: University of Chicago Press, 1992.

Hawthorn, Geoffrey. *Enlightenment and Despair: A History of Sociology*. New York: Cambridge University Press, 1976.

Hayden, Tom. "The Politics of the Movement." In *The New Left: A Documentary History*, ed. Massimo Teodori, 202–9. Indianapolis, Ind.: Bobbs-Merrill, 1969.

Hicks, Heather. "Striking Cyborgs: Reworking the 'Human' in Marge Piercy's *He, She, and It*." In *Reload: Rethinking Women and Cyberculture*, ed. Mary Flanagan and Austin Booth, 85–106. Cambridge, Mass.: MIT Press, 2002.

Hirsch, Jerrold. *Portrait of America: A Cultural History of the Federal Writers' Project*. Chapel Hill: University of North Carolina Press, 2003.

Hoberek, Andrew. *The Twilight of the Middle Class: Post–World War II American Fiction and White Collar Work*. Princeton, N.J.: Princeton University Press, 2005.

Hofstadter, Richard. *The Age of Reform: From Bryan to F. D. R.* New York: Knopf, 1955.

Horowitz, Irving Louis. *C. Wright Mills: An American Utopian*. New York: Free Press, 1983.

Howe, Irving. *A World More Attractive: A View of Modern Literature and Politics*. New York: Horizon Press, 1963.

Huaco, George. "Ideology and General Theory: The Case of Sociological Functionalism." *Comparative Studies in Society and History* 28 (1996): 34–54.

Inter-University Consortium for Political and Social Research. "Census Data for the Year 1940." Available at http://fisher.lib.virginia.edu/cgi-local/censusbin/census/cen.pl?year=940.

Jackson, Lawrence. "Ralph Ellison, Sharpies, Rinehart, and Politics in *Invisible Man*." *Massachusetts Review* 49 (Spring 1999): 71–95.

Jackson, Walter. *Gunnar Myrdal and America's Conscience: Social Engineering and Racial Liberalism, 1938–1987*. Chapel Hill: University of North Carolina Press, 1990.

Jameson, Fredric. *Archaeologies of the Future: The Desire Called Utopia and Other Science Fictions*. London: Verso, 2005.

Jancovich, Mark. *The Cultural Politics of the New Criticism*. Cambridge, U.K.: Cambridge University Press, 1993.

Jarrell, Randall. *Pictures from an Institution, a Comedy*. New York: Knopf, 1954.

Jurca, Catherine. *White Diaspora: The Suburb and the Twentieth-Century American Novel*. Princeton, N.J.: Princeton University Press, 2001.

Kampf, Louis and Paul Lauter. "Introduction." In *The Politics of Literature: Dissenting Essays on the Teaching of English*, ed. Louis Kampf and Paul Lauter, 3–54. New York: Pantheon, 1972.

Kant, Immanuel. *Critique of Judgment*. Trans. Werner S. Pluhar. Indianapolis, Ind.: Hackett, 1987.

——. *Critique of Pure Reason*. Trans. Norman Kemp Smith. New York: St. Martin's Press, 1965.

Katz, Michael. *The Undeserving Poor: From the War on Poverty to the War on Welfare*. New York: Pantheon Books, 1989.

Keesey, Douglas. *Don DeLillo*. New York: Twayne, 1993.

Kernan, Alvin. *The Death of Literature*. New Haven, Conn.: Yale University Press, 1990.

Kesey, Ken. *One Flew over the Cuckoo's Nest*. New York: New American Library, 1962.

Kristol, Irving. "Irving Kristol Writes." *Commentary* 78, no. 4 (October 1984): 15–17.

——. *Neoconservativism: The Autobiography of an Idea*. New York: Free Press, 1995.

——. *Reflections of a Neoconservative: Looking Back, Looking Ahead*. New York: Basic Books, 1983.

——. *Two Cheers for Capitalism*. New York: Basic Books, 1978.

Kuklick, Henrika. "A 'Scientific Revolution': Sociological Theory in the United States, 1930–1945." *Sociological Inquiry* 43, no. 1 (1973): 3–22.

Land, Mary. "Whatever Happened to 'the Ooze at the Bottom of the Mass Mind'?" *Journal of Popular Culture* 9, no. 2 (Fall 1975): 423–32.

Larsen, Nella. *Quicksand and Passing*. Ed. Deborah E. McDowell. New Brunswick, N.J.: Rutgers University Press, 1986.

Lasch, Christopher. *The Culture of Narcissism: American Life in an Age of Diminishing Expectations*. New York: W. W. Norton, 1978.

——. *The New Radicalism in America, 1889–1963: The Intellectual as a Social Type*. New York: Vintage, 1967.

Laskin, David. *Partisans: Marriage, Politics, and Betrayal Among the New York Intellectuals*. New York: Simon and Schuster, 2000.

Latham, Michael. *Modernization as Ideology: American Social Science and "Nation Building" in the Kennedy Era*. Chapel Hill: University of North Carolina Press, 2000.

Layton, Edwin. *The Revolt of the Engineers: Social Responsibility and the American Engineering Profession.* Baltimore: John Hopkins University Press, 1986.

LeClair, Tom. *In the Loop: Don DeLillo and the Systems Novel.* Urbana: University of Illinois Press, 1987.

Le Guin, Ursula K. *Always Coming Home.* New York: Harper and Row, 1985.

———. *Dancing at the Edge of the World: Thoughts on Words, Women, Places.* New York: Grove Press, 1989.

———. *The Dispossessed: An Ambiguous Utopia.* New York: Harper and Row, 1974.

———. *The Wind's Twelve Quarters.* Toronto: Bantam Books, 1976.

Lepenies, Wolf. *Between Literature and Science: The Rise of Sociology.* Trans. R. J. Hollingdale. Cambridge, U.K.: Cambridge University Press, 1988.

Levine, Donald. *Visions of the Sociological Tradition.* Chicago: University of Chicago Press, 1995.

Lipset, Seymour Martin and Everett Carll Ladd Jr. "The Politics of American Sociologists." *American Journal of Sociology* 78 (1972): 67–104.

Liu, Alan. *The Laws of Cool: Knowledge Work and the Culture of Information.* Chicago: University of Chicago Press, 2004.

Lynd, Robert. *Knowledge for What? The Place of Social Science in American Culture.* Princeton, N.J.: Princeton University Press, 1939.

Mailer, Norman. *The Armies of the Night: History as a Novel, the Novel as History.* 1968. Reprint. New York: Penguin, 1994.

Malamud, Bernard. *A New Life.* 1961. Reprint. New York: Avon, 1980.

Mattson, Kevin. *Intellectuals in Action: The Origins of the New Left and Radical Liberalism, 1945–1970.* University Park: University of Pennsylvania Press, 2002.

McCann, Sean. *Gumshoe America: Hard-Boiled Crime Fiction and the Rise and Fall of New Deal Liberalism.* Durham, N.C.: Duke University Press, 2000.

———. *A Pinnacle of Feeling: American Literature and Presidential Government.* Princeton, N.J.: Princeton University Press, 2008.

McCann, Sean and Michael Szalay. "Do You Believe in Magic? Literary Thinking After the New Left." *Yale Journal of Criticism* 18, no. 2 (2005): 435–68.

McCarthy, Mary. *Birds of America.* 1971. Reprint. New York: Harcourt Brace Jovanovich, 1992.

———. *Conversations with Mary McCarthy.* Ed. Carol Gelderman. Jackson: University of Mississippi Press, 1991.

———. *The Groves of Academe.* 1952. Reprint. New York: Harcourt Brace, 1992.

———. *Ideas and the Novel.* New York: Harcourt Brace Jovanovich, 1980.

———. *On the Contrary.* New York: Farrar, Straus and Cudahy, 1961.

——. *The Seventeenth Degree: How It Went, Vietnam, Hanoi, Medina, and Sons of the Morning.* New York: Harcourt Brace Jovanovich, 1974.

——. *The Writing on the Wall and Other Literary Essays.* New York: Harcourt, Brace and World, 1970.

McClure, John. *Partial Faiths: Postsecular Fiction in the Age of Pynchon and Morrison.* Athens: University of Georgia Press, 2007.

McGurl, Mark. *The Novel Art: Elevations of American Fiction After Henry James.* Princeton, N.J.: Princeton University Press, 2001.

——. *The Program Era: Postwar Fiction and the Rise of Creative Writing.* Cambridge, Mass.: Harvard University Press, 2009.

McKee, James. *Sociology and the Race Problem: The Failure of a Perspective.* Urbana: University of Illinois Press, 1993.

Melley, Timothy. *Empire of Conspiracy: The Culture of Paranoia in Postwar America.* Ithaca, N.Y.: Cornell University Press, 2000.

Menand, Louis. *Discovering Modernism: T. S. Eliot and His Context.* New York: Oxford University Press, 1987.

Miller, James. *Democracy Is in the Streets: From Port Huron to the Siege of Chicago.* Cambridge, Mass.: Harvard University Press, 1994.

Mills, C. Wright. *The Causes of World War Three.* 1958. Reprint. London: Secker & Warburg, 1959.

——. *The New Men of Power: America's Labor Leaders.* 1948. Reprint. Urbana: University of Illinois Press, 2001.

——. *The Power Elite.* London: Oxford University Press, 1956.

——. *Power, Politics, and People: The Collected Essays of C. Wright Mills.* Ed. Irving Louis Horowitz. New York: Oxford University Press, 1963.

——. *The Sociological Imagination.* 1959. Reprint. Oxford, U.K.: Oxford University Press, 2000.

——. *White Collar: The American Middle Classes.* Oxford, U.K.: Oxford University Press, 1951.

Myrdal, Gunnar. *An American Dilemma: The Negro Problem and Modern Democracy.* 1944. Reprint. New York: Pantheon Books, 1972.

Nabokov, Vladimir. *Pnin.* 1957. Reprint. New York: Vintage, 1989.

Newfield, Christopher. *Ivy and Industry: Business and the Making of the American University, 1880–1980.* Durham, N.C.: Duke University Press, 2003.

Novak, Michael. *The Spirit of Democratic Capitalism.* New York: Simon and Schuster, 1982.

Nye, Russel. *The Unembarrassed Muse: The Popular Arts in America.* New York: Dial Press, 1970.

O'Connor, Alice. *Social Science, Social Policy, and the Poor in Twentieth-Century U.S. History.* Princeton, N.J.: Princeton University Press, 2001.

O'Kane, Karen. "Before the New Criticism: Modernism and the Nashville Group." *Mississippi Quarterly* 51, no. 4 (Fall 1998): 683–97.

Olster, Stacey. "*White Noise.*" In *The Cambridge Companion to Don DeLillo,* ed. John N. Duvall, 79–93. Cambridge, U.K.: Cambridge University Press, 2008.

Orwell, George. *Nineteen Eighty-Four.* 1949. Reprint. Harmondsworth, U.K.: Penguin Books, 1954.

Osteen, Mark. "DeLillo's Dedalian Artists." In *The Cambridge Companion to Don DeLillo,* ed. John N. Duvall, 137–50. Cambridge, U.K.: Cambridge University Press, 2008.

Owsley, Frank Lawrence. "The Irrepressible Conflict." In *I'll Take My Stand: The South and the Agrarian Tradition,* by Twelve Southerners (John Crowe Ransom and others), 61–91. 1930. Reprint. New York: Harper, 1962.

Park, Robert and Ernest Burgess. *Introduction to the Science of Sociology.* 1921. Reprint. Chicago: University of Chicago Press, 1924.

Parsons, Talcott. *The Social System.* Glencoe, Ill.: Free Press, 1951.

——. *The Structure of Social Action: A Study in Social Theory with Special Reference to a Group of Recent European Writers.* 1937. Reprint. New York: Free Press, 1968.

——. *The System of Modern Societies.* Englewood Cliffs, N.J.: Prentice-Hall, 1971.

Parsons, Talcott and Edward Shils. *Toward a General Theory of Action.* Cambridge, Mass.: Harvard University Press, 1951.

Pease, Donald. *Visionary Compacts: American Renaissance Writings in Cultural Context.* Madison: University of Wisconsin Press, 1987.

Phillips, William (a.k.a. Wallace Phelps). "Three Generations." *Partisan Review* 1, no. 4 (September–October 1934): 49–55.

Phillips, William and Philip Rahv. "Criticism." *Partisan Review* 2, no. 7 (April–May 1935): 16–25.

——. "Editorial Statement." *Partisan Review* 19, no. 3 (May 1952): 282–86.

——. "Literature in a Political Decade." In *New Letters in America,* ed. Horace Gregory, 170–80. New York: W. W. Norton, 1937.

——. "Problems and Perspectives in Revolutionary Literature." *Partisan Review* 1, no. 3 (June–July 1934): 3–10.

Piercy, Marge. *Braided Lives.* New York: Summit Books, 1982.

——. "The Grand Coolie Damn" (1969). In *Sisterhood Is Powerful: An Anthology of Writings from the Women's Liberation Movement,* ed. Robin Morgan, 421–38. New York: Random House, 1970.

——. *He, She, and It*. New York: Fawcett Crest, 1991.

——. *The High Cost of Living*. New York: Harper and Row, 1978.

——. *Parti-colored Blocks for a Quilt*. Ann Arbor: University of Michigan Press, 1982.

——. *Small Changes*. New York: Fawcett Crest, 1973.

——. *Woman on the Edge of Time*. New York: Fawcett Books, 1976.

Piercy, Marge and Robert Gottlieb. "Movement for a Democratic Society: Beginning to Begin to Begin" (1968). In *The New Left: A Documentary History*, ed. Massimo Teodori, 403–10. Indianapolis, Ind.: Bobbs-Merrill, 1969.

Pizer, Donald. *Twentieth-Century American Literary Naturalism: An Interpretation*. Carbondale: Southern Illinois University Press, 1982.

Podhoretz, Norman. *Breaking Ranks: A Political Memoir*. New York: Harper and Row, 1979.

Poirier, Richard. "*Herzog*, or Bellow in Trouble." In *Saul Bellow: A Collection of Critical Essays*, ed. Earl Rovit, 81–89. Englewood Cliffs, N.J.: Prentice-Hall, 1975.

Rahv, Philip. "Our Country and Our Culture." *Partisan Review* 19, no. 3 (May 1952): 304–10.

——. "A Season in Heaven." *Partisan Review* 3 (June 1936): 11–14.

Rainwater, Lee and William Yancey, eds. *The Moynihan Report and the Politics of Controversy: A Trans-action Social Science and Public Policy Report*. Cambridge, Mass.: MIT Press, 1967.

Rampersad, Arnold. *Ralph Ellison: A Biography*. New York: Alfred A. Knopf, 2007.

Ransom, John Crowe. *God Without Thunder: An Unorthodox Defense of Orthodoxy*. 1930. Reprint. Hamden, Conn.: Archon, 1965.

——. *Poems and Essays*. New York: Vintage, 1955.

——. "Reconstructed but Unregenerate." In *I'll Take My Stand: The South and the Agrarian Tradition*, by Twelve Southerners (John Crowe Ransom and others), 1–27. 1930. Reprint. New York: Harper, 1962.

——. *Selected Essays of John Crowe Ransom*. Ed. Thomas Daniel Young and John Hindle. Baton Rouge: Louisiana State University Press, 1984.

——. *Selected Letters of John Crowe Ransom*. Ed. Thomas Daniel Young and George Core. Baton Rouge: Louisiana State University Press, 1985.

——. "A Statement of Principles." In *I'll Take My Stand: The South and the Agrarian Tradition*, by Twelve Southerners (John Crowe Ransom and others), xxxvii–xlviii. 1930. Reprint. New York: Harper, 1962.

——. *The World's Body*. 1938. Reprint. Baton Rouge: Louisiana State University Press, 1968.

Readings, Bill. *The University in Ruins.* Cambridge, Mass.: Harvard University Press, 1996.

Reising, Russell. *The Unusable Past: Theory and the Study of American Literature.* New York: Methuen, 1986.

Riesman, David, with Nathan Glazer and Reuel Denney. *The Lonely Crowd: A Study of the Changing American Character.* 1950. Reprint. New Haven, Conn.: Yale University Press, 2001.

Robbins, Bruce. *Upward Mobility and the Common Good: Toward a Literary History of the Welfare State.* Princeton, N.J.: Princeton University Press, 2007.

Rossinow, Doug. *Visions of Progress: The Left-Liberal Tradition in America.* Philadelphia: University of Pennsylvania Press, 2008.

Rostow, Walt Whitman. *The Stages of Economic Growth: A Non-Communist Manifesto.* London: Cambridge University Press, 1960.

Russ, Joanna. *The Female Man.* 1975. Reprint. Boston: Beacon Books, 1986.

Russell, Mariann. "White Man's Black Man: Three Views." *CLA Journal* 17 (1973): 93–100.

Savio, Mario. "An End to History." In *The New Left: A Documentary History,* ed. Massimo Teodori, 158–61. Indianapolis, Ind.: Bobbs-Merrill, 1969.

Schaub, Thomas Hill. *American Fiction in the Cold War.* Madison: University of Wisconsin Press, 1991.

Schumpeter, Joseph. *Capitalism, Socialism, and Democracy.* 1940. Reprint. London: Unwin University Books, 1943.

Scott, Daryl Michael. *Contempt and Pity: Social Policy and the Image of the Damaged Black Psyche, 1880–1996.* Chapel Hill: University of North Carolina Press, 1997.

Sedgwick, Peter. *Psychopolitics.* London: Pluto Press, 1982.

Seguin, Robert. *Around Quitting Time: Middle-Class Fantasy in American Fiction.* Durham, N.C.: Duke University Press, 2001.

Shils, Edward. *Center and Periphery: Essays in Macrosociology.* Chicago: University of Chicago Press, 1975.

Siegel, Ben. "Saul Bellow and the University as Villain." In *Saul Bellow in the 1980s: A Collection of Critical Essays,* ed. Gloria Cronin and L. H. Goldman, 137–59. East Lansing: Michigan State University Press, 1989.

Snyder, Gary. *Earth House Hold: Technical Notes and Queries to Fellow Dharma Revolutionaries.* New York: New Directions, 1969.

Southern, David. *Gunnar Myrdal and Black–White Relations: The Use and Abuse of "An American Dilemma," 1944–1969.* Baton Rouge: Louisiana State University Press, 1987.

Staley, Eugene. *The Future of Underdeveloped Countries: Political Implications of Economic Development.* Rev. ed. New York: Harper and Brothers, 1961.

Steinfels, Peter. *The Neoconservatives.* New York: Simon and Schuster, 1979.

Stewart, John. *The Burden of Time: The Fugitives and the Agrarians.* Princeton, N.J.: Princeton University Press, 1965.

Strychacz, Thomas. *Modernism, Mass Culture, and Professionalism.* New York: Cambridge University Press, 1993.

Sumner, William Graham. *Folkways: A Study of the Sociological Importance of Usages, Manners, Customs, Mores, and Morals.* 1907. Reprint. New York: Dover, 1959.

Szalay, Michael. *New Deal Modernism: American Literature and the Invention of the Welfare State.* Durham, N.C.: Duke University Press, 2000.

Tate, Allen. "The Present Function of Criticism." *Southern Review* 6 (1940–1941): 236–46.

Taylor, Mark C. *The Moment of Complexity: Emerging Network Culture.* Chicago: University of Chicago Press, 2001.

Teres, Harvey. *Renewing the Left: Politics, Imagination, and the New York Intellectuals.* New York: Oxford University Press, 1996.

Trilling, Lionel. *Beyond Culture: Essays on Literature and Learning.* 1965. Reprint. London: Secker & Warburg, 1966.

——. "'Elements That Are Wanted.'" *Partisan Review* 7, no. 5 (September–October 1940): 367–79.

——. *A Gathering of Fugitives.* 1956. Reprint. London: Secker & Warburg, 1957.

——. *The Journey Abandoned: The Unfinished Novel.* Ed. Geraldine Murphy. New York: Columbia University Press, 2008.

——. *The Liberal Imagination: Essays on Literature and Society.* 1950. Reprint. Garden City, N.Y.: Doubleday, 1957.

——. *The Middle of the Journey.* 1947. Reprint. New York: New York Review of Books, 2002.

——. "Our Country and Our Culture." *Partisan Review* 19, no. 3 (May 1952): 318–26.

——. *Sincerity and Authenticity: The Charles Eliot Norton Lectures, 1969–1970.* Cambridge, Mass.: Harvard University Press, 1972.

Urbanowicz, Victor. "Personal and Political in *The Dispossessed.*" In *Ursula K. Le Guin,* ed. Harold Bloom, 145–54. New York: Chelsea House, 1986.

U.S. Census Bureau. "No. 673: Occupation of Employed Workers, by Sex, 1960 to 1980." In *1981 Statistical Abstract.* Available at http://www2.census.gov/prod2/statcomp/documents/1981–07.pdf.

——. "QT-P27: Occupation by Sex." In *Census 2000 Summary File 3, Matrix P50.* Available at http://factfinder.census.gov/servlet/QTTable?_bm=y&-geo_id=01OoUS&-qr_name=DEC_2000_SF3_U_QTP27&-ds_name=DEC_2000_SF3_U&-redoLog=false.

Vickers, George R. *The Formation of the New Left: The Early Years*. Lexington, Mass.: Lexington Books, 1975.

Wald, Alan. *The New York Intellectuals: The Rise and Decline of the Anti-Stalinist Left from the 1930s to the 1980s*. Chapel Hill: University of North Carolina Press, 1987.

Warren, Kenneth. *So Black and Blue: Ralph Ellison and the Occasion of Criticism*. Chicago: University of Chicago Press, 2003.

Warren, Robert Penn. "The Briar Patch." In *I'll Take My Stand: The South and the Agrarian Tradition*, by Twelve Southerners (John Crowe Ransom and others), 246–64. 1930. Reprint. New York: Harper, 1962.

Watts, Jerry Gafio. *Heroism and the Black Intellectual: Ralph Ellison, Politics, and Afro-American Intellectual Life*. Chapel Hill: University of North Carolina Press, 1994.

Whyte, William H. *The Organization Man*. New York: Simon and Schuster, 1956.

Wiebe, Robert. *The Search for Order, 1877–1920*. New York: Hill and Wang, 1967.

Wilford, Hugh. *The New York Intellectuals: From Vanguard to Institution*. Manchester, U.K.: Manchester University Press, 1995.

Wilson, Christopher. *The Labor of Words: Literary Professionalism in the Progressive Era*. Athens: University of Georgia Press, 1985.

——. *White Collar Fictions: Class and Social Representation in American Literature, 1885–1925*. Athens: University of Georgia Press, 1992.

Wilson, Edmund. *Axel's Castle: A Study in the Imaginative Literature of 1870–1930*. 1931. Reprint. London: Fontana, 1984.

Wolters, Raymond. *The New Negro on Campus: Black College Rebellions of the 1920s*. Princeton, N.J.: Princeton University Press, 1975.

Wright, Erik Olin. *Classes*. London: Verso, 1985.

——. *Class Structure and Income Determination*. New York: Academic, 1979.

Wright, Richard. *Black Boy*. 1945. Reprint. New York: Harper Perennial, 2007.

——. *Native Son*. 1940. Reprint. New York: Perennial Classics, 1998.

Young, Thomas Daniel. *Gentleman in a Dustcoat: A Biography of John Crowe Ransom*. Baton Rouge: Louisiana State University Press, 1976.

Zinn, Howard. *The Southern Mystique*. New York: Knopf, 1964.

INDEX

Bush, George W., 201
business elite, 133–35;
neoconservative alliance with,
114–15, 125, 132, 138

campus fiction, campus satire,
168–69, 175, 178
canon of U.S. writers, 172, 205n14
capital, capitalism, 6, 25, 52, 93, 114,
135, 191; anti-, 165; in *Birds of
America*, 96; corporations and,
133–34; disillusionment with, 88;
global, 92, 185, 194; Le Guin on,
156–57; in *Mr. Sammler's Planet*,
137–38; neoconservatives and, 125;
post-, 206n17; Protestant work
ethic and, 132. *See also* cultural
capital; economic capital;
free-market capitalism
Capitalism, Socialism, and Democracy
(Schumpeter, 1940), 134
Cappetti, Carla, 33; *Writing
Chicago*, 20
Carlyle, Thomas, 88
Cash (character in *Woman on the Edge of
Time*), 155
Castro, Fidel, 94
categorical imperative (Kant), 62, 97,
228n21
Catholicism, Catholics, 88, 125, 188,
189
Causes of World War III, The (Mills,
1958), 12–13
charisma, 22, 147, 155
Chicago, 20–21, 22, 33; naturalism of,
9, 36
Chicago School of Sociology, 9,
33–34, 220n16; criticism of,
35–36; as dominant paradigm, 20,
33; members of, 24; methodology
and style of, 39, 40; midwestern
dominance of, 34; Parsons and, 31,
35–36; Wright and, 218n8
Chick (character in *Ravelstein*), Bellow
as, 129

children: in *Mr. Sammler's Planet*, 118,
136; of middle-class professional
homes, 142; new class and, 25; in
Woman on the Edge of Time, 152, 156;
younger generation, 124
Christianity, 43, 88, 125, 126, 238n9.
See also Catholicism, Catholics;
Protestantism, Protestants
citizens, citizenry, 14, 85, 169,
192, 193
City University of New York, 150
civil rights, 81, 96, 99, 100
class, classes, 22, 144; of authors, 9;
consciousness of, 142; divisions
between, 12, 15; identity of, 19,
167; intellectual, 104; relations
between, 12, 115; sociology and, 56;
spirit of, 6; tourism and, 101–2. *See
also under individual classes*
close reading: New Critics and,
29–30, 41; Ransom and, 31,
48, 49
Closing of the American Mind, The
(Bloom, 1987), 116, 129
cold war, 117, 178; anti-Communists
in, 109, 176; cultural criticism of,
85; humanists of, 100, 172;
literature of, 5; social science in,
89; in *Underworld*, 191; university
in, 179
Coleridge, Samuel Taylor, 47, 88
collective politics of 1930s, 5, 205n14
College-on-the-Hill (in *White Noise*),
170, 174–80, 189; popular culture
studies at, 172–73; reform mission
of, 171; tuition of, 188
Columbia University, 207n30
Commentary (magazine), 15, 113
commercialism, commercialization,
96, 100, 115
Committee for the Free World,
226n9
Committee on Social Thought
(University of Chicago), Bellow
and, 116